Communities of Practice

'Communities of practice' has become an increasingly influential model of learning, organization and creativity, and is informing current debates about learning processes, managerial control of organizational knowledge, and general and vocational education. This benchmark text provides a critical but accessible introduction to the theory and application of communities of practice and their use in a diverse range of managerial and professional contexts, from education to human resource development. The book charts the development of the idea of communities of practice and explores the key relationship between learning and identity among newcomers and 'old timers', male and female workers, the low-skilled and the high-skilled, professionals and managers, adults and adolescents.

Drawing on international empirical studies, and adopting a multidisciplinary approach, this book will be of interest to all students, researchers, practitioners and policy makers with an interest in work, employment, labour markets, learning, training or education.

Jason Hughes is a Senior Lecturer at Brunel University, London. His current research interests include emotional reflexivity in the 'new' workplace, emotional and aesthetic labour, and new managerial discourses. His book *Learning to Smoke: Tobacco Use in the West* (2003) was the winner of the 2006 international Norbert Elias Amalfi Prize.

Nick Jewson is a Senior Research Fellow in the School of Social Sciences at Cardiff University. He has published widely on equal opportunities, non-standard forms of employment, spatial transformations in patterns of work and employment, and learning in the workplace.

Lorna Unwin is Professor of Vocational Education at the Institute of Education, University of London. Her interests include the changing meaning and role of skill and vocational knowledge. Her most recent book, *Improving Workplace Learning*, was published by Routledge in 2006.

Communities of Practice

Critical perspectives

Edited by Jason Hughes, Nick Jewson and Lorna Unwin

Routledge
Taylor & Francis Group

LONDON AND NEW YORK

First published 2007
by Routledge
2 Park Square, Milton Park, Abingdon, Oxon, OX14 4RN

Simultaneously published in the USA and Canada
by Routledge
711 Third Avenue, New York NY 10017

Routledge is an imprint of the Taylor & Francis Group, an informa business

Typeset in Times New Roman by
RefineCatch Limited, Bungay, Suffolk

British Library Cataloguing in Publication Data
A catalogue record for this book is available from the British Library

Library of Congress Cataloging in Publication Data
Communities of practice : critical perspectives / edited by Jason Hughes,
    Nick Jewson, and Lorna Unwin.
        p. cm.
    Includes bibliographical references and index.
    1. Organizational learning.   2. Communities of practice.   3. Knowledge
management.   I. Hughes, Jason.   II. Jewson, Nick, 1946–   III. Unwin,
Lorna.
    HD58.82.C64 2007
    302.3′5—dc22
    2007007163

ISBN13: 978-0-415-36473-7 (hbk)
ISBN13: 978-0-415-36474-4 (pbk)

Contents

Notes on contributors

Vanessa Beck is a Lecturer in Employment Studies at the Centre for Labour Market Studies, University of Leicester. She previously worked as a researcher on European Commission funded projects on barriers to employment for women and workers with ethnic minority backgrounds. Vanessa's main research and publications have been in the area of unemployment, redundancy and employability and a lot of this was conducted in post-unification Germany. She is also interested in the impact of gender and ethnicity on individuals' situation within VET and the labour market.

Stephen Billett is an Associate Professor in the Faculty of Education, Griffith University, Nathan QLD. He has previously worked as a vocational educator, educational administrator, teacher educator, professional development practitioner and policy developer within the Australian vocational education system. His research interests include the social and cultural contributions to vocational knowledge and its learning by individuals. Learning in and through working life has been the focus of his research work, particularly how vocational practice can be developed in workplace settings. In addition, he has a broad interest in policy and practice within adult and vocational education.

Matthew J. Brannan is a lecturer in Management at the School of Economic and Management studies, Keele University. He has also held a post at the Centre for Labour Market Studies, University of Leicester. His research focuses upon the contemporary experience of control processes at work, with particular emphasis given to emotional labour, misbehaviour and service work. He has published on recruitment and selection practices, and on gender and sexuality in the context of service interactions. He has a particular interest in ethnographic research methodologies.

Yrjö Engeström is Professor of Communication at the University of California, San Diego, and Professor of Adult Education and Director of the Centre for Activity Theory and Development Work Research at the University of Helsinki. He studies transformations in work and organizations, combining micro-level analysis of discourse and interaction with modelling of organizations as networks of activity systems going through developmental contradictions. His recent books include *Cognition and Communication at Work* (edited with David Middleton, 1996), and *Perspectives on Activity Theory* (edited with Reijo Miettinen and Raija-Leena Punamaki, 1999).

Alison Fuller is Professor of Education and Work in the School of Education, University of Southampton, and has held previous research posts at the Universities of

Leicester and Lancaster. She has long-standing research interests in a variety of areas, including: changing patterns of participation in education, training and work; school to work initiatives; apprenticeship, and workplace learning. Alison is currently co-directing two ESRC funded studies: 'Non-participation in HE' and 'Learning as Work'. Her recent publications include a book, *Workplace Learning in Context*, co-edited with Helen Rainbird and Anne Munro; and the articles 'The gendered nature of apprenticeship: employers' and young people's perspectives', *Education and Training*, 47 (4/5): 298–311, with Vanessa Beck and Lorna Unwin, and 'Learning as apprentices in the contemporary UK workplace: creating and managing expansive and restrictive participation', with Lorna Unwin, *Journal of Education and Work*, 16 (4): 407–26.

John Goodwin is a Senior Lecturer and Head of Department of the Centre for Labour Market Studies, University of Leicester (UK). He obtained a BSc degree in Sociology and Social Psychology from Loughborough University (UK) and a PhD in Sociology, specialising in masculinity and work from the University of Leicester. His principal research interests include young workers and the transition from education to work; young worker restudies and the secondary analysis of qualitative data; life histories and work narratives; figurational sociology and the works of Norbert Elias. He is currently working on articles exploring issues such as youth transitions as 'shock experiences', learning at work during the last 50 years, and 'fantasy and reality' in the transition to retirement. He is co-authoring a book entitled *Key Concepts in HRM* with Jason Hughes (Brunel University) and he is also writing articles exploring the correspondence between Ilya Neustadt and Norbert Elias (1962–1964) and Neustadt's role in the development of sociology at Leicester.

Jason Hughes is a Senior Lecturer at Brunel University, London. He previously was a lecturer at the Centre for Labour Market Studies, University of Leicester. His current research interests include emotional reflexivity in the 'new' workplace; emotional labour and aesthetic labour; new managerial discourses, particularly emotional intelligence, knowledge management, and organizational learning; risk and leisure commodities (particularly tobacco); corporate social responsibility and 'neat capitalism'; figurational sociology and communities of practice. His book *Learning to Smoke: Tobacco Use in the West* (2003) was the winner of the 2006 international Norbert Elias Prize. He is currently working on two other books: *Sociology and its Discontents: Norbert Elias and Contemporary Social Theory* (with E. Dunning, 2007), and *Key Concepts in HRM* (with J. Goodwin, 2007).

Nalita James is Lecturer in Employment Studies in the Centre for Labour Market Studies at the University of Leicester. Her research interests include: identity, work and learning, in particular academics' identity development and their learning transitions in higher education, and the use of the Internet in qualitative research. She recently has published in *Qualitative Research* and the *British Educational Research Journal* (2007). She is currently exploring and writing about the impact of the creative arts, particularly drama, on young adults' skills development and learning transitions. She is also co-authoring a book entitled *Online Interviews: Epistemological, Methodological and Ethical Considerations in Qualitative Research* (2007).

Nick Jewson is a sociologist. He is a Senior Research Fellow in the School of Social Sciences at Cardiff University and is currently part of a team carrying out a large-scale ESRC funded study of learning in the workplace, entitled 'Learning as Work'. He has published widely on equal opportunities, non-standard forms of employment, spatial transformations in patterns of work and employment, and learning in the workplace. His book publications include, *inter alia*, *Global Trends in Flexible Labour* (with Alan Felstead, 1999), *In Work, At Home: Towards an Understanding of Homeworking* (with Alan Felstead, 2000) and *Changing Places of Work* (with Alan Felstead and Sally Walters, 2005). Now in his senior years, he anticipates that his next community of practice will be a residential home for senile skint sociologists.

Valerie Owen-Pugh is a university lecturer and chartered psychologist. She currently teaches undergraduate and postgraduate courses in counselling and psychotherapy for the Institute of Lifelong Learning at the University of Leicester. Prior to joining the institute she taught courses on training and development and HRM for the University of Leicester's Centre for Labour Market Studies. She writes and researches on topics including: theories of learning; the social dimensions of learning, working, training and development; figurational sociology; team work and group processes; coaching and mentoring; stress and conflict in organizations; the training of counsellors and psychotherapists; and career development in sport.

Lorna Unwin is Professor of Vocational Education at the Institute of Education, University of London. She has taught in further education colleges and adult community education, and has held academic posts at the Open University and University of Sheffield. From 2003 to 2006 she was Director of the Centre for Labour Market Studies at the University of Leicester. Professor Unwin currently co-directs (with Professor Alan Felstead, Cardiff University, and Professor Alison Fuller, University of Southampton) a multi-sector study of the relationship between workplace learning, the organization of work, and performance. Her most recent book, *Improving Workplace Learning*, co-authored with Karen Evans, Phil Hodkinson and Helen Rainbird, was published by Routledge in 2006.

1 Introduction

Communities of practice: a contested concept in flux

Jason Hughes, Nick Jewson and Lorna Unwin

This book is a critical introduction to one of the most influential concepts to have emerged within the social sciences during recent years. The concept of 'communities of practice', and the associated concept of 'legitimate peripheral participation', arose out of a paradigm shift centring on the notion of 'situated learning'. Together, these ideas have transformed the assumptions and metaphors guiding the study of learning, opened up new areas of empirical research and investigation, reinvigorated existing fields of enquiry and facilitated interdisciplinary exchanges of knowledge and expertise. Their impact can be measured by the growth and focus of academic publications, journals, conferences and networks since the early 1990s. Moreover, the concept of communities of practice has also had great influence outside academia. It has been developed as a managerial tool that is widely recommended by consultants as a beneficial aspect of the functioning of contemporary organizations (in both the public and private sector) characterized by an overt commitment to empowered collaborative working.

For students and practitioners who have little previous knowledge or experience of the notion of communities of practice, this book provides an introduction to, and familiarization with, the key arguments underpinning the concept. Those who already have some background in the area will find that the chapters offer substantial critiques of the key themes and their implications. These include, on the one hand, theoretical and conceptual evaluations of the assumptions and arguments embedded in this model of learning and, on the other, empirical studies which explore the relevance of these ideas to an understanding of diverse learning contexts. Thus, as the title implies, the book offers a *critical* approach rather than simply a descriptive exposition. Furthermore, the book does not seek to represent a single or unified line of argument. Rather, scholars with contrasting views and agendas have been brought together in this volume. This, then, is a collection of critical *perspectives*, in the plural. We hope that readers will find this diversity intellectually stimulating and that it will encourage them to reflect on their own learning practices and experiences. Hence, in working through the chapters, readers may themselves become participants in an on-going debate that, at least in some respects, is itself a community of practice. To aid navigation through the text, each chapter is prefaced by a brief guide to its main themes and concludes with a list of suggested issues for further thought and discussion.

This chapter is divided into two parts. First, we outline and consider the implications of the paradigm shift associated with the emergence of the concept of situated learning, and the subsequent articulation of the idea that learning takes place within 'communities of practice'. The second section considers some of the theoretical directions in which these original ideas have been carried forward and their usefulness in interpreting the findings of recent research. This will enable us to introduce each of the chapters in turn.

Making sense of a new paradigm

Readers of this book could well be forgiven for believing that a 'community of practice' is some kind of organizational tool or managerial stratagem. Indeed, to a great extent this is what the term has come to mean in popular usage. Type the phrase into your favourite internet search engine and you will immediately be swamped with millions of hits. On the first page or so the names of Jean Lave and Etienne Wenger, and their groundbreaking book, *Situated Learning: Legitimate Peripheral Participation* (1991), will figure prominently. Thereafter, you will encounter references to articles on the link between communities of practice and organizational performance, including topics such as communities of practice as a knowledge management solution, as an alternative to formal training and as a new vehicle for collaboration distinct from work-based teams. You will encounter a vast array of consultancy organizations offering assistance in 'establishing' communities of practice. There will be links to online 'virtual communities', advertisements for dedicated software, details of forthcoming workshops, and a host of religious, governmental, medical, educational, corporate and other interest group networks consciously adopting the communities of practice moniker as a means of expressing their common association.

It is clear, then, that the idea of communities of practice has had a huge impact in the fields of management, organizations and what is known as Human Resource Management (HRM). It has launched what can only be called an industry of academic and applied research and consultancy practice, focused on organizational productivity, creativity and flexibility. The term has come to signify, variously, a knowledge management solution, an inexpensive alternative to training and a 'toolkit' for human resource development practitioners. It has become, in short, emblematic of an ostensibly new consultancy movement. To a large extent, this project was spurred on by Wenger's later publications (see, in particular, Wenger 1998; Wenger *et al.* 2002). In this context, Wenger brought the concept of communities of practice directly to the forefront of his analysis and was more explicit about the specific attributes of the social relationships that constitute communities of practice than had been the case in his work with Jean Lave. Our book certainly does not ignore or discount this way of thinking about communities of practice, and chapters by Hughes and Engeström comment on and take forward the managerial perspective. However, our aim is also to give weight to other forms of enquiry and other lines of thought that have developed the original ideas of Lave and Wenger (1991) and taken them in different directions.

Jean Lave and Etienne Wenger's seminal text (1991) offered a new theorization of learning, one which, as will be discussed below, was initially aimed at a specialist academic audience, particularly those within the field of education studies. *Situated Learning* represented nothing short of a paradigm shift (Kuhn 1996) in the study of learning. Lave and Wenger's thesis arose out of growing dissatisfaction, expressed by several commentators, with the pre-existing, 'standard' paradigm of learning, and built on Lave's (1998) earlier work in the field of situated cognition. Exemplars of the standard paradigm include the classical learning theory of behaviourism and cognitivism (Hager 2004). These characteristically conceived of learning as an individual process, involving the acquisition of a formal body of knowledge from a teacher or expert. What Lave and Wenger proposed was in many ways a new paradigm of learning, one in which active social participation was not so much an adjunct to learning processes, or a context to frame them, as their primary condition – the vehicle for learning itself. Lave and Wenger's work also exposed and directly challenged some of the shortcomings of formal education in its reliance upon the teacher–learner dyad as the principal educational form. Indeed, situated learning raised important questions about the institutional context of education, in particular the extent to which the school-based classroom as a 'situation' offered limited possibilities for learning. By extension, formal training and trainer-centric models of workplace learning were called into question. Since its earliest articulation there has been a parallel, and subsequently convergent, strand of writing concerning how communities of practice might offer an alternative model of learning, innovation, and collaboration within the knowledge-intensive workplace (see, for example, Brown and Duguid 1991).

The concept of situated learning, and its focus on individuals as social beings, is part of a long tradition of philosophical concern about the character of the educational process and the role of learning in people's lives and development. The eighteenth-century French philosopher Rousseau drew attention to the need for children to be active learners so that they could, from an early age, start to make sense of their surroundings and make their experiences the basis of their education. In the modern era, the American philosopher John Dewey also emphasized the importance of learning from real life experience:

> I believe that the only true education comes through the stimulation of the child's powers by the demands of the social situations in which he finds himself. Through these demands he is stimulated to act as a member of a unity, to emerge from his original narrowness of action and feeling, and to conceive of himself from the standpoint of the welfare of the group to which he belongs.
>
> (Dewey 1897: 77)

In the 1970s, Ivan Illich advocated the abolition of schools, arguing that the most effective learning was self-directed and took place outside formal educational institutions. His ideas align, to some extent, with those of the radical adult educators of the 1970s and 1980s. The Brazilian radical educationalist, Paulo Freire (Freire 1972), developed a critique of what he called the 'banking concept' of education, in which learners were thought to be empty vessels waiting passively to have facts and ideas poured into their heads by teachers.

Lave and Wenger's work, therefore, followed on a from long critical debate, and further challenged the field of educational studies, which had traditionally positioned learning as a psychological process located in the heads of individuals. Furthermore, the majority of educational research had focused on learning in schools. As Young (1998: 179) notes, Lave and Wenger turned this 'school-centric' approach on its head by revealing that learning takes place in many settings beyond the school classroom and is not, necessarily, associated with teaching. The conceptualization of learning as 'social participation' also offered a profoundly different vision from the school-centric concept as a form of 'social selection' (Young 1998: 179). By placing emphasis upon the social community as the primary unit of analysis, Lave and Wenger shifted and broadened the lens of educational enquiry from its often fixed focus upon 'the individual' so that it now embraced the context in which learning took place. Harrison *et al.* (2002: 5) argue that this shift also challenged traditional notions of the role of knowledge as a 'stable commodity that belongs to an individual and can be transmitted, assessed and accredited'.

Lave and Wenger's (1991) book has all the attributes – inspiring and frustrating – of a paradigm-defining text. The book established new metaphors and assumptions that redefined the field of enquiry, generating new agendas of debate and research. It not only overturned established ideas but opened up a new territory that was previously a largely unrecognized area of investigation. It took an aspect of individual and social life that was widely regarded as obvious, commonsense and of little interest and elevated it into a subject of serious and exciting academic study. It provided a lens that rendered visible what had previously been invisible, ignored or neglected. Partly this entailed the introduction of new terminology as well as new concepts. The impact of the book was to erode established subdisciplinary boundaries and create crossovers between scholars studying labour processes and learning processes. It broke down some of the silos between the study of education, sociology, organizations and business. It is no accident that the editors of this book are variously located within a business school, school of social sciences and institute of education.

However, *Situated Learning* is a slim volume that is heuristic, controversial and provocative rather than exhaustive and definitive. Lave and Wenger give the distinct impression of wrestling with ideas that were taking form, and of doing so within an intellectual context in which debates about learning '*in situ*', and the concept of 'situatedness' more generally, were at the fore. It has many loose ends, not least of which concern key features of the concept of communities of practice. The authors (1991: 42) describe the idea as 'a largely intuitive notion', one that they adopt as a useful working tool but have not systematically developed. They themselves anticipate some of the key criticisms that have been levelled at the concept since its earliest inception – for example, the failure to adequately conceptualize relations of power – undertaking an auto-critique even as they unfold their thesis. Lave and Wenger's paradigm was, then, indistinct and underdeveloped in crucial respects. There were many opportunities to work on ambiguities, lacunae, puzzles, anomalies and knots. It was open to development in a number of different ways, and authors of differing backgrounds and inclinations saw divergent potentialities within it.

In later publications Wenger articulated and firmed up the notion of communities of practice in important respects. He was addressing both an academic and practitioner audience in introducing three definitional criteria: 'mutual engagement', 'joint enterprise' and 'shared repertoire'. However, Wenger's managerialist interpretation is only one way to go. Indeed, the concept has been applied so widely that, on occasion, it has seemed in danger of losing specificity and analytical edge, sliding into a catch-all descriptive term. It is the objective of this book to recognize the full spread of the development of the paradigm, whilst, at the same time, highlighting contributions that sharpen its focus.

Critical perspectives

This book examines key developments in the concept of communities of practice by exploring both theoretical and empirical articulations of the original paradigm. Chapters 2–7 are devoted to contrasting conceptual arguments. Each of these explores a different approach, or in some cases variety of approaches, to the critique and further development of the concept. Readers will not find consensus here but, rather, will encounter more or less competing explanations, theoretical frameworks and modes of argument. None is dismissive of the concept and many agree about where shortcomings lie. However, their prescriptions for fixing these weaknesses lead them off in different directions. For example, Billett seeks to restore the proactive agent or personal subject to centre stage, whereas Jewson develops a more structural and relational perspective. Owen-Pugh, in reviewing both psychological and sociological theories, sees value in retaining a range of different kinds of approaches, blending the best elements of each. Readers must judge for themselves where they stand on these issues and the extent to which the perspectives reviewed here are compatible or mutually exclusive.

Chapter 2 by Alison Fuller sets the scene for many of the later contributions. Fuller maps out the paradigm of learning from which the concept of community of practice emerged and charts a way through the substantial thickets of literature that have grown up around the idea. She provides an overview of the contribution of the work of Lave and Wenger to the study of learning, including the impact of their work on the metaphors and fundamental assumptions that guide research in the field. Of major importance here is the shift from metaphors based around notions of 'learning as acquisition' to those rooted in 'learning as participation'. She spells out the conceptual and theoretical transformations that Lave and Wenger initiated, thereby reminding us of the intellectual contributions their book made. Fuller goes on to remind us that the notion of community of practice was, to a significant degree, underdeveloped and latent within Lave and Wenger (1991), although they did highlight the historical and developmental cycle of relationships between novices and knowledgeable practitioners, or 'old-timers'. Fuller acknowledges the strengths of this approach but also its weaknesses. She goes on to draw out six themes within the extensive literature that constitute key aspects of development of the model. They include: concerns about the adequacy of the 'learning as participation' metaphor; ambiguities surrounding the definition of communities of practice; doubts about the innovative and transformative capacities of communities of practice; oversimplification of relationships between novices and knowledgeable practitioners; failure to specify the full range of trajectories of participation experienced by members, including both novices and old-timers; and failure sufficiently to recognize the implications of multiple settings and networks of relationships for learning processes. The chapter concludes with a plea for research to move forward by adopting a more nuanced and sophisticated conceptualization of layered contexts of learning that goes beyond merely specifying individual and organizational levels of analysis.

Following Fuller's overview, in Chapter 3 Jason Hughes explores one of the specific directions in which the communities of practice model has been developed. In particular, he tackles the most well-known line of development, that of the application of the model as a consultancy tool. One source of this approach is in the later publications of Wenger (1998) and Wenger *et al.* (2002), which have inspired many other subsequent applications by consultants within the field. However, parallel to these contributions has been a stream of literature exploring the links between the idea of communities of practice and cognate management philosophies, such as organizational learning and, later, knowledge management (see, for example, Brown and Duguid 1991, 2001; Easterby-Smith *et al.* 1998). It may seem ironic that a perspective on learning that seeks to advance the autonomous and self-directed activities of reflexive participants should evolve into a tool through which organizational elites seek ultimately to exercise control and regulation over their work forces. However, Hughes argues that even in the original (Lave and Wenger 1991) text there is some ambiguity over the status of the model. He suggests that Lave and Wenger oscillate between positing communities of practice as an analytical heuristic of learning and presenting the model as an ideal for educational practitioners. That is to say, they switch between analysis and prescription, between presenting a model of how learning 'actually is' and an idealized projection of how learning 'ought to be'. As a result, Hughes proposes, the critical and academic edge of the original model has become in some ways lost by its translation into a social technology.

The theme of communities of practice as a toolkit for organizational design and knowledge management is further developed in Chapter 4 by Yrjö Engeström. Engeström's work in the field of 'activity theory' has been of major importance in seeking to assimilate the contribution of the communities of practice model within a broader conceptual framework. He highlights the significance of multiple and complex divisions in active work groups, their historical evolution, and the part played by social contradictions as driving forces for change in their constitution and functions (Engeström 2001). In the chapter presented here he acknowledges the salience of Lave and Wenger's (1991) contribution, not least in its focusing on apprenticeship as the paradigmatic form of situated learning. However, he extensively criticizes their approach for its failure to adopt an historical perspective on the development of organizational forms and managerial strategies. He argues that recent developments in the production of value and new arrangements in the labour process have created radically new patterns of social relationships at work which are typically dispersed, fluctuating and shifting in response to rapidly changing markets and technologies. As a result, what he calls 'new forms of peer production' are coming into being, exemplified by the Open Source Project in the field of software development. The model of community of practice proposed by Lave and Wenger, he suggests, reflects earlier socio-economic conditions in which work groups were tightly bounded, local and directed from central sources of authority. These principles were enshrined in relations between novices and knowledgeable practitioners. In contrast, Engeström develops an alternative conceptualization of contemporary work groups that emphasizes processes of negotiation, flexibility, innovation and potentiality for development in multiple directions. He traces the organic texture of the lived experience of participants in these modes of production and exchange.

Another direction in which discussions of the model have developed is within the context of theoretical debates which hinge around notions of 'structure' and 'agency' (Giddens 1984). In this context, a number of authors have sought to highlight the importance of 'the reflexive individual subject' within learning processes, stressing the active role of self-directed agents in responding to the 'learning affordances' they encounter and perceive in workplaces (Billett 2001). This perspective highlights the complex and diverse character of individual biographies and their relevance to becoming a learner in the workplace. It stresses that workplace learners bring with them pre-formed sets of attitudes, experiences, identities, life histories and ways of working learned elsewhere. These attributes, then, are seen as constitutive of agentic actors (Hodkinson and Hodkinson 2004; Billett 2006).

In Chapter 5, Stephen Billett argues that the popularity of the concept of communities of practice has served to downplay what he sees as the most powerful contribution of Lave and Wenger's (1991) text. For Billett the lasting legacy of the book lies in its discussion of the relationship between the personal and immediate social experience in learning through participation. Billett is not disregarding the concept of communities of practice, but instead he calls for the reinstatement of the individual agent as equal in importance to the community in which they are situated. For Billett the relationship between the individual and the social, through the act of participation, is symbiotic in character. Hence both the situation (community) and the individual are shaped by and, in turn, help to shape each other. This insight draws our attention to the individual learner as an agentic being, one whose actions are influenced by their biography, life history and sense of identity. Billett's discussion finds some echo in Unwin's chapter, where the experience of individual apprentices throughout history is used to critique the concept of community as experienced by young workers. There are echoes too in Goodwin's chapter in which retired workers look back on the impact that joining a workforce community as teenagers had on their transition towards adulthood. Similarly, the chapters by James and by Beck also explore the relationship between personal agency and social networks of support.

In contrast, a number of authors have noted the potential for developing our understanding of workplace learning through the lens of actor-network theory (see Mutch 2002; Edwards and Nicoll 2004). Others have explicitly drawn on this theory to critique and develop the notion of communities of practice (Fox 2000). Actor-network theory has diverse and extensive roots (see Callon 1986; Law and Hassard 1999). It adopts a relational, generative and processual perspective on social interaction. Power is conceived as the capacity of key participants in social networks to enrol and mobilize others into their web of actions, often through the dissemination of collective mythologies or rhetorically persuasive interpretations of the situation. Included within, and constitutive of, these webs of influence and action are animals and objects as well as human beings; these include items of 'shared repertoire', such as tools, natural resources, transport technologies, weapons, domesticated animals, and so on. Networks are conceived as potentially fragile, in need of constant reproduction and repair, subject to collapse, betrayal and reformation. Owen-Pugh, in this volume, illustrates the cross-cutting circumstances in which alliances are made and broken in professional sport. The meanings, activities and experiences of individual participants, human and non-human, are derived from their positions and functions within the context of the network itself, rather than from essential intrinsic qualities. Subjectivity and the subject are, thus, relationally constituted in participation, not pre-given.

In many ways, the community of practice model has significant parallels with actor-network theory. However, Fox (2000) draws attention to the concept of power embedded in actor-network theory, which he sees as having more in common with that of Foucault than Lave and Wenger. In actor-network theory, power is not conceived as a possession or thing but as an attribute of the functioning of networks. It is shaped by the localized connections within networks, not diffused from above or centrally. Actor-network theory explores how processes such as legitimate peripheral participation gradually incorporate novices into the webs of old-timers. Furthermore, the theory draws attention to the way people act in, through and with non-human aspects of networks so as to build chains of influence over space and time. Non-human elements are thought of as not merely pragmatically selected means to an end but as part of the overall web of constraints and opportunities that constitute the network. Arguably, however, actor-network theory suffers from some of the limitations of theories of communities of practice. Both have difficulty in identifying the boundaries of social groupings, lack a theory of overall societal development and have a tendency to view widely disparate social entities through one theoretical lens.

In Chapter 6, Nick Jewson draws on a number of sources, including actor-network theory, in developing his argument that social network analysis has much to offer in developing the concept of community of practice. In so doing he seeks to address some of the limitations of both theories identified above. He begins by examining the provenance of the term 'community' as it is deployed in the community of practice literature. He argues that the predominant reading has drawn on one particular theoretical perspective that highlights a shared sense of belonging, expressed in morally valued symbolic forms. He points out that there are other schools of thought in the sociology of community that might prove fruitful, most notably those which develop network models of community relationships. Adopting this perspective generates a wide range of relational concepts that provide a structural theoretical basis for specifying, analysing and explaining many of the characteristics of communities of practice that are described by Lave and Wenger (1991) and Wenger (1998) but which remain vague or contingent within their texts. Jewson argues that incorporating the framework fostered by actor-network theory avoids falling into a static, reified notion of network. He goes on to suggest that network analysis offers the possibility of developing a badly needed historical dimension to the notion of community of practice (an issue also highlighted by Engeström in his chapter). Long-term processes of societal change may be conceptualized in terms of the structural differentiation, vertical and horizontal, of network interdependences. This interpretation of the changing macro-societal context has fundamental implications for the forms and functions of smaller groups and communities.

Chapter 7 by Valerie Owen-Pugh shifts our focus towards a related set of theoretical possibilities. She compares Lave and Wenger's model of communities of practice with, on the one hand, psychological theories of skill transmission and, on the other, relational theories of psycho-social development, with a principal focus on the work of Norbert Elias. Her analysis evaluates the utility of these theories through a discussion of relationships between elite athletes and their coaches, specifically within the field of British basketball. She identifies complex and contradictory tensions in coach–athlete relationships, thereby presenting an account which is sensitive to the Janus-faced character of interactions between novices and old-timers. In many ways, this formulation goes beyond the model of generational displacement which is at the heart of Lave and Wenger's perspective. It is interesting to note that, while the psychologistic 'transmission' model of training elite athletes appears to have considerable success in improving performance, it, nevertheless, fails to provide a convincing explanation of the dynamic interplay between social and psychological processes that underpin athletic training. It is tempting to draw parallels here with the consultancy model of communities of practice within organizations, which also may produce 'results' in terms of performance gains whilst simultaneously offering only limited possibilities for understanding and explanation (see Hughes in this volume). A further valuable contribution of this chapter is that it provides an introduction to the theoretical framework of Norbert Elias. Owen-Pugh finds Elias's work to be compatible with Lave and Wenger's model. However, she suggests that it offers a much broader perspective that encompasses macro social processes at the global level through to micro psychological processes at the level of individuals. Moreover, Eliasian models of power provide a more subtle explanation for the two-way and shifting character of interdependences between coaches and athletes and, by conceptual extension, novices and old-timers. Nevertheless, the chapter concludes by suggesting that all three types of theory have something to offer in setting agendas and investigating processes of learning.

Another direction of development has been to locate the concept of community of practice within theories of language, literacy and discourse (see Holmes and Meyerhoff 1999; Barton and Tusting 2005). This perspective suggests that central to an understanding of the lived experience and practical outcomes of communities of practice are relationships of power, framed within the dynamics of language. Barton and Tusting (2005: 6) suggest that these processes represent a crucial aspect that is not sufficiently developed in the work of Wenger (1998). This approach offers a particular perspective on sources of resistance, inequality and division. It focuses on how the linguistic negotiation of meanings within small-scale social interactions generate, communicate and constitute relationships of conflict, rivalry and tension as well as co-operation, co-ordination and harmony. It is suggested that in and through the use of language, spoken and textual, power relations are established and maintained, resented and challenged (Barton and Hamilton 2005; Tusting 2005). Struggles are played out in the clash of alternative discourses. Some command high-status cultural recognition; others are marginalized, suppressed or silenced (see Creese 2005). The capacity convincingly to command and deploy material and symbolic discourses, and to prove membership of significant speech communities, both establishes the credibility of individuals within communities of practice and enables members to extend their remit into wider social spheres (Rock 2005). Thus, in this perspective, what Wenger (1998) calls 'shared repertoire' becomes conceptualized as shared language and discourse. Similarly, 'situated learning' and 'legitimate peripheral participation' can be framed in terms of access to, and sanctioned membership of, speech communities. Inequalities within communities of practice reflect socio-linguistically mediated practices of inclusion and exclusion. Positions of subordinate and superordinate authority – such as novice and old-timer – are coded and legitimated in and through the implicit and explicit uses of language. Divisions between multiple communities of practice reflect hierarchies of cultural prestige and moral value that are embedded in modes of talk. Struggles over the distribution of resources and bids for autonomy are conducted through interpretations and counter-interpretations of ambiguities in language and meanings (Harris and Shelswell 2005; Myers 2005).

Although Barton and Tusting (2005) do not draw on the work of Judith Butler (1994), there are interesting parallels between these authors (and, ultimately, to that of Michel Foucault). Butler's work is philosophically complex and any summary is bound to simplify. However, it is worth picking out some key points. Butler eschews all notions of a pre-existing subject that acts, feels, thinks or performs. For her, 'performativity', as opposed to 'performance' (Butler 1994: 33), refers to discursive practices of power, in and through which subjectivity and the subject are formed. Identity does not prefigure action but is constituted through action, discourses and language. She further argues that, 'The more fully a practice is mastered, the more fully subjection is achieved' (Butler 1995: 45). This would imply, for example, that as individual subjects achieve recognition in communities of practice as 'old-timers' they incorporate and 'submit' to one particular way of being, feeling, thinking and doing. The existence of discourses that shape thought, emotion and desires are the condition of 'performativity'. As Foucault (1994: 341) notes, 'To govern . . . is to structure the possible field of action of others.' However, Butler does not conceive subjects as passive products of deterministic forces. Rather, they may, in certain instances, reflexively and critically examine the conditions of their own possibility, radically subverting or reconfiguring them. Discourses, thus, are never chosen but, paradoxically, initiate and sustain agency (Butler 1997: 2). Moreover, performances are typically experienced by subjects as less than they ought to be. There is a gap between ideal and reality that has to be psychologically negotiated.

Whilst none of the contributors to this book overtly position their work within this school of thought, powerful echoes of this approach are to be found in a number of chapters. Indeed, whenever power relations are theorized, the framing of inequality, division and control within language, discourse and speech communities quickly comes to the fore. The chapter by Brannan, on the gendering of social relationships within call centres and between call centre operatives and their clients, demonstrates vividly how membership was constructed through participation in linguistic forms and communities of talk based on stereotyped notions of gender and sexuality. Owen-Pugh's analysis of relationships between athletes and coaches within basketball draws on the concept of 'established/outsider' relationships developed by Elias and Scotson (1994). She notes that a key feature of the power struggles between 'established' and 'outsiders' concerns the mobilizing and symbolizing of speech communities in the form of 'praise' gossip and 'blame' gossip that define boundaries of inclusion and exclusion. James, in her chapter about the learning trajectories of British academics within multiple communities of practice, explores how the redefinition and renegotiation of the powers and status of 'old-timer' are enacted through shifts in the words that constitute key signifiers of identity. Her work also throws light on the experience of a gap between ideal and actual performances, as reflected in the ambiguous and shifting character of membership within a community of practice.

The theoretical roots of several, though by no means all, lines of development of the communities of practice paradigm tap into the work of Foucault. His work is of increasing interest in understanding workplace learning, not merely because of its general intellectual influence in the social sciences in recent years, but also because of its particular relevance to understanding contemporary corporate governance. As centrally driven, bureaucratic and hierarchical managerial strategies fade in at least some economic sectors, the question of how managerial regulation and control are maintained within 'decentred', 'empowered', 'post-Fordist' organizations comes increasingly to the fore (Gabriel 2003; Casey 1995; Rose 1990, 1999; du Gay 1996). Foucaldian notions of power, knowledge, subjectivity and discipline offer one possibility (Fox 2000; Zemblyas 2006).

Foucault (1983) conceives power to be relational and productive. It is not a mechanism, institution or attribute wielded by some groups or individuals over others. Rather power is localized, diffuse and ubiquitous. The learning, practice and legitimation of knowledge are crucial aspects of power; knowledge and power go hand in hand. The concept of 'governmentality' is achieved through the acquisition of disciplines, practices, techniques, procedures and bodies of expertise. Compliance with this regime is policed through external surveillance devices but also through inner docility and self-regulation (Edwards and Nicoll 2004). We learn to govern ourselves and even, through acquiring 'technologies of the self', we *learn how to learn* to govern ourselves (Foucault 1990a, b). Power does not merely control subjects, it produces 'the self' in a web of practices and discourses. Hence workplace learning is not merely an empowerment of the worker but a colonization of the self and a seduction into submission (Garrick and Usher 2000). In the post-Fordist era, power, discipline and surveillance diminish in visibility as they become incorporated into the emotional, bodily and cognitive regimes of individual workers. Power is exercised non-coercively through educating workers to accept the pastoral authority of the organization (Rose 1990, 1999).

In this volume the chapter by Brannan illustrates these processes in operation. He shows, in his research site, how cultivating and demonstrating masculine and feminine sexual practices and identities involved call centre staff simultaneously in learning disciplined workplace behaviour and submitting to close managerial surveillance. Jewson's chapter on recent changes in the spatial locations of employment draws attention to a heightened requirement for diverse and complex forms of self-control and self-motivation in the conduct of work, both in virtual and in real time/space. Learning these 'technologies of the self' becomes a crucial generic aspect of participation in communities of practice and the conduct of employment relationships.

It goes without saying that theoretical analysis and empirical evidence march hand in hand. However, the chapters outlined thus far are predominantly conceptual and theoretical in their focus. In contrast, the following six contributions are directed towards an empirically based understanding of specific learning situations. These chapters enable us to tease out general conclusions and conceptual insights through an examination of detailed investigations into particular cases, issues and circumstances. This empirical work throws up new challenges for theory and gives a 'real world' context for the more abstract points made by analytical commentators. Thus, for example, whereas the chapter by Owen-Pugh refers to 'power asymmetries' in social relationships, that of Brannan identifies how gender inequalities and stereotypes play out in a specific workplace. Whereas the chapters by Fuller and by Hughes call for greater sophistication in specifying interdependent levels of theoretical and empirical analysis, those by Brannan and James explore how multiple communities of practice interconnect in real occupational contexts. Research-based contributions, therefore, enable us to situate situated learning.

The contribution of Norbert Elias to the understanding of communities of practice, introduced in this volume by Owen-Pugh, is further elaborated in Chapter 8 by John Goodwin. Goodwin's analysis is devoted to a discussion of the transition of young people to work and adulthood. Like Owen-Pugh, Goodwin emphasizes the stretch of Elias's theory, which, as he suggests, incorporates the broad sweep of historical development and the minutiae of personal emotional and cognitive processes. In Eliasian terms, these are encapsulated in the concepts of 'sociogenesis' and 'psychogenesis' respectively. The chapter is informed by detailed historical data on school-to-work transitions in mid-twentieth century Britain. In this context, Goodwin emphasizes that the entry and progress of young people into work-based communities of practice has both generated, and been predicated upon, a simultaneous transition from the social status of 'child' to 'adult'. This change in social standing comprised progress through a series of liminal and transitory states characterized by a sense of being 'in between' and 'neither–nor'. Goodwin, then, elucidates the specific processes of change involved in entering into, taking up and assuming the identity of 'novice'. Drawing upon Elias, he highlights the psycho-emotional processes of adjustment and 'shock' entailed in legitimate peripheral participation and places this within the context of generational transition. Hence, for many young workers at least, participation in communities of practice is not merely a matter of occupational socialization but, in addition, demands and entails a reconstruction of the self. Generalizing from the example of young workers, therefore, Goodwin is bringing into sharp relief the nexus of relationships and interdependences that mediate between social and psychological processes of learning within communities of practice, and those beyond it.

In Chapter 9, Lorna Unwin offers a further perspective on the experience of young workers by re-examining apprenticeship, a concept which is central to Lave and Wenger's (1991) thesis on both situated learning and communities of practice. She compares Lave and Wenger's interpretation with historical and contemporary accounts of apprenticeship in England. Unwin reminds us that Lave and Wenger began their book with a concern that the concept of apprenticeship had become so broadly and loosely used in debates and common parlance that it was in danger of losing its meaning. Yet, as Unwin argues, Lave and Wenger's own empirical examples reveal that apprenticeship does indeed take many forms. Unwin discusses the extent to which this was always the case by examining the evolution of apprenticeship as a model of skill formation in England, a country which experienced the world's first industrial revolution and that, as a consequence, shifted much more rapidly than others to mass production and away from craft-based working. Apprenticeship became used as means of controlling the large number of child workers drafted in to service the new mills and factories. The chapter then moves to the contemporary manifestation of apprenticeship in England where government policies in the area of vocational education and training for young people over the past thirty years have similarities with the social control agendas of the past. At the same time, Unwin highlights the impact of economic change on the appropriateness of the apprenticeship model and the meaning of the term 'communities of practice', particularly in relation to the service sectors of the economy.

Matthew J. Brannan, in Chapter 10, also explores the theme of communities of practice within service employment. His examination of the practices and lived experience of call centre representatives develops a number of themes that are found in the work of Lave and Wenger (1991) and Wenger (1998) as well as several that are relatively neglected in the key paradigmatic texts. First, he demonstrates the difficult hurdles that novices sometimes face in getting a foothold within communities of practice, as well as the complex and sometimes contradictory demands placed on them. Second, he suggests that one of the sources of this complexity concerns how multiple communities of practices, or 'constellations', may emerge within a single workplace, sometimes nested one within another. A third major theme of Brannan's chapter concerns the significance of the performance of managerially approved and prescribed gender and sexual roles for the successful completion of the work tasks of customer service representatives. The community of practice described by Brannan is fundamentally gendered. This finding draws attention to the surprising neglect of issues of gender within the paradigmatic texts – as well as age, ethnicity, class, creed, nationality and other critical social bonds. Much of the theoretical literature treats members of communities of practice as differentiated around the novice/old-timer divide but does not focus on other dimensions of inequality. It is worth noting, in this context, that whilst participants undoubtedly bring with them pre-formed notions of sexual and gender identities, they may also learn to confirm, develop or change these identifications in the course of participating in legitimate peripheral participations (cf. chapter by Goodwin in this volume).

Chapter 11, by Nalita James, also highlights how contrasting constraints and opportunities of multiple communities of practice shape and compete for the identifications of members. She explores the competing demands of research, teaching, institutional and professional roles on academics in British higher education, developing her analysis through two biographical case studies. Thus an emerging theme of the empirical studies reported in this book concerns the often complex and fragmented character of participation in workplace communities of practice. As James argues, this draws attention to issues such as the relative prestige and material rewards afforded by different spheres of participation, and shifting alliances between co-workers who encounter one another in the context of different types of practice. The two biographical accounts presented by James also suggest that affiliation with several communities of practice creates potential opportunities for vertical and horizontal mobility. Thus, when continued participation within one community of practice is threatened, for whatever reasons, it may be possible to shift personal identifications and professional participation into another sphere. James notes that, in recent years, academics in British universities have experienced the impact of new managerial strategies which have shifted and specified the definition, and quantitative measures, of their productivity. These developments are, in turn, a function of globalization, state educational policies and the marketization of British universities. She argues that these innovations have narrowed and constrained the opportunities of some old-timers, such as the two academics profiled, to continue participating in their favoured communities of academic practice, precipitating them to seek to negotiate lateral moves. Here, then, is another theme of both theoretical analysis and empirical research, that is, the impact of forces outside the control, or possibly even perception, of members of communities of practice on their on-going modes of participation. In fast-moving contemporary societies this often means that the learning trajectories of old-timers are not fixed or stable but are subject to ambiguity, insecurity and renegotiation.

From the outset, it was argued that communities of practice are not confined to work situations but may be found more widely. Vanessa Beck, in Chapter 12, explores these possibilities by asking whether the unemployed can form communities of practice. She examines this question within the specific historical setting of post-unification East Germany, following the collapse of the state socialist regime of the old German Democratic Republic. In a manner similar to James, she develops her analysis via biographical accounts of the lives of two of her research respondents, in this case two unemployed women. Both experience a sense of disruption and disturbance in their lives as a result of being made redundant and as a result of the disappearance of the collective moral values and practices associated with the socialist era. However, one reacts with positive coping responses that create a sense of stability and direction in her life, even if they do not necessarily yield a new job. The other, despite her efforts, is less successful in building a network of protective social relationships. This chapter, then, explores the effects of expulsion or exclusion from intense social networks. These include those found in the workplace among colleagues and the 'imagined community' (Anderson 1983) of the political and economic regime that was the German Democratic Republic. In addition, the chapter considers the circumstances that enable individuals to respond positively to the stresses of such circumstances. Here both individual resources of personal agency and social resources of family and friendship circles are relevant. Beck argues that network resources and personal agency go hand in hand, reinforcing one another.

In recent years the impact of new information and communication technologies (ICTs) on the conduct of communities of practice has become a subject of considerable interest within managerial and academic circles. A growing literature has addressed the possibility that communities of practice might be wholly or substantially maintained through channels such as e-mail, web cams, conference calls, mobile phones and the like. This is the subject of Chapter 13 on virtual communities of practice by Nick Jewson. These issues came to the fore during the 1990s, when access to virtual reality and cyberspace became affordable and ubiquitous, the same era in which theories of communities of practice were being developed. By the time Wenger *et al.* (2002: 113–38) published, these possibilities were the subject of serious consideration and merited a chapter on 'the challenge of distributed communities' in which face-to-face interaction was not the primary mode of connection among the members. A central concern has been whether the attenuated channels of sociability and sensory experience afforded by ICT are sufficient to sustain the levels of trust, involvement, commitment, sharing, reciprocity, mutuality and solidarity characteristic of effective communities of practice. Since it is often assumed virtual reality is the workplace of the future, the fear is that communities of practice may become increasingly superficial, stretched and fragile. Most commentators have suggested that overcoming these problems depends upon technical aspects of the design of ICT facilities and/or how participants conduct themselves online. Jewson argues that this approach is sociologically limited and focuses too narrowly on the intrinsic characteristics of the technology. He argues that an appreciation of the broader picture requires us to put virtual communities of practice into the context of overall changes in the spatial location of work. Two insights emerge from such a perspective. First, the emphasis on virtual communities of practice has overshadowed other changes in places of work – such as the rise of offices without personal spaces – that arguably increase rather than diminish the intense forms of sociability that foster communities of practice. Virtual working does not replace physical workplaces but rather supplements them. Secondly, virtual communications always take place in real times and places, such as at home, in a car or waiting for a plane. The real space/time contexts of virtual communities of practice vary widely and each places its own distinctive demands and limitations on participants. Commanding these diverse situations calls for members to develop 'technologies of the self' that shape their subjectivities around self-discipline, self-motivation and self-criticism. These are generic and transferable aspects of learning required for participation in communities of practice located in a decentred, fragmented and rapidly changing economic and social world.

In the concluding contribution to the book, Chapter 14, the editors assess the key strengths and weaknesses of the communities of practice model. In the light of this critique, they identify a series of themes and issues that call for further clarification or empirical research. They conclude that communities of practice are a rich, useful and potentially fruitful concept, but one which requires considerable further development, specification and illustration. Much remains to be done!

References

Anderson, B. (1983) *Imagined Communities: Reflections on the Origin and Spread of Nationalism*, New York: Verso.

Barton, D. and Hamilton, M. (2005) 'Literacy, reification and the dynamics of social interaction', in Barton, D. and Tusting, K. (eds) *Beyond Communities of Practice: Language, Power and Social Context*, Cambridge: Cambridge University Press, pp. 14–35.

Barton, D. and Tusting, K. (eds) (2005) *Beyond Communities of Practice: Language, Power and Social Context*, Cambridge: Cambridge University Press.

Billett, S. (2001) 'Learning through work: workplace affordances and individual engagement', *Journal of Workplace Learning*, 13 (5): 209–14.

Billett, S. (2006) 'Relational interdependence between social and individual agency in work and working life', *Mind, Culture and Activity*, 13 (1): 53–69.

Brown, J. S. and Duguid, P. (1991) 'Organizational learning and communities-of-practice: toward a unified view of working, learning, and innovation', *Organization Science*, 2 (1): 40–57.

Brown, J. S. and Duguid, P. (2001) 'Knowledge and organization: a social practice perspective', *Organization Science*, 12 (2): 198–213.

Butler, J. (1994) 'Gender as performance', *Radical Philosophy*, 67: 127–43.

Butler, J. (1995) 'Contingent foundations: feminism and the question of postmodernism', in Benhabib, S., Butler, J., Cornell. D. and Fraser, N. (eds) *Feminist Contentions: A Philosophical Exchange*, New York: Routledge, pp. 35–57.

Butler, J. (1997) *The Psychic Power of Life*, Stanford, CA: Stanford University Press.

Callon, M. (1986) 'Some elements in a sociology of translation: domestication of the scallops and fishermen of St Brieuc Bay', in Law, J. (ed.) *Power, Action and Belief*, London: Routledge.

Casey, C. (1995) *Work, Self and Society after Industrialism*, London: Routledge.

Creese, A. (2005) 'Mediating allegations of racism in a multiethnic London school: what speech communities and communities of practice tell us about discourse and power', in Barton, D. and Tusting, K. (eds) *Beyond Communities of Practice: Language, Power and Social Context*, Cambridge: Cambridge University Press, pp. 55–76.

Dewey, J. (1897) 'My pedagogic creed', *School Journal*, 54 (3): 77–80.

du Gay, P. (1996) *Consumption and Identity at Work*, London: Sage.

Easterby-Smith, M., Snell, R. and Gheradi, S. (1998) 'Organizational learning: diverging communities of practice', *Management Learning*, 29 (3): 259–72.

Edwards, R. and Nicoll, K. (2004) 'Mobilizing workplaces: actors, discipline and governmentality', *Studies in Continuing Education*, 26 (2): 159–73.

Elias, N. and Scotson, J. (1994) *The Established and the Outsiders* (rev. edn, first published 1965), London: Sage.

Engeström, Y. (2001) 'Expansive learning at work: toward an activity theoretical reconceptualisation', *Journal of Education and Work*, 14 (1): 133–56.

Foucault, M. (1983) 'The subject and power: afterward', in Dreyfus, H. and Rabinow, P. (eds) *Michel Foucault: Beyond Structuralism and Hermeneutics*, Chicago: University of Chicago Press, pp. 208–27.

Foucault, M. (1990a) *The History of Sexuality* I, *An Introduction*, New York: Vintage Books.

Foucault, M. (1990b) *The History of Sexuality* III, *The Care of the Self*, New York: Vintage Books.

Foucault, M. (1994) 'The subject and power', in J. Faubion (ed.) *Michel Foucault: Power*, pp. 326–48, New York: New Press.

Fox, S. (2000) 'Communities of practice, Foucault and actor-network theory', *Journal of Management Studies*, 37 (6): 853–67.

Freire, P. (1972) *Pedagogy of the Oppressed*. Harmondsworth: Penguin.

Gabriel, Y. (2003) 'Glass palaces and glass cages: organizations in times of flexible work, fragmented consumption and fragile selves', *Ephemera*, 3 (3): 166–84.

Garrick, J. and Usher, G. (2000) 'Flexible learning, contemporary work and enterprising selves', *Electronic Journal of Sociology* 5 (1): available at www.sociology.org/content/vol005.001/garrick-usher.html

Giddens, A. (1984) *The Constitution of Society*, Cambridge: Polity Press.

Hager, P. (2004) 'The conceptualization and measurement of learning at work', in Rainbird, H., Fuller, A. and Munro, A. (eds) *Workplace Learning in Context*, London: Routledge, pp. 242–58.

Harris, S. R. and Shelswell, N. (2005) 'Moving beyond communities of practice in adult basic education', in Barton, D. and Tusting, K. (eds) *Beyond Communities of Practice: Language, Power and Social Context*, Cambridge: Cambridge University Press.

Harrison, R., Reeve, F., Hanson, A. and Clarke, J. (2002) 'Introduction: perspectives on learning', in Harrison, R., Reeve, F., Hanson, A. and Clarke, J. (eds) *Supporting Lifelong Learning* I, London: Routledge.

Hodkinson, P. and Hodkinson, H. (2004) 'A Constructive Critique of Communities of Practice: Moving beyond Lave and Wenger', paper presented at OVAL Research Group, University of Technology, Sydney, 11 May.

Hodkinson, P., Hodkinson, H., Evans, K., Kersh, N., Fuller, A., Unwin, L, and Senker, P. (2004) 'The significance of individual biography in workplace learning', *Studies in the Education of Adults*, 36 (1): 6–24.

Holmes, J. and Meyerhoff, M. (1999) 'The community of practice: theories and methodologies in language and gender research', *Language in Society*, 28 (2): 173–83.

Illich, I. (1971) *De-schooling Society*, Harmondsworth: Penguin.

Kuhn, T. (1996) *The Structure of Scientific Revolutions*, 3rd edn, Chicago: University of Chicago Press.

Law, J. and Hassard, J. (eds) (1999) *Actor Network Theory and After*, Oxford: Blackwell.

Lave, J. (1998) *Cognition in Practice: Mind, Mathematics, and Culture in Everyday Life*, Cambridge: Cambridge University Press.

Lave, J. and Wenger, E. (1991) *Situated Learning: Legitimate Peripheral Participation*, Cambridge: Cambridge University Press.

Mutch, A. (2002) 'Actors and networks or agents and structures: towards a realist view of information systems', *Organization*, 9 (3): 477–96.

Myers, G. (2005) 'Communities of practice, risk, and Sellafield', in Barton, D. and Tusting, K. (eds) *Beyond Communities of Practice: Language, Power and Social Context*, Cambridge: Cambridge University Press.

Rock, F. (2005) '"I've picked some up from a colleague": language, sharing and communities of practice in an institutional setting', in Barton, D. and Tusting, K. (eds) *Beyond Communities of Practice: Language, Power and Social Context*, Cambridge: Cambridge University Press, pp. 77–104.

Rose, N. (1990) *Governing the Soul: The Shaping of the Private Self*, London: Routledge.

Rose, N. (1999) *Inventing Ourselves: Psychology, Power and Personhood*, Cambridge: Cambridge University Press.

Tusting, K. (2005) 'Language and power in communities of practice', in Barton, D. and Tusting, K. (eds) *Beyond Communities of Practice: Language, Power and Social Context*, Cambridge: Cambridge University Press, pp. 36–54.

Wenger, E. (1998) *Communities of Practice: Learning, Meaning and Identity*, Cambridge: Cambridge University Press.

Wenger, E., McDermott, R. and Snyder, W. M. (2002) *Cultivating Communities of Practice: A Guide to Managing Knowledge*, Boston, MA: Harvard Business School Press.

Young, M. F. D. (1998) *The Curriculum of the Future*, London: Falmer Press.

Zemblyas, M. (2006) 'Work-based learning, power and subjectivity: creating space for a Foucauldian research ethic', *Journal of Education and Work*, 19 (3): 291–303.

2 Critiquing theories of learning and communities of practice

Alison Fuller

Key themes in this chapter

- Received assumptions about learning
- Contrasting theories of and metaphors for learning
- Ideas underpinning communities of practice
- Dimensions for development
- Further questions

In the aftermath of the tsunami disaster of 2004 in South East Asia a radio journalist reporting from a devastated community in Sri Lanka interpreted the reopening of a school as the first sign of a return to 'normal life'. He observed: 'the children can start to learn again.' His comment was a stark reminder of the received assumptions that surround the concept of learning. First, in relation to space or place, learning is recognized (only) if it happens in a formal educational setting such as a school, college or university. Second, it is assumed that learning is dependent on the presence of a recognized (qualified) teacher. Third, it is believed that learning (always) involves a process of knowledge transmission from an expert (the teacher) to a novice (usually conceived of as a child or young adult). Fourth, learning is conceived as a 'product' to be acquired. The product takes the form of codified and stable knowledge, reified in textbooks and distributed to those in receipt of 'formal schooling'. Fifth, it is assumed that learning is essentially an individual matter. From a cognitive perspective, learning is associated with changes in 'mental state', which occur when the individual mind processes information. From a behaviourist perspective learning is associated with observable changes in a person's behaviour. In their analysis of approaches to learning, Beckett and Hager (2002) suggest that such assumptions can be clustered together as the 'standard paradigm' of learning. It was dissatisfaction with the tenets associated with this paradigm that underpinned Lave and Wenger's (1991) seminal book and which has made such an influential contribution to the emergence in recent years of an alternative theorization of learning or to what Beckett and Hager call 'the emerging paradigm'.

This chapter supports Lave and Wenger's view that conventional behavioural and cognitive theories of learning provide an inadequate understanding of learning and downplay the role of learning as an integral feature of growing up, living and working with others in-the-world. In particular, Lave and Wenger's focus on 'participation in social practice' as a condition for (all) learning provides a concept which enables learning to be studied in a wide range of social settings, including the workplace, domestic and recreational sites. To return to the journalist's remark, once participation is seen as an important, or in Lave and Wenger's terms *the* central condition for learning, it becomes ludicrous to imply that those returning school children have somehow been inhabiting a 'learning-free zone' during their enforced absence from school. The idea that learning occurs only in formal educational settings appears particularly perverse and fallacious in the context of the tsunami, when learning to adapt and cope with an entirely new set of circumstances, in which 'participation' was not optional, has been key to survival.

This chapter locates its discussion of learning and communities of practice primarily in the context of workplace learning. It has a number of aims, including:

1   To sketch out contrasting perspectives on learning and to indicate how a social theory has appeal for those interested in researching and understanding learning at work.
2   To outline the idea of community of practice proposed by Jean Lave and Etienne Wenger and to indicate the areas in which it is underdeveloped.
3   To identify some of the shortcomings in the concept of community of practice that have emerged from the findings of workplace learning researchers.
4   To suggest ways in which the concept needs to be developed to meet the challenges that have been posed.

The discussion is organized in two broad sections. The first introduces the main approaches to understanding learning and the ideas underpinning the notion of community of practice. The second identifies a range of themes which illustrate the extent to which the concept requires further analysis and elaboration. The conclusion discusses how the debate on communities of practice can be taken forward, particularly with regard to its empirical operationalization. Overall, the chapter argues that conceptualizing learning as a social practice provides a strong theoretical foundation from which to research learning in a variety of workplace settings. However, it also raises a number of questions which help expose the weaknesses in the notion of community of practice in relation to its application to contemporary workplaces.

Learning and communities of practice

It is not the intention of this chapter to provide a comprehensive or detailed review of learning theories, these can be found in textbooks (*inter alia* Leonard 2002; Mower and Klein 2001). Instead, the aim is to draw attention to the sorts of theoretical ideas which underpin the concept of community of practice and which increasingly inform analyses of informal and workplace learning. This shift has grown from dissatisfaction with the ability of more traditional theories such as cognitivism and behaviourism adequately to account for how people learn in formal and non-formal educational settings. In their recent review of learning theories Beckett and Hager (2002) make a broad distinction between theories which focus on learning as 'product' and as 'acquisition', and those which conceive learning as 'process' and as 'participation'. In the former approach knowledge is hierarchically structured, with complex ideas being built on basic foundations. This 'safe knowledge' is transmitted to the student through the mediation of qualified teachers who are subject specialists. As Beckett and Hager suggest, the metaphor of acquisition highlights the:

individual human mind steadily being stocked with ideas . . . The focus of learning as a product is on the stock of accumulated ideas that constitute a well furnished mind, the structure of those ideas, how various ideas relate to one another and so on.

(Beckett and Hager 2002: 97)

Such learning is seen as superior to tacit or 'informal' learning, as it is seen to be certain, more or less stable and readily articulated. In this latter regard, the learning can be assessed by examinations which test how much the individual candidate has acquired.

Lave and Wenger's theory of learning as participation in a community of practice provides a very different concept of learning. First, their theorization promotes the collective or group as the important unit of analysis rather than the individual. Individuals are important in so far as they learn by being in social relation to others. For Lave and Wenger it is the relational network, associated in the case of workplace learning with the social relations of production, which is key to understanding learning and not the before, during and after (learning) states of individual minds. Second, their analysis foregrounds the notion of social practice. People learn through their co-participation in the shared practices of the 'community' or the 'lived-in world'. Individuals are conceived as constituting and as constituted by the social world and not as separate beings who determine when they move in and out of the practice arena. Third, for Lave and Wenger the question of *what* is learned by participants is answered in terms of identity formation (rather than the acquisition of knowledge products). People learn (through participation) to become full members of, or 'knowledgeable practitioners' in, the relevant community(s) of practice. Fourth, although Lave and Wenger's approach promotes the concepts of novice and expert, there is no expectation or inevitability that the 'expert' should be a qualified or recognized teacher. The novice is not conceived as a (passive) recipient of codified knowledge made available through formal instruction; rather the 'curriculum' is available to newcomers through their increasing participation (with others) in the relevant and inevitably structured social practices (activities, tasks, habits) of the community. Making the connection between social practice and an explicit theorization of learning is one of Lave and Wenger's main achievements and helps to distinguish them from other social practice theorists such as Bourdieu (e.g. 1977), whose notion of social space (field) does not include an explicit notion of learning.

Overall, the concept of community of practice invites a focus on learning as a collective, relational and, in short, a social process. This perspective is at odds with traditional theories of learning preoccupied either with the mind and the ways in which learning results in changed mental states or with behaviour and how changes in behaviour can be brought about through the formula of stimulus–response. From the 'standard' viewpoint on learning, the individual is conceived as separate from the world and as able to acquire (context-free) knowledge through instruction by a teacher. This position is based on dualistic distinctions between mind and body, and person and world, in which learning is a question of learning about the world. Jean Lave succinctly states her alternative position: 'theories of situated everyday practice insist that persons acting and the social world of activity cannot be separated' (1993: 5).

Communities of practice: an underdeveloped concept

It is important to remember that the central purpose of Lave and Wenger's (1991) monograph was to propose a new 'situated' theorization of learning, the main tenets of which have been outlined in the introductory chapter to this book. Whilst the notion of community of practice is an integral component of this theory, Lave and Wenger acknowledge that it is undeveloped and highlight areas for further elaboration:

> The concept of 'community of practice' is left largely as an intuitive notion, which serves a purpose here but which requires a more rigorous treatment. In particular, unequal relations of power must be included more systematically in our analysis . . . It would be useful to understand better how these relations generate characteristically interstitial communities of practice and truncate possibilities for identities of mastery.
>
> (Lave and Wenger 1991: 42)

Lave and Wenger acknowledge that 'practice' is socially, historically and politically organized. Participation in communities of practice give rise to the opportunity for people to become 'knowledgeable practitioners' through their co-participation but this outcome is not inevitable. Indeed, Lave and Wenger appear to recognize that communities of practice can create conditions which inhibit, or give rise to alternative learning outcomes.

> Conditions that place newcomers in deeply adversarial relations with masters, bosses, or managers; in exhausting over-involvement in work; or in involuntary servitude rather than participation distort, partially or completely the prospects for learning in practice.
>
> (Lave and Wenger 1991: 64)

Commentators have often failed to notice Lave and Wenger's acknowledgement that less than benign effects can be associated with communities of practice, particularly as the concept is applied to the workplace. There are at least two reasons why this part of their analysis has been overlooked. First, although such insights are located in the book's theoretical discussion they are not followed through in the examples. These are used to illustrate the authors' analysis of learning as a social process which occurs through legitimate peripheral participation in a community of practice. With the exception of the 'meat cutters', counter-examples to show how the 'centripetal' movement of the legitimate peripheral participant can be halted, impeded or thrown off track are not included. Second, the use of the term 'community' is far from neutral, as it carries connotations of harmony and togetherness (see Jewson elsewhere in this volume). With regard to the workplace, the gloss of 'community' is highly questionable, as it implies that all workers, work groups and managers share common interests. This is a perspective which the history of industrial disputes and conflicts as well as Marxist and neo-Marxist theorizations of workplace relations would clearly contradict (Lloyd and Payne 2004).

In addition, the lack of attention Lave and Wenger devote to defining communities of practice has, on the one hand, given others the latitude to use the concept flexibly. On the other, it has made it difficult to operationalize in any sort of consistent fashion.

How then is the concept defined by Lave and Wenger? Their primary lens for defining a community of practice is its 'temporal delineation':

> It is possible to delineate the community that is the site of a learning process by analyzing the reproduction cycles of the communities that seem to be involved and their relations.
>
> (Lave and Wenger 1991: 98)

The focus on the temporal dimension coheres with the concept of the legitimate peripheral participant's learning journey, which culminates in the displacement of 'old-timers'. Consequently, 'communities of practice have histories and developmental cycles, and reproduce themselves in such a way that the transformation of newcomers becomes remarkably integral to the practice' (Lave and Wenger 1991: 98).

The other lens with which community of practice can be delineated is through a focus on its socio-spatial dimension. For Lave and Wenger, this relates to their primary focus on the relational networks in which learning occurs. A difficulty with this approach lies not so much in the underpinning theorization of learning as in its operationalization. For researchers who adopt a social practice perspective on learning, at what point (if any) should or can the socio-spatial boundaries be drawn for analysing the learning process? Lave and Wenger implicitly acknowledge the subtlety and subjectivity that such decisions will involve:

> Nor does the term community imply necessarily co-presence, a well-defined identifiable group, or socially visible boundaries. It does imply participation in an activity system about which participants share understandings concerning what they are doing and what that means in their lives and for their communities.
>
> (Lave and Wenger 1991: 98)

Wenger (1998) has attempted to develop his and Lave's earlier thinking. He takes the view that communities of practice are instantly recognizable but argues that there are a range of indicators (e.g. 'shared ways of engaging in doing things together; local lore, shared stories, inside jokes, knowing laughter; specific tools, representations and other artefacts') which provide evidence of their existence (1998: 124–5). These indicators revolve around the nature and quality of social relations and interaction and their links to practice and can be categorized in terms of three dimensions (Wenger 1998: 72ff):

1   Mutual engagement.
2   A joint enterprise.
3   A shared repertoire.

For Wenger, then, the difference between a community of practice and any social network is that social relations are formed, negotiated and sustained around the activity that has brought people together. The next section of the chapter identifies and outlines some of the main issues which have been raised in response to Lave and Wenger's (1991) and Wenger's (1998) community of practice concept. These have emerged largely as a consequence of the research into workplace learning that followed their original contribution.

Questioning learning as participation in communities of practice

The six themes identified and discussed below emanate from researchers who are interested in theorizing and analysing workplace learning. They are sympathetic to Lave and Wenger's social theorization of learning and to aspects of the concept of community of practice, but on the basis of empirical work in contemporary work organizations have identified weaknesses and areas for development.

Adequacy of 'learning as participation'

The first section of this chapter distinguished between two broad metaphors for learning. The first, learning as acquisition, was associated with the standard paradigm of learning, whilst the second, learning as participation, was associated with an emerging social paradigm of learning. Lave and Wenger's work has been central to shifting the focus from acquisition to participation, particularly among workplace learning researchers. However, Hager (2005) argues that the two approaches are not mutually exclusive and that the participation metaphor can be seen as including notions of learning as both process and product:

> This is because while participation itself is a process, the learner belongs more and more to the community of practice by acquiring the right characteristics (products of learning).
>
> (Hager 2005: 23)

Hager goes on to suggest that there are three main limitations to Lave and Wenger's concept of participation. First, it overlooks the importance of the process of 'construction' in the social world in which learning, the self and the world are mutually constituted and reconstituted. Second, he points out that there is something inherently conservative about the notion of participation, in that it aligns with continuity and reproduction rather than discontinuity and transformation. Hence, in Lave and Wenger's terms, a successful path from legitimate to full participation typically appears to occur with minimal changes to practice or social relations. In an early commentary on Lave and Wenger's perspective, Seely Brown and Duguid (1991) observed that 'they [legitimate peripheral participants] acquire that particular community's subjective viewpoint and learn to speak its language. In short, they are enculturated'. Finally, Hager, in similarity with Hodkinson and Hodkinson (2004), objects to the idea that 'participation' (or for that matter any other factor) can provide an explanation for learning that has universal applicability.

Edwards (2005) is also concerned about the use of the learning as participation perspective in research into workplace learning. Although there is not the space in this chapter to outline her arguments in full, she makes the important point that 'participation', on its own, fails to account for how new learning comes about and how new knowledge is produced. In short, she suggests that the learning as participation approach has become associated with a wholly 'non-cognitive' approach to understanding learning. This is at odds with the roots of the perspective in Vygotskyan cultural psychology. As Edwards reminds us, Lave, at least in her earlier work (1988), was strongly concerned with cognition.

Defining communities of practice

In their critique of communities of practice Hodkinson and Hodkinson (2004) address the ambiguity surrounding the socio-spatial delineation of the concept. In essence they suggest that there are two interpretations of the idea, one broad and one narrow, and that there are strengths and weaknesses in adopting either. The broad perspective foregrounds the notions of participation, belonging and social relations: 'we need to belong to learn, and what it is that we belong to, can be called a community of practice' (2004: 8). The narrower view, as exemplified in the vignettes included in Lave and Wenger's book, focuses on the learning that takes place in small 'tight-knit' groups. Hodkinson and Hodkinson find some value in both the broad and narrower conceptions. A strength of the former is its elasticity and ability, rather like a Russian doll, to include within its compass smaller manifestations of communities of practice. Hence an individual can simultaneously belong to a continuum of communities starting small and becoming progressively larger. For example, a hairdresser belongs to a tightly drawn community which consists only of the hairdressers in a particular salon; as well to ones which (growing progressively wider) consist of all the salon's employees; all hairdressers practising in a particular category of salons (e.g. men's barbers or 'up-market, creative'); all people who work in 'customer-facing' roles, and so on.

A strength of the narrower conception is in the attention it draws to the small community of practice, such as the hairdressing salon, which has everyday relevance for particular groups. To illustrate this point, Hodkinson and Hodkinson use the example of schoolteachers, whose primary (tight-knit) community of practice is the subject departments/teams within which they work. The authors conclude that both narrow and broad versions are helpful but suggest that they should be distinguished by different terminology, with the broader version captured as 'situated learning or learning as social participation' and only the narrower version as communities of practice (2004: 14).

Whilst Hodkinson and Hodkinson's analysis provides an approach to delineating community of practice, it does not completely solve what is probably an intractable problem in the sense that the concept, either in its broader or in its narrower versions, still essentially involves a 'container notion' of context. The researcher is always left with making decisions about what is inside or outside the container as well as how large it should be. Lave has addressed this issue to some extent by indicating that context is treated differently in different theoretical orientations, and that the choice of theoretical perspective can guide decisions about delineating context. She uses the examples of 'activity theory' and 'interactionism' to illustrate her argument. For proponents of activity theory, 'the central theoretical relation is historically constituted between persons engaged in socioculturally constructed activity and the world with which they are engaged' (1993: 17). For proponents of interactionism, the 'central theoretical tradition is the intersubjective relation among coparticipants' (1993: 17). Their narrow delineation of context follows from their focus on interaction as the context of activity. Activity theory with its focus on the historical dimension produces a broader delineation of what constitutes context. However, neither of the two orientations is definitive about where the boundaries should be drawn and neither has much to say about the spatial dimension of where the boundaries might fall. Elmholdt's reminder that there is a distinction between 'situation' and 'situatedness' is helpful when thinking about the ways in which context can be delineated. He points out:

The understanding of learning as situated social practice exceeds the immediate situation. Situation refers to the surface of what goes on right here and now, whereas situatedness emphasizes how the present situation is related within a social and historical context.

(Elmholdt 2004: 82)

Transforming communities of practice

The chapter has already indicated that the ability of communities of practice to transform is inadequately dealt with by Lave and Wenger. One of the reasons why this issue requires further attention relates to the connotations of harmony and stability, which are associated with community (of practice), but which cannot be taken for granted. Contemporary industrial workplaces are dynamic and often conflictual environments, where reorganizations, take-overs and buy-outs are relatively common occurrences. Eraut (2002) draws on empirical findings on workplace learning to dismiss the concept of communities of practice as empirically unhelpful in that the conditions of stability and predictable temporal cycles of reproduction based on the newcomer to old-timer trajectory are rarely in place in the contemporary context of advanced industrial economies.

Once then the political and economic realities of contemporary organizations are foregrounded, the use of the term 'community of practice' appears to be a less accurate or helpful descriptor of the phenomenon which is being studied. Moreover if, paradoxically, change is a constant feature of many 'situations' then the question of how new knowledge is created and 'acquired' can be viewed as an (inevitable) effect of settings-in-flux.

Engeström (e.g. 2001) has developed the theory of expansive learning to explain how organizational transformation can occur. He starts from an acknowledgement that the community of practice or what he prefers to term the activity system is the proper unit of analysis. However, he is concerned that the type of learning implied by the participation metaphor will not bring about organizational change or new learning because it is associated too strongly with 'first order' learning types such as imitation and socialization (1994). In contrast, learning which focuses on the solving of emerging 'contradictions' requires 'second order' investigative learning. Where this learning involves collective questioning of how the problem can be conceptualized, and a collaborative approach to finding a novel solution, the associated transformation provides evidence that a 'third order' expansive learning process has taken place. Engeström (2004) uses the example of inter-professional collaborations in the care sector to illustrate how expansive learning can bring about system-level changes in patient care.

Challenging the concepts of novice–expert

Fuller and Unwin (2004) have argued that the concepts of novice and expert are not stable or uniform concepts and that the pedagogy they imply cannot simply be characterized as one-way transmission. In contrast to the accounts given by Lave and Wenger, they have found that not all novices are the same and not all experts are the same. For example, they found that apprentices were considerably more expert in some tasks (e.g. activities associated with information technology) than their older and more experienced colleagues. In order to understand this finding, Fuller and Unwin researched the backgrounds of the participants in their study and found a wide variety of differences in the richness and extent of their individual 'learning territories' (Fuller and Unwin 2004, 2005). The learning territory consists of a range of regions in which the individual has had the opportunity to learn and gain expertise. This could include those relating to home life and hobbies as well as prior educational experiences. In addition, and in relation to their work with Hodkinson and others, they found that the learning and work dispositions of their subjects differed and that this had an effect on the extent to which they identified and engaged in opportunities to learn at work (Fuller *et al.* 2005; Hodkinson *et al.* 2004).

Different types of trajectory

Lave and Wenger have been criticized for focusing only on one kind of participation – that experienced by legitimate peripheral participants engaged on an 'inbound' journey from newcomer to old-timer in a community of practice. This type of trajectory is inadequate to explain the different patterns of participation associated with individuals, groups and workplaces. Wenger (1998: 154) recognized this limitation in his later work when he identified five trajectories of participation:

1 *Inbound* trajectory. Newcomers are joining the community with the prospect of becoming full participants in its practice.
2 *Peripheral.* By choice or by necessity, some trajectories never lead to full participation.
3 *Insider.* The formation of an identity does not end with full membership.
4 *Boundary.* Some trajectories find their value in spanning boundaries and linking communities of practice.
5 *Outbound.* Some trajectories lead out of a community, as when children grow up.

In recognizing the limitations of a single form of participation (learning), Wenger observes, 'we go through a succession of forms of participation our identities form trajectories, both within and across communities of practice' (1998: 154).

However, despite moving the debate on, Wenger (1998) still foregrounds the importance of participation (of whichever type) in and in relation to communities of practice. Dreier (1999) approaches the issue from a different perspective. He focuses on the notion of 'trajectory' as the organizing and explanatory principle of individual learning and identity formation. As individuals develop a trajectory that will enable them to realize their personal goals they find themselves operating in (and learning through their participation in) 'cross-contextual structures of social practice'. This perspective has been explored empirically by Nielsen (1997) in his study of students attending an academy of music. He used the concept of trajectories of participation to explain students' different experiences and perceptions in terms of their individual backgrounds and changing personal and career aspirations. The different trajectories developed by students helped to explain their perceptions and contextualized the different ways in which they engaged in and identified learning opportunities as part of an on-going process of identity formation. Fuller *et al.* (2005) develop this theme when they highlight the importance of researching individuals' backgrounds and dispositions:

> equally important is what the worker brings to that community, from outside . . .

prior learning, including education, has helped construct the whole person who arrives. This embodied person learns to belong in their new setting, adapting, developing and modifying their whole person in that process.

(Fuller *et al.* 2005: 66)

Learning across communities of practice

Österlund (1996) argues that the notion of learning as participation in communities of practice places too much emphasis on the learning that takes place 'inside the community' and does not reflect the importance of the learning that takes place through participation in multiple social spaces and in the process of crossing between contexts. He draws on evidence of a study of salespeople to illustrate his argument and concludes:

> in order to understand what salespeople's learning at work involves it is essential to study how salespeople's social relations in multiple contexts/communities change over time . . . First, salespeople adapt and elaborate their participation in relation to specific contexts of action. Second, salespeople improve their ability to make use of their environment's cross-contextual structures and establish cross-contextual connections, barriers, and intersections. Third, salespeople develop identities and generalized standpoints as they gain experience in their job.
>
> (Österlund 1996: 151)

In some similarity, Fuller and Unwin (2003) found that apprentices who had the opportunity to participate in multiple settings and networks of social relations enjoyed a more 'expansive' experience than their peers who were confined to a single site. In particular, they found that those whose apprenticeship included the opportunity to participate in formal educational institutions as well as in different departments at work were afforded the most chances to make connections between different types of learning and experience. A wider literature examining the relevance of 'boundary crossing' for individual and collective learning and the implications for the organization of work and organizational performance is growing (see, *inter alia*, Engeström 2004, Nonaka and Takeuchi 1995).

Conclusions and taking the debate forward

The critiques of communities of practice outlined above reflect the starting points and interests of researchers. Some are more interested in theorizing and researching how the individual learns as 'person-in-world', some are more interested in organizational or group learning, where the individual is left relatively untheorized. However, the bulk of the attention devoted to communities of practice stems from a primary interest in 'learning' irrespective of whether this interest revolves more around individual or organizational (learning) concerns. There are also related differences in how commentators conceive the importance and scope of context. Hence Engeström and Lave and Wenger are most interested in the relevance of the historical and temporal dimension of communities of practice to explaining learning. Others, including Hodkinson and Hodkinson, Dreier and Österlund, seem more interested in how the individual learns through participation in social practice, or through the socio-spatial dimension of context. However, what has tended to be missing from debates on the workplace as a community of practice is an hierarchical dimension to what constitutes the relevant context for research and analysis. By this I mean that context can be seen as a series of interdependent levels consisting of the unit, organizational, sectoral and wider social, economic and political dimensions, which all influence the shape and character of the workplace as a learning environment. As the chapter pointed out earlier, Lave and Wenger hint that the wider levels are important but do not elaborate.

With regard to delineating the phenomenon for research, then, it seems that the debate about unit of analysis needs to move beyond deciding between the individual or the collective to identifying and researching a wider range of contextual dimensions. The evidence base on workplace learning would be strengthened by more studies which attempt to incorporate a multi-level conception of context into their design. This would open up opportunities to first map and then theorize the relationships between the diverse factors that influence the extent and nature of learning opportunities available to different groups of workers in different settings. This type of approach is starting to gain ground among interdisciplinary groups of researchers (Rainbird *et al.* 2004) and in current research which is bringing together sociological perspectives from the organization of work, management perspectives on organizational performance and educational perspectives on workplace learning (http://learningaswork.cardiff.ac.uk/). This research indicates that the notion of context requires analysing on a range of levels, including the micro (unit or department), meso (organization) and macro (sectoral and wider levels) (Unwin *et al.* 2007). Moreover, it is also important to take up the challenge, identified but not addressed by Lave and Wenger (1991), critically to explore the meanings of community of practice in the sorts of conflictual social settings which characterize many contemporary work organizations.

Key questions to consider

1   To what extent is community of practice a meaningful unit of analysis in workplace learning research?
2   What meanings does the notion of community of practice have to employees at different levels and in different types of workplaces?
3   In what ways can the concept of 'community of practice' be operationalized in workplace learning research?
4   To what extent can organization theories (as well as learning theories) shed light on the concept of community of practice?

References

Beckett, D. and Hager, P. (2002) *Life, Work and Learning: Practice in Postmodernity*, London: Routledge.

Bourdieu, P. (1977) *Outline of a Theory of Practice*, Cambridge: Cambridge University Press.

Dreier, O. (1999) 'Personal trajectories of participation across contexts of social practice', *Outlines, Critical Social Studies*, 1: 5–32.

Edwards, A. (2005) 'Let's get beyond community and practice: the many meanings of learning by participating', *Curriculum Journal*, 16 (1): 49–65.

Elmholdt, C. (2004) *Landscapes of Learning in ICT Workplaces: Learning as an Aspect of Change in Social Practice*, Aarhus: Psykologisk Institut, Aarhus Universitet, Denmark.

Engeström, Y. (1994) *Training for Change: New Approach to Instruction and Learning in Working Life*, Geneva: International Labour Office.

Engeström, Y. (2001) 'Expansive learning at work: toward an activity theoretical reconceptualization', *Journal of Education and Work*, 14 (1): 133–55.

Engeström, Y. (2004) 'The new generation of expertise: seven theses', in Rainbird, H., Fuller, A. and Munro, A. (eds) *Workplace Learning in Context*, London: Routledge.

Eraut, M. (2002) 'Conceptual Analysis and Research Questions: Do the Concepts of "Learning Community" and "Community of Practice" provide Added Value?' Paper presented at the annual meeting of the American Educational Research Association, New Orleans, LA, 1–5 April.

Fuller, A. and Unwin, L. (2003) 'Learning as apprentices in the contemporary UK workplace: creating and managing expansive and restrictive participation', *Journal of Education and Work*, 16 (4): 407–26.

Fuller, A. and Unwin, L. (2004) 'Young people as teachers and learners in the workplace: challenging the novice–expert dichotomy', *International Journal of Training and Development*, 8 (1): 31–41.

Fuller, A. and Unwin, L. (2005) 'Older and wiser? Workplace learning from the perspective of experienced employees', *International Journal of Lifelong Education*, 24 (1): 1–19.

Fuller, A., Hodkinson, H., Hodkinson, P. and Unwin, L. (2005) 'Learning as peripheral participation in communities of practice: a reassessment of key concepts in workplace learning', *British Educational Research Journal*, 31 (1): 49–68.

Hager, P. (2005) 'Current theories of workplace learning: a critical assessment', in Bascia, N., Cumming, A., Dannow, A., Leithwood, K. and Livingstone, D. (eds) *International Handbook of Education Policy*, Dordrecht, Boston MA and London: Kluwer.

Hodkinson, P. and Hodkinson, H. (2004) 'A Constructive Critique of Communities of Practice: Moving beyond Lave and Wenger', paper presented at OVAL Research Group, University of Technology, Sydney, 11 May.

Hodkinson, P., Hodkinson, H., Evans, K., Kersh, N., Fuller, A., Unwin, L. and Senker, P. (2004) 'The significance of individual biography in workplace learning', *Studies in the Education of Adults*, 36 (1): 6–24.

Lave, J. (1988) *Cognition in Practice: Mind, Mathematics, and Culture in Everyday Life*, Cambridge: Cambridge University Press.

Lave, J. (1993) 'The practice of learning', in S. Chaiklin and J. Lave, *Understanding Practice: Perspectives on Activity and Context*, Cambridge: Cambridge University Press.

Lave, J. and Wenger, E. (1991) *Situated Learning: Legitimate Peripheral Participation*, Cambridge: Cambridge University Press.

Leonard, D. C. (2002) *Learning Theories A to Z*, Westport, CT: Oryx Press.

Lloyd, C. and Payne, J. (2004) 'The political economy of skill: a theoretical approach to developing a high skills strategy in the UK', in C. Warhurst, I. Grugulis and E. Keep (eds) *The Skills that Matter*, Basingstoke: Palgrave Macmillan, pp. 207–24.

Mower, R. and Klein, S. (eds) (2001) *Handbook of Contemporary Learning Theories*, Mahwah, NJ: Erlbaum.

Nielsen, K. (1997) 'Musical apprenticeship: trajectories of participation at the Academy of Music', *Journal of Nordik Educational Research*, 17 (3): 160–8.

Nonaka, I. and Takeuchi, H. (1995) *The Knowledge-creating Company: How Japanese Companies create the Dynamics of Innovation*, Oxford and New York: Oxford University Press.

Österlund, C. (1996) *Learning across Contexts: A Field Study of Salespeople's Learning at Work*, Aarhus: Psykologisk Institute, Aarhus Universitet, Denmark.

Rainbird, H., Fuller, A. and Munro, A. (eds) (2004) *Workplace Learning in Context*, London: Routledge.

Seely Brown, J. and Duguid, P. (1991) 'Organizational learning and communities-of-practice: toward a unified view of working, learning and innovation', *Organization Science*, 2 (1): 50–7.

Unwin, L., Felstead, A., Fuller, A., Lee, T., Butler, P. and Ashton, D. (2007) 'Worlds within worlds: the relationship between context and pedagogy in the workplace', in Nijhof, W. J. and Nieuwenhuis, L. F. M. (eds) *The Learning Potential of the Workplace*, Rotterdam: Sense Publishers.

Wenger, E. (1998) *Communities of Practice: Learning, Meaning and Identity*, Cambridge: Cambridge University Press.

3 Lost in translation: communities of practice

The journey from academic model to practitioner tool

Jason Hughes

Key themes in this chapter

- The conceptual development of the concepts of legitimate peripheral participation and communities of practice
- The tensions between empirical and rational components of the model
- Applications of the model within the workplace
- Conceptual ambiguities in the communities of practice model
- Communities of practice as an analytical device and a consultancy tool

This chapter investigates the conceptual development of the community of practice model, from its origins in debates surrounding learning theory to its application, and subsequent transformation, by workplace practitioners. The chapter begins by identifying the community of practice model as related to the quest for a fundamentally social and relational perspective on learning. Here the genesis of the concept as a response to individual-centred, nominalist theories of learning is briefly explored. The chapter centrally focuses on Lave and Wenger's (1991) text, and commences with a consideration of the authors' aims and intentions in developing their distinctive theorization of learning. In relation to this analysis, the chapter considers the extent to which the community of practice model is intended as a theory of how learning *ought to be* or whether it is more a model of how learning *actually is*. The discussion critically examines certain important differences between the theory as it is espoused at an abstract level, on the one hand, and how it is used in relation to concrete cases of apprenticeship, on the other. The chapter argues that there are problems concerning the status of evidence in Lave and Wenger's work, and in the relationship between the empirical and rational components of their approach.

The chapter examines the application of the communities of practice concept by workplace practitioners and considers the extent to which the concept has been influenced by demands from practitioners for theoretical models which have utility to those involved in human resource development and management consultancy interventions. It is suggested that, through its application, the model has become transformed in some important respects such that it may be in danger of losing its analytical and critical purpose, its theoretical centre, and is at risk of being 'hi-jacked' for short-term commercial interests.

The intellectual foundations of the communities of practice model

As has been discussed in the previous chapter and the introduction, the communities of practice model has its origins in a growing dissatisfaction with the 'standard paradigm' of learning (Beckett and Hager 2002). Within this paradigm, 'the individual' is characteristically posited as the primary unit of analysis, and the notion of learning as centrally involving a process of *acquisition* is centrally promoted. The work of Lave and Wenger (1991) can be understood as part of a more general intellectual movement, counter to this paradigm, to develop a properly social understanding of learning; a movement which would also include the work of writers such as Engeström (1987), Marsick and Watkins (1990), Nicolini and Meznar (1995) and Gherardi *et al.* (1998). While, for some time, theorists have attempted to take account of the social dimensions of learning (see, for example, Mead 1934; Bandura 1977; Vygotsky 1978), the work of Lave and Wenger marks a more fundamental break from the standard paradigm by proposing that learning *consists of* social participation – of the whole person in the lived-in world. That is to say, Lave and Wenger wish to forward a reorientation of the primary theoretical object of learning: from the notion of learning as a 'product' to be 'acquired' by an individual (albeit in a social 'context'), to the conceptualization of learning as itself primarily social – as 'participation' within communities of practice. In this sense, human activity and shifting social relationships are not so much what contextualize learning as the stuff of learning itself.

Central concepts and their primary aims

A full introduction to the communities of practice model has been provided in the opening chapters of this book. However, it is worth reviewing Lave and Wenger's key conceptual schema. Essentially, they posit three central concepts: (1) situated learning (the umbrella concept of learning); legitimate peripheral participation (the form that situated learning takes); and (3) communities of practice (the locus or site of learning). The concept of situated learning expresses Lave and Wenger's reworking of a term that had come to gain some currency at the time of their writing (particularly in relation to the study of apprenticeship as both a model for, and site of, learning). Lave and Wenger define their concept of 'situatedness' in direct opposition to simplistic readings of the term. They are keen to stress that situatedness is not simply an 'empirical attribute' expressive of the indexicality of any given activity, as it refers primarily to 'activity in and with the world' (1991: 33). As their arguments unfold, however, the term 'situated' becomes almost redundant because, they propose, it would be impossible for an activity not to be 'situated', since activity always implies individuals in the plural, it always implies human social relationships. Thus a primary aim of Lave and Wenger's discussion of situatedness is to stress that learning and knowledge can never be 'decontextualized'. Even the most abstract representations of knowledge – say, for example, 'general knowledge' or 'trivia' – are essentially meaningless without application and situation in the lives of people who make such knowledge possible (1991: 34).

These guiding insights concerning 'situatedness' in turn undergird the centre-stage concept of Lave and Wenger's work, legitimate peripheral participation, with the cognate concept of communities of practice left relatively underdeveloped and ambiguous. In the concept of legitimate peripheral participation Lave and Wenger sought to avoid the reification of learning as somehow an independent process ontologically distinct from activity, and to use it to act as a 'descriptor of engagement in social practice that entails learning as an integral component' (1991: 35). The concept of legitimate peripheral participation formed the cornerstone of Lave and Wenger's attempt to develop an approach to learning which, they hoped, could more adequately encapsulate the kinds of learning that they had encountered in their work on approaches to technological development, craft apprenticeship, intelligent tutoring, and cybernetics. Attention to such learning in and of itself highlighted some of the key problems of the standard paradigm of learning and, by connection, its exemplar – formal education in schools. However, while the focus on legitimate peripheral participation did indeed bring into sharp relief the paucity of the 'teacher/learner dyad' as a model of learning, Lave and Wenger's intention was explicitly not to attribute the concept a 'prescriptive value' or to propose techniques for 'implementing' or 'operationalizing' it as an 'educational form' or 'pedagogical strategy' (1991: 41–2). In short, therefore, Lave and Wenger's primary aim was not to construct a treatise on how learning *ought to be* but, rather, to develop an approach which could help reveal learning as it *actually is*.

Between theory and practice

While Lave and Wenger are clear as to their aims and intentions in developing their approach to learning, questions remain as to the extent to which these are consonant with the analysis in the (1991) text, their later work, and subsequent applications of their approach by others. Their proposed reorientation towards a properly situated, social and contextualized approach to learning demands a substantial reorientation in how to think about, articulate and theorize learning, one which has broad-ranging implications for the practice of researching and writing of academics themselves. In particular, their arguments relating to abstraction/ generalization and their stress on the embeddedness of learning in the lived-in world raise questions about the status of theory, abstraction and the treatment of evidence, including that of their own work. As Lave and Wenger state, the dilemma can be expressed thus: 'How can we purport to be working out a *theoretical conception* of learning without, in fact, engaging in just the project of abstraction rejected above?' (1991: 38). Phrased in another way, it can be expressed as the extent to which there is an inherent tension between the medium and message of their approach: on the one hand they argue for a consideration always of 'context', of 'situatedness', of 'activity', of 'application', and, on the other, their endeavour has involved the formulation of a highly abstract and ostensibly 'decontextualized' theorization of learning.

Lave and Wenger's arguments in response to this dilemma draw much from the work of Marx. They argue that it is important to move away from conceiving of 'abstract' and 'concrete', 'general' and 'particular', 'theories of the world' and 'the world itself' as 'dualisms', as binary oppositions. *A la* Marx, they suggest that these are best conceived not so much as competing poles of interest, but as different points of departure from which to 'ascend (from both the particular and the abstract) to the concrete' (1991: 38). Legitimate peripheral participation, they propose, constitutes an 'analytical perspective' which is more than a mere 'distillation of apprenticeship'; it is a concept which should provide purchase on any 'educational form' (1991: 38). While Lave and Wenger are right to challenge stale dichotomies between 'abstract' and 'concrete' and 'general' and 'particular', a number of key concerns remain. Positioning their approach as 'analytical' effectively sidesteps, but by no means obviates, important questions concerning the relationship between theory and research in their work or, more precisely, the relationship between the empirical and rational components of their analytical perspective, particularly the degree of congruence between these. It is clear that Lave and Wenger's perspective is intended to offer more than a distillation of apprenticeship, however, the question remains as to whether their theoretical conception of learning is something that *emerges from* their research into apprenticeship or is more something that is *projected on to* concrete cases of apprenticeship. While their position is somewhat equivocal on this point, the overriding treatment of apprenticeship is not so much as an empirical testing ground for their conceptual schema as its exemplar to demonstrate the insights it can reveal. This in turn raises further questions regarding the status of evidence in their work: whether the enterprise of using their analytical approach to explore different cases of learning is solely to demonstrate its utility or whether, indeed, this enterprise also involves exploring the object adequacy of their theoretical conception of learning. Put another way, this question concerns the extent to which theory is relatively autonomous from research in the work of Lave and Wenger or, to use their language, whether their theoretical conception of learning is, in the final analysis, treated as 'context-independent'.

Lave and Wenger's position oscillates between, on the one hand, suggesting that their conceptual schema constitutes a kind of 'lens' that can be applied, independent of context, and, on the other, positing general theoretical conceptions of learning predicated on highly context-bound observations from a narrow empirical base. To provide an example, it is worth quoting from their (1991: 108) text:

> In a community of practice, there are no special forms of discourse aimed at apprentices or crucial to their centripetal movement towards full participation that correspond to the marked genres of the question–answer–evaluation format of classroom teaching, or the lecturing of college professors or midwife-training course instructors.

In this short extract, Lave and Wenger stylistically render communities of practice as standing in opposition to formal/conventional modes of education, but doing so is problematic in a number of respects. Immediately this practice raises the question of whether the absence of, say, a 'question–answer–evaluation' format is characteristic only of the few concrete cases of apprenticeship examined by Lave and Wenger. Indeed, it appears that they are suggesting that an absence of this format is what *defines* a community of practice. Whether or not this is the case, the statement does not square easily with discussions in other parts of the text where they suggest that all educational modes are communities of practice, albeit that some offer better opportunities for centripetal progression than others (see, for example, the discussion of schools, 1991: 39–40). Moreover, the above passage also serves to highlight that while Lave and Wenger start out by expressing concern with how learning actually is – an interest in developing a more adequate academic model of learning – the analysis that follows from this starting point seems, at times, to be more concerned with prescribing how learning *should* be. The same can be said of their concept of legitimate peripheral participation. For example, they write:

> Conditions that place newcomers in deeply adversarial relations with masters, bosses, or managers; in exhausting overinvolvement in work; or involuntary

servitude *rather than* participation distort, partially or completely, the prospects for learning in practice.

(Lave and Wenger 1991: 64, emphasis added)

Here Lave and Wenger discursively position 'participation' in opposition to 'exhausting overinvolvement in work', 'involuntary servitude', and so forth. It is almost as if over-involvement in work or involuntary servitude were not themselves forms of participation. Again, the above assertions are hard to reconcile with statements in other parts of the text that learning is 'as an aspect of all activity' (1991: 38) and that 'legitimate peripheral participation takes place no matter which educational form provides a context for learning' (1991: 40). While it may not be their intention, Lave and Wenger's concepts of 'participation' and, ultimately, 'community' appear to take on normative overtones within their analysis, and again are often positioned more to define what learning should be than what learning actually is.

The dilemma concerning application and abstraction, the empirical and rational components of their analysis, extends to what we might call their exposition strategy. The organization of their text does little to facilitate the shift in orientation that is central to their arguments. The book begins with a highly abstracted 'theory' section, which comes before its application to selected case studies, only one of which is based on the primary empirical research of Lave and Wenger themselves; the text then returns to abstracted theoretical conceptions once more. So, again, the relationship between theory and research is unclear, and the question presents itself as to why Lave and Wenger had to look to the research of others to exemplify their approach, particularly given that they explain the genesis of their model as residing in their own previous work on intelligent tutoring systems, technological change, and so forth. Their separation of theory and research is, thus, both textual and analytical. Such separation leaves relatively unchecked the degree of congruence between, to borrow Argyris and Schön's (1978) terminology, Lave and Wenger's *espoused theory* and their *theory-in-use*.

For example, at the level of espoused theory, Lave and Wenger argue that 'Any given attempt to analyze a form of learning through legitimate peripheral participation must involve analysis of the political and social organization of that form, its historical development, and the effects of both of these on sustained possibilities for learning' (1991: 64). However, at the level of theory-in-use such analysis is rarely provided. There is a discussion of the case of Vai and Gola tailors in relation to the increasing diversification of the division of labour in West Africa, but even this analysis is adopted wholesale from the work of Goody (1989), and is not developed by Lave and Wenger themselves. Given the Marxist underpinnings of their approach, and Lave and Wenger's stress on the importance of considering the political and social organization of legitimate peripheral participation, one might have expected, for instance, a political economy of the communities of practice considered or, for example, discussions of *legitimation* processes that went beyond the *prima facie* relationships of old-timers and newcomers – particularly when considering, say, entrance into relatively senior positions within the US military.

Similarly, Lave and Wenger are critical of attempts to theorize the knowledge and skill development characteristic of apprenticeship as 'informal learning', with their inevitable recourse to standard paradigm notions of 'acquisition', classically through the mechanism of 'observation or imitation' (1991: 95). According to this viewpoint, they argue, 'apprentices are supposed to acquire the "specifics" of practice through "observation and imitation". But this view is in all probability wrong in every particular, or right in particular circumstances, but for the wrong reasons' (1991: 95). And yet, to exemplify their theory of legitimate peripheral participation, they cite Lave's own work on Vai and Gola tailors, which describes subdivisions in the tailoring curriculum thus: 'The learning of each operation is subdivided into phases I have dubbed 'way in' and 'practice'. 'Way in' refers to the *period of observation* and attempts to construct a first approximation of the garment . . . ' (1991: 72, emphasis added). In a similar manner, the 'mechanism' of learning of, for example, a Yucatan midwife (another of the exemplar cases of apprenticeship considered by Lave and Wenger) from her mother appears remarkably dependent on processes of observation and behavioural modelling. Again, these ostensible gaps between espoused theory and theory-in-use are compounded by the textual over-separation of theory and research. Lave and Wenger present a potential reconciliation between these seemingly contradictory positions by suggesting that 'newcomers' legitimate peripherality provides them with more than an "observational" lookout post: it crucially involves *participation* as a way of learning – of both absorbing and being absorbed in – the "culture of practice"' (1991: 95). However, this raises as many problems as it addresses: what, for example, is the difference between a process of 'absorption' and a process of 'acquisition'– the very metaphor of learning to which Lave and Wenger are responding? If anything, the term 'absorption' would appear to imply a greater degree of passivity, less 'activity', than the 'acquisition' of the standard paradigm.

Even where examples immediately follow theory, these do not always square well with one another. For example, Lave and Wenger argue that there are often discrepancies between what a community of practice claims to be 'about' and its actual practice. A particular case in point is that of physics students at a high school. They ask, 'What community of practice is in the process of reproduction?' (1991: 99). Lave and Wenger suggest it may be only the reproduction of the high school itself; and even if the practice of physics is being reproduced in some way, there are 'vast differences' between high-school students and professional physicists in the activities they pursue and meanings they attribute to this. They write, 'The actual reproducing community of practice, within which schoolchildren learn about physics, is not the community of physicists but the community of schooled adults . . . The reproduction cycles of the physicists' community start much later, possibly only in graduate school' (1991: 99–100). However, this ontological delineation between 'professional physicists' and 'schoolchildren studying physics' is highly problematic, particularly given that Lave and Wenger intend their approach to be fundamentally a processual one. It is as if professional physicists were never schoolchildren. While it may be possible to distinguish these groups temporally, particularly in relation to their age, it is somewhat artificial to discount the profound importance that, for instance, having learned to read, write, make sense of plastic models of atoms, use mathematical abstractions, indeed, having developed the full cultural repertoire necessary even to commence communication with other physicists, has to the reproductive cycles both of high schools and the professional physicist community itself.

Lost in translation

Given the above problems relating to the relationship between the empirical and rational components of Lave and Wenger's work, the discrepancies between their 'theory-in-use' and 'espoused theory', their oscillation between a theory of learning as it actually is and a model of how learning should be, we are left with a certain ambiguity relating to the status and enduring purpose of Lave and Wenger's conceptual scheme. This ambiguity presents a further dilemma: how can – indeed, how should – subsequent researchers and practitioners use this approach? Should it be superimposed on to other concrete learning contexts? Should it be used as a model of practice? Or should it be revised with recourse to further research in a way that is different from how it has been 'practised' and presented in Lave and Wenger's work? These are questions to which I return in the conclusion, however; for the moment it is worth considering how Lave and Wenger's work actually has been applied, particularly by consultancy practitioners in the field. While of course Lave and Wenger should not be held responsible for how others have applied their work, it is fair to say that since the publication of their (1991) text, Wenger's subsequent (1998) book, and indeed Wenger *et al.*'s (2002) text, the community of practice model has come to take on considerable practitioner significance, to the extent that we might now refer to a community of practice 'consultancy movement'. Indeed, as the very title of this book would suggest, it is the concept of communities of practice, more than legitimate peripheral participation, that has gained currency within a range of fields. That this is so may be revealing.

In relation to the workplace, we might envisage a community of practice thus:

> Workers organize their lives with their immediate colleagues and customers to get their jobs done. In doing so, they develop or preserve a sense of themselves they can live with, have some fun, and fulfil the requirements of their employers and clients. No matter what their official job description may be, they create a practice to do what needs to be done.
>
> (Wenger 1998: 6)

Following from Wenger's definition, we can understand communities of practice at work as defined not so much by the organization chart as by how people 'work around' a job, how people collaborate irrespective of their job description, how they 'live their lives' at work. Such a definition would appear to have a certain currency with management consultancy practitioners who seek, ostensibly, to transform the workplace into a 'community' in the normative sense, to get rid of a 'command and control structure', and instead pursue the envisaged ideal of a unitarist workplace where like-minded colleagues creatively and collaboratively develop together. In this sense the concept has considerable resonance with models of organizational learning, the learning organization, knowledge management, and indeed, since its earliest exposition, it has been discussed in relation to this literature (see, for example, Brown and Duguid 1991). The shift is subtle but, following the arguments above, the concept of communities of practice, particularly the 'version' that has been received by the workplace practitioner community, has come to take on the status of a kind of 'ideal model' of how learning should be – the archetype of a 'group that learns'. Consider, for example, the following extract from *Training Top 100* newsletter, a publication which features bulletins on 'best practice'. The extract is based upon an interview with the vice-president of Sprint Corporation, Jed Dodd:

> 'If workers simply need assistance while learning on the job, there is no reason to bring them into a class.' It is in such instances, he says, that communities of practice

(CoPs) become a logical choice. These communities, which exist primarily online, offer a way for employees with similar working responsibilities or information needs to learn from each other. At Sprint, the primary purpose of CoPs is to put users into environments that provide a 'safety net' while they learn on the job from both peers and subject-matter experts (SMEs). At other times, says Dodd, CoPs are used as post-training resources. They provide ongoing learning support after employees leave the classroom. Since fall 2003, Sprint Corp. has instituted more than 150 of these CoPs . . . While Sprint's CoPs have delivered significant results in numerous areas of the business, says Dodd, they have yielded better knowledge management, increased time savings, reduction in redundancy and enhanced cross-departmental collaboration as well.

(Training Top 100, 2005)

The article continues with a list of 'best practices' for 'starting' communities of practice which includes 'Tie your CoP to business needs', 'Choose your membership carefully', 'Monitor the community to ensure accuracy', 'Measure your successes and failures', 'Talk the right talk'. What this extract serves to demonstrate is a growing disparity between the carefully formulated exposition of Lave and Wenger's approach to learning, on the one hand, and the translated, transformed version of 'how we might achieve communities of practice' on the other. Indeed, the very notion that communities of practices constitute a 'managerial option', that they can in any simple sense be 'instituted', or created by fiat, stands in stark contrast to Lave and Wenger's nuanced discussion of a community's reproductive cycles, pathways of centripetal progression via legitimate peripheral participation (with the latter concept characteristically not mentioned in the extract cited above), and so forth. In one section of the *Training Top 100* article readers are instructed to 'Find an expert on communities of practice who understands every aspect of the process – from technology and administration to measurement and analysis – and appoint that individual to lead the charge for CoPs in your organization'. There would perhaps be few people better to consult than Etienne Wenger himself, who, according to his web site, 'has been making a living helping people and organizations apply these ideas' (Wenger 2005). And yet this emphasis on learning for commercial gain, this emphasis on the administration, measurement, monitoring and evaluation of a community of practice in relation to business needs, seems profoundly at odds with the origins of the concept in which Lave and Wenger (1991: 112) argued, for example, that 'The commoditization of learning engenders a fundamental contradiction between the use and exchange values of the outcome of learning.'

Articles on communities of practice similar to the *Training Top 100* example discussed above are simply too numerous to cite. To get a sense of the communities of practice consultancy movement, as we might begin to call it, one could consider, for example, the knowledge management resource web site www.brint.com, where 'communities of practice' is included as a sub-topic under the heading 'knowledge flow', or, for example, Lesser and Storck's (2001) discussion of 'Communities of practice and organizational performance', which seeks to elucidate how communities of practice within organizations can add 'value' through, for example, 'decreasing the learning curve of new employees', 'responding more rapidly [than formal "teams"] to consumer needs and inquiries', 'reducing rework and preventing the "reinvention of the wheel" ', 'spawning new ideas for products and services' (Lesser and Storck 2001: 836).

In these ways, and numerous others, the communities of practice model has come to constitute in and of itself an emergent managerial discourse relating to workplace development and performance; it has made the transition from analytical model to practitioner tool, and appears to have lost much of its critical centre through this translation.

Conclusion

Moving forward with the communities of practice model

A central aim of this chapter has been to raise questions about the status and purpose of Lave and Wenger's approach to learning in terms of how it was initially conceived and later applied by management consultants in the workplace. Lave and Wenger's declared intention was to establish a more adequate approach to understanding learning, one which could help facilitate a paradigm shift: a move from viewing learning as 'acquisition' and towards understanding learning as 'participation', a shift in orientation away from 'learning from' and towards 'learning to' (1991: 109). However, it has been argued, there are significant differences between Lave and Wenger's espoused theory and their theory-in-use within their original work which also extend to differences between their original and later work. For example, in Wenger's 1998 text he describes communities of practice as the 'locus for the *acquisition* of knowledge' (1998: 214, original emphasis). This chapter has found Lave and Wenger to switch from at times arguing that learning is an aspect of *all* activity to, at others, proposing that learning is a *particular kind* of activity; and, in a similar manner, from arguing in places that *all* educational forms inevitably constitute communities of practice to suggesting that communities of practice are a *distinctive* learning context. In parallel, Lave and Wenger fluctuate between developing an approach to understanding learning as it *actually is* and positing a model of how learning *ought to be* – a problem compounded by subsequent applications of the concept of 'community of practice' as the 'consultancy ideal' of collaborative learning.

It may in fact be possible to reconcile the apparent ambivalence of Lave and Wenger's position. After all, a more adequate understanding of learning could indeed yield insights that have utility, that are of value to educational and workplace practitioners; as Wenger himself recognizes, theory can be 'practical' (Wenger 1998: 9). However, if we follow this course of reconciliation, a model of how learning 'should be' would need to be predicated upon, not conflated with, an approach to understanding, first and foremost, what learning 'actually is'. Moreover, the inherent danger in the extensive application of the communities of practice model by human resource development practitioners in the workplace is that the concept will become 'hi-jacked'. Put another way, the danger is that Lave and Wenger's paradigm shift from 'learning from' towards 'learning to' will be extended a step further such that the communities of practice model will come to exemplify 'learning for'; particularly 'learning for' productive gain. As such, the communities of practice model is in danger of losing its analytical purpose, and could indeed come to be used to implement precisely the kind of 'commoditized learning' against which Lave and Wenger were reacting. For example, a 'community of practice' might become a place where employees are 'indoctrinated' and where knowledge, ideas, innovations become 'appropriated' by those who hold the most power resources within that community.

Ultimately, this chapter has found important problems relating to the relationship between the empirical and rational components of Lave and Wenger's work which raise the question of whether the theory really can be said to speak beyond the cases examined. Without a sustained two-way *dialogue* with evidence, Lave and Wenger's approach risks replacing a one-sided view of learning with another equally one-sided version: from one in which formal education in schools is privileged as the guiding metaphor for learning to another in which the same is true of apprenticeship. Must, for example, all communities of practice necessarily have no 'question–answer–evaluation' equivalents? Must they all involve lengthy cycles of reproduction of the type that may, indeed, be on the wane in an advanced industrial workplace characterized by short-termism and ephemerality (see, for example, Sennett 1998)? Throughout their work, Lave and Wenger position their approach not so much as a final answer to the problem of learning, but more as a hopeful conceptual bridge which has the potential to help facilitate the broader paradigm shift that is necessary. In their 1991 book they explicitly recognized that the concept of communities of practice is left largely 'intuitive' and requires further development (1991: 42). In keeping with the spirit of their work it is thus pertinent to ask how such development may take place. How, indeed, does any theory develop? It is argued here that superimposing or force-fitting the conceptual scheme on to concrete cases of learning is an approach which offers limited prospects for the amendment and revision of theory. Instead, an important step in moving forward with the community of practice model, perhaps moving beyond it, is the development of a sustained and rigorous dialogue between theory and research by an intergenerational body of social scientists, by an academic community of practice. As yet, the trajectory of conceptual development of the community of practice model has arguably been one marked more by increasing paradigmatic heterogeneity than by increasing coherence, revision, amendment and refinement via conceptual and empirical extension. It is the latter enterprise – critically extending and developing the model, rescuing its coherence and analytical purpose – that is central to this book.

Key questions to consider

1 How useful is the concept of legitimate peripheral participation to facilitating an understanding of the contemporary workplace?
2 Are communities of practice distinctive social forms?
3 What is the relationship between observation and learning in communities of practice?
4 How are communities of practice different from formal work-based teams?
5 To what extent is the current consultancy model of community of practice faithful to Lave and Wenger's original concept?

References

Argyris, C. and Schön, D. (1978) *Organizational Learning: a Theory of Action Perspective*, Reading, MA: Addison-Wesley.

Bandura, A. (1977) *Social Learning Theory*, Englewood Cliffs, NJ: Prentice-Hall.

Beckett, D. and Hager, P. (2002) *Life, Work and Learning: Practice in Postmodernity*, London: Routledge.

Brown, J. S. and Duguid, P. (1991) 'Organizational learning and communities-of-practice: toward a unified view of working, learning, and innovation', *Organization Science*, 2 (1): 40–57.

Engeström, Y. (1987) *Learning by Expanding*, Helsinki: Orienta-Konsultit.

Gherardi, S., Nicolini, D. and Odella, F. (1998) 'Toward a social understanding of how people learn in organizations: the notion of a situated curriculum', *Management Learning*, 29 (3): 273–97.

Goody, E. (1989) 'Learning and the division of labor', in Coy, M. (ed.) *Anthropological Perspectives on Apprenticeship*, New York: SUNY Press.

Lave, J. and Wenger, E. (1991) *Situated Learning: Legitimate Peripheral Participation*, Cambridge: Cambridge University Press.

Lesser, E. L. and Storck, J. (2001) 'Communities of practice and organizational performance', *IBM Systems Journal*, 40 (4): 831–62.

Marsick, V. J. and Watkins, K. (1990) *Informal and Incidental Learning in the Workplace*, London: Routledge.

Mead, G. H. (1934) *Mind, Self, and Society: From the Standpoint of a Social Behaviourist*. Chicago: University of Chicago Press.

Nicolini, D. and Meznar, M. B. (1995) 'The social construction of organizational learning: concepts and practical issues in the field', *Human Relations*, 48 (7): 727–46.

Sennett, R. (1998) *The Corrosion of Character: The Personal Consequences of Work in the New Capitalism*, New York: Norton.

Training Top 100 (2005), 23 August, www.trainingmag.com/training/reports_analysis/top100/index.jsp.

Vygotsky, L. (1978) *Mind in Society*, Cambridge, MA: Harvard University Press.

Wenger, E. (1998) *Communities of Practice: Learning, Meaning, and Identity*, Cambridge: Cambridge University Press.

Wenger, E. (2005) 'Etienne Wenger's Home Page', http://www.ewenger.com/, Accessed 18 November 2005.

Wenger, E., McDermott, R. and Snyder, W. M. (2002) *Cultivating Communities of Practice: A Guide to Managing Knowledge*, Boston, MA: Harvard Business School Press.

4 From communities of practice to mycorrhizae

Yrjö Engeström

Key themes in this chapter

- Critiquing the ahistorical approach of communities of practice
- Fluctuating and weakly bounded forms of community
- Impact of co-configuration and peer production on communities in knowledge-intensive sectors
- Contribution of activity theory and knotworking to advance the community concept
- Emergent and new landscapes of learning

When Jean Lave and Etienne Wenger (1991) introduced the notion of communities of practice in their book, *Situated Learning: Legitimate Peripheral Participation* their ideas had a widespread refreshing impact on studies of learning. Acquisition was replaced by participation as the key metaphor and mechanism of learning. Analysis was extended beyond the skin of the individual, to encompass the entire community involved in a given productive practice. Learning was shown to be an inevitable aspect of all productive practices, not a specific process mainly or exclusively limited to schools and other institutions of formal learning.

Subsequently Wenger's (1998) work brought the notion of communities of practice to the consciousness and vocabulary of management practitioners and organization scholars. Wenger developed a rich conceptual framework around the concept of community of practice and turned it into a toolkit for organization design and knowledge management (Wenger *et al.* 2002).

Despite its virtues, the notion of community of practice is a quite ahistorical way to conceptualize work communities. In this chapter I will first assess some strengths and limitations of the notion. I will then discuss the attempt of Paul Adler and Charles Heckscher (2006) to analyse firms as historically evolving communities. After that I will push the historical view further, to identify some emergent features in human activities that seem to open up a radically new landscape of widely dispersed, fluctuating and weakly bounded community forms. These features are particularly evident in new forms of peer production or social production, most prominently in the open source movement of software production, that have emerged along with the evolution of the internet. I will introduce the concept of mycorrhizae to capture the quality of these new forms. I will conclude with a discussion of the potentials of mycorrhizae-like activities to take root and spread in domains such as medicine.

Communities of practice: promise and limits

A key strength of *Situated Learning* (Lave and Wenger 1991) was its presentation of five case studies of apprenticeship. These examples made the notion of community of practice concrete and grounded in empirical data. They helped educational researchers redirect their gaze to partially forgotten forms of learning-by-participating in apprenticeship arrangements, often surprisingly robust even in advanced industrial economies (Ainley and Rainbird 1999).

On the other hand, making apprenticeship the paradigmatic form of situated learning in a community of practice had a heavy cost. It fixed the idea of community of practice to the following historically quite limited and limiting aspects of prototypical apprenticeship:

1   A community of practice is a fairly well bounded local entity which has clear boundaries and membership criteria.
2   A community of practice has a single centre of supreme skill and authority, typically embodied in the master.
3   A community of practice is characterized mainly by centripetal movement from the periphery toward the centre, from novice to master, from marginal to fully legitimate participation; opposite centrifugal movement may occur, but is not foundational.

The last point was noted by Lave and Wenger at the end of their book (Lave and Wenger, 1991: 113–17). However, after recognizing this 'contradiction between continuity and displacement', the authors soften it by concluding:

> Shared participation is the stage on which the old and the new, the known and the unknown, the established and the hopeful, act out their differences and discover their commonalities, manifest their fear of one another, and come to terms with their need for one another. . . . Conflict is experienced and worked out through a shared everyday practice in which differing viewpoints and common stakes are in interplay.
>
> (Lave and Wenger 1991: 116)

This is more wishful apology than historically or empirically informed analysis. It overlooks the history of oppression by masters and individual and collective rebellions by apprentices against their masters (see Rorabaugh 1986). More generally, it glorifies a historically limited form of community as a general model for all times. Putting decisive emphasis on the movement from periphery to the centre is a foundationally conservative choice. It marginalizes the creation of novelty by means of rejecting, breaking away from and expanding the given activity.

In his book *Communities of Practice* Wenger (1998) distanced himself from the original apprenticeship notion. He realized that communities have increasingly problematic and permeable boundaries, and adopted the complementary notion of 'constellations of practices'. This refers to multiple communities of practice that are somehow connected to another. The analytical power of this notion is limited by the fact that the structure of a constellation 'depends on the perspective one adopts' (Wenger 1998: 127), and 'a given constellation may or may not be recognized by participants; it may or may not be named' (1998: 128). In other words, it may be practically anything.

In sum, neither Lave and Wenger (1991) nor Wenger (1998) situate their communities of practice in the history of real societies and patterns of organizing work. Wenger (1998: 87–9) does take up history, but only as a general and abstract issue of remembering and forgetting, reification and participation. One looks in vain for discussions on the conditions of implementing communities of practice in highly rationalized hierarchical mass-production organizations, or in settings driven by financialization, outsourcing and fragmentation of work, or in various networks, partnerships and strategic alliances.

Towards collaborative community?

Within organization studies, Adler and Hecksher (2006) put the notion of community in its historical context. Building on the classic sociological distinction between traditional hierarchical *Gemeinschaft* community and modern market-oriented *Gesellschaft* community, the authors argue that a third historical form is currently emerging, particularly in knowledge-intensive firms. This third historical type of community is called 'collaborative community' or 'collaborative interdependence':

> Collaborative community in modern industry needs to coordinate interactions that span a wide range of competencies and knowledge bases, and that shift constantly to accommodate the evolving nature of knowledge projects. The challenges it faces cannot be met through 'teamwork' in the usual sense of small, homogeneous, and informal groups.
>
> (Adler and Heckscher 2006: 44)

Adler and Heckscher list four challenges that this emerging third type of community must meet (Adler and Heckscher 2006: 44):

1 The boundaries of solidary groups must be far less fixed than in traditional communities, far more capable of being bridged and merged.
2 It must accommodate a very high level of technical division of labour and diversity of knowledge and skills.
3 It must allow for authority based not on status but on knowledge and expertise – that is, 'value rationality' – meaning that people must in many cases be accountable to peers or those below them in the hierarchy, rather than to their formal superiors.
4 It must bring values into the realm of public discussion, so that they can become common orienting and motivating elements for all the members of the community.

Interestingly enough, the authors suggest that 'process management' in corporations is a key ingredient and enabler of collaborative community. Process management is seen as the avenue to transparent co-ordination of large, diverse communities and high levels of complexity. Process management has two aspects, namely developing shared purpose across organizational units and divisions, and co-ordinating work among various skills and competences along the value chain:

> These new formalisms are sometimes experienced as oppressive, and indeed the language of process management can become a cover for coercive bureaucratic

control; but when it is successful, people experience the rules of process management as enabling rather than constraining, as helping to structure new relations
rather than limiting them.

(Adler and Heckscher 2006: 44)

I have no problem accepting the progressive potential of process management in many
cases. But I do not think it can be the core co-ordinating mechanism of historically new
forms of community at work. Process management is foundationally a linear view of
work and production. In its linearity it follows, albeit in expanded and more sophisticated forms, the same basic logic that was the core of standardized industrial mass
production. Mastering and updating this logic may be a necessary precondition for
successful introduction of more interactive and flexible forms of production, such as
process enhancement, mass customization and co-configuration (to use the terms of
Victor and Boynton 1998). But, as I will try to show shortly, particularly in conditions
of co-configuration and social production, the linear logic of process management is
simply not enough.

From co-configuration to social production

Each historical type of work generates and requires a certain type of knowledge and
learning. At present, the most demanding and promising developments are associated
with the emergence of *co-configuration work*. A critical prerequisite of co-configuration is
the creation of customer-intelligent products and services which adapt to the changing
needs of the user and evolve in use over long periods of time.

(Victor and Boynton 1998: 195)

We may provisionally define co-configuration as an emerging historically new type
of work that relies on (1) adaptive 'customer-intelligent' product–service combinations, (2) continuous relationships of mutual exchange between customers,
producers and the product–service combinations, (3) on-going configuration and
customization of the product–service combination over lengthy periods of time, (4)
active customer involvement and input into the configuration, (5) multiple collabor-
ating producers that need to operate in networks within or between organizations,
and (6) mutual learning from interactions between the parties involved in the configuration actions. These characteristics have commonalities with von Hippel's (2005)
notion of 'user innovations', as well as with Prahalad and Ramaswamy's (2004)
notion of 'co-creation of value'. In their different ways, both emphasize the growing
role of users in the creation of innovations and in the shaping of products and
services.

My research groups have been particularly interested in what we call *negotiated
knotworking* as an emerging way of organizing work in settings that strive toward
co-configuration (Engeström *et al.* 1999; Engeström 2005). In knotworking,
collaboration between the partners is of vital importance, yet takes shape without
rigid predetermined rules or a fixed central authority. However, the notion of
co-configuration does not capture the profound implications of what is called social
production or peer production. Benkler (2006: 59) summarizes this phenomenon as
follows:

A new model of production has taken root; one that should not be there, at least according to our most widely held beliefs about economic behavior. It should not, the intuitions of the late-twentieth-century American would say, be the case that thousands of volunteers will come together to collaborate on a complex economic project. It certainly should not be the case that these volunteers will beat the largest and best-financed business enterprises in the world at their own game. And yet, this is precisely what is happening in the software world.

The open source movement in software production (DiBona *et al.* 1999) is usually used as the prime example of new forms of community-based work and knowledge creation that go beyond the limits of bounded firm-based models (Lee and Cole 2003; Weber 2004; Feller *et al.* 2005). According to Lee and Cole (2003), the key to the 'knowledge expansion' witnessed in the Linux kernel development is, besides its openness and non-proprietary nature, the norm of critique:

> In the Linux development community we observe a peer review process as a struc-
> tured approach to generating criticism of existing versions, evaluating these criti-
> cisms, and eliminating 'error', while retaining those solutions that cannot be
> falsified.
>
> (Lee and Cole 2003: 639)

Lee and Cole (2003: 641) report that between 1995 and 2000 they found 2,605 people in the Linux community 'development team' which adds features and fixes bugs. Over the same period they found 1,562 people on the 'bug reporting team' which reports, docu-ments or characterizes bugs. In addition, the authors found that 49 per cent of the 'bug reporting team' also performed tasks of the 'development team', while 29 per cent of the 'development team' performed tasks of the 'bug reporting team'. The sheer size, openness and fluctuation across boundaries of this community makes the use of the term 'team' somewhat ludicrous.

Independently of the open source movement, authors like Howard Rheingold (2002) have began to prophesy 'smart mobs' as radically new forms of community organiza-tion made possible by mobile technologies. Initial conditions of such 'swarm' or 'amoeba' organizations were nicely captured by Rafael in an essay where he discusses the overthrowing of President Estrada in the Philippines in 2001:

> Bypassing the complex of broadcasting media, cell phone users themselves
> became broadcasters, receiving and transmitting both news and gossip and often
> confounding the two. Indeed, one could imagine each user becoming a broadcast-
> ing station unto him- or herself, a node in a wider network of communication
> that the state could not possibly even begin to monitor, much less control. Hence,
> once the call was made for people to mass at Edsa, cell phone users readily
> forwarded messages they received, even as they followed what was asked of them
> . . . Cell phones then were invested not only with the power to surpass crowded
> conditions and congested surroundings brought about by the state's inability to
> order everyday life. They were also seen to bring a new kind of crowd about,
> one that was thoroughly conscious of itself as a movement headed towards a
> common goal.
>
> (Rafael 2003)

Clearly such a 'smart mob' has no single, permanent centre. Mobile technologies make it possible that each participant is potentially a momentary centre. Rafael's example underlines the importance of a shared goal. But the emphasis on goal also implies the problem. Since goals are relatively short-lived, also 'smart mobs' seem to be very temporary organizational forms.

However, there are amoeba-like collective activities which are not limited to the pursuit of short-term goals. Two quite resilient examples are the activities of bird-watching (Obmascik 2004) and skateboarding (Borden 2001). These may be also called 'wildfire activities', as they have the peculiar capacity to disappear or die in a given location and suddenly reappear and develop vigorously in a quite different location, or in the same location after a lengthy dormant period. While participants in these activities commonly use mobile technologies to communicate with one another and to broadcast information about their objects (rare birds, good skating spots), these activities are much older than mobile phones and the internet. Bird-watching has a history of several hundred years, and skateboarding dates back at least to the early 1970s. Two additional features need to mentioned. Both birdwatch-ing and skateboarding are peculiar combinations of leisure, work, sport and art. And they both have consistently defied attempts at full commercialization, offering ample opportunities for entrepreneurship, but not becoming themselves dominated by commercial motives.

Movement and learning in the new landscape

What might be the nature of agency, co-ordination and learning in social production and amoeba-like wildfire activities? What are the basic patterns of movement in such a landscape? I'd like to note, in this connection, that the importance of movement for an activity-theoretical analysis of development was stressed by Davydov and Zinchenko (1981), who put forward the concept of 'living movement' as a foundational starting point for a developmentally oriented psychology. Space does not allow a thorough discussion of this concept in this chapter. Table 1 sketches a first answer to these questions by presenting rough historical characterizations of dominant features of craft, mass production, and social production. Co-configuration as described by Victor and Boynton (1998) would appear to be a transitional form between mass production and social production.

In craft-based organizations, when each individual practitioner is focused on his or her own object or fragment of the object, practitioners are commonly held together by externally imposed or tradition-based identification and subordination. In industrial organizations, teams emerged as units for co-operative solving of problems. Their efforts are typically co-ordinated by various forms of explicit process management. However, teams run into trouble and find their limits when faced with objects which require constant questioning and reconfiguration of the division of labour, rules and boundaries of the team and the wider organization – in short, negotiation across horizontal and vertical boundaries of the given process.

Negotiation is a central co-ordinating mechanism of the distributed agency required in knotworking within social production. Negotiation is required when the very object of the activity is unstable, resists attempts at control and standardization, and requires rapid integration of expertise from various locations and traditions. On the other hand, as noted above by Lee and Cole (2003), social production such as the open source

Table 1 Framework for conceptualizing social production as a new landscape of learning

Form of production	Nature of object	Locus of agency	Co-ordinating mechanism	Learning movement
Craft	Personal object	Individual actor	Identification and subordination	Peripheral participation, gradual transition towards the centre
Mass production	Problematic object	Team	Process management	Focal involvement, linear and vertical improvement
Social production	Runaway object	Knots in mycorrhizae	Negotiation and peer review	Expansive swarming engagement, multi-directional pulsation

software movement is dependent on constant, publicly accessible critical commentary and peer review.

In the second column of Table 1 the notion of 'runaway object' requires further elaboration at this point. The notion is related to the concept of 'runaway world', coined by Giddens (1991, 2000). Claudio Ciborra (2002: 98) characterizes the phenomenon as follows:

> We experience control in the age of globalization as more limited than ever. We are creating new global phenomena (global warming and greenhouse effects, nuclear threats, global production processes, and so on) that we are able to master only in part. Although information infrastructures appear to be important instruments for governing global phenomena, they possess ambiguities which make their eventual outcome difficult to determine. Consequently, they may serve to curb our control capabilities just as much as they enhance them.

Runaway objects typically have the potential to escalate and expand up to a global scale of influence. They are objects that are poorly under anybody's control and have far-reaching unexpected side effects. Actor-network theorists (Law 1991) point out that such objects are often monsters: they seem to have a life of their own that threatens our security and safety in many ways. They are contested objects that generate opposition and controversy. They can also be powerfully emancipatory objects that open up radically new possibilities of development and well-being, as exemplified by the Linux operating system.

Contrary to mega-projects (Altshuler and Luberoff 2003; Flyvbjerg *et al.* 2003), most runaway objects do not start out as big and risky things. More commonly they begin as small problems or marginal innovations, which makes their runaway potential difficult to predict and utilize. They often remain dormant, invisible or unseen for lengthy periods of time, until they break out in the form of acute crises or breakthroughs (Vickers 2001).

In the third column of Table 1 the most demanding concept is 'mycorrhizae'. I use it to some extent in the same general sense in which Deleuze and Guattari (1987) proposed the concept of 'rhizome'. They wanted to highlight the importance of horizontal and multidirectional connections in human lives, in contrast to the dominant vertical, tree-like images of hierarchy. Originally a biological concept, rhizome refers to a horizontal underground stem, such as found in many ferns, where only the leaves may stick up into the air. As such, I find the implications of 'rhizome' too limited.

I am more interested in the invisible organic texture underneath visible fungi. Such a formation is called 'mycorrhizae' (Allen 1991; Sharma and Johri 2002). It is a symbiotic association between a fungus and the roots or rhizoids of a plant. Fungi are not able to ingest their food like animals do, nor can they manufacture their own food the way plants do. Instead, fungi feed by absorption of nutrients from the environment around them. They accomplish this by growing through and within the substrate on which they are feeding. This filamentous growth means that the fungus is in intimate contact with its surroundings; it has a very large surface area compared with its volume. Most plants rely on a symbiotic fungus to aid them in acquiring water and nutrients from the soil. The specialized roots which the plants grow and the fungus which inhabits them are together known as mycorrhizae, or 'fungal roots'. The fungus, with its large surface area, is able to soak up water and nutrients over a large area and provide them to the plant. In return, the plant provides energy-rich sugars manufactured through photosynthesis.

The visible mushrooms are reproductive structures. Even these structures are sometimes quite large, but the invisible body of the fungus, mycorrhizae, can be truly amazing. When molecular techniques were used, one Michigan fungus (*Armillaria bulbosa*) which grew in tree roots and soil and had a body constructed of tubular filaments was found to extend over an area of thirty-seven acres and to have a weight of 110 tons, equivalent to a blue whale. An even larger fungal clone of *Armillaria ostoyae*, reported earlier in the state of Washington, covered over 1,500 acres. Each clone began from the germination of a single spore over a thousand years ago. Although they probably have fragmented and are no longer continuous bodies, such organisms give us cause to think about what constitutes an individual.

Mycorrhizae are difficult if not impossible to bound and close, yet not indefinite or elusive. They are very hard to kill, but also vulnerable. They may lie dormant for lengthy periods of drought or cold, then generate again vibrant visible mushrooms when the conditions are right. They are made up of heterogeneous participants working symbiotically, thriving on mutually beneficial or also exploitative partnerships with plants and other organisms.

As I see it, knotworking eventually requires a mycorrhizae-like formation as its medium or base. Such a formation typically does not have strictly defined criteria of membership. But its members can be identified by their activism. The 2,605 'development team' members and 1,562 'bug reporting team' members of the Linux mycorrhizae mentioned by Lee and Cole (2003) were identified on the basis of their publicly available contributions to the development and perfection of the object, the Linux operating system. It is very likely that mycorrhizae include quite a variety of members, ranging from grass-roots activists or clients or victims to certified professionals, researchers, entrepreneurs and spokespersons.

A mycorrhizae formation is simultaneously a living, expanding process (or bundle of developing connections) *and* a relatively durable, stabilized structure; both a mental landscape and a material infrastructure. In this it resembles the 'cognitive trails' of Cussins (1992) and the 'flow architecture' described by Knorr-Cetina (2003: 8) as 'a reflexive form of coordination that is flat (non-hierarchical) in character while at the same time being based on a comprehensive summary view of things – the reflected and projected global context and transaction system'.

The model of an activity system (Engeström 1987: 78) is a functioning tool for the analysis of individuals and teams. But does it have any use when we step into the fluid world of mycorrhizae? The answer is that horizontal and invisible mycorrhizae do not eliminate visible, erect, bounded and institutionalized activity systems. As I pointed out above, mycorrhizae depend on plants and generate mushrooms, both visible, vertical and more or less durable. Knorr-Cetina (2003: 18) points out that the mycorrhizae-like formation of global financial markets is crucially dependent on institutionalized, stable 'bridgehead centres'. Without these relatively stable and well bounded 'plants' and 'mushrooms' the knotworking mycorrhizae will not take shape. Careful analyses of the structures and dynamics of the activity systems involved are more important than ever before.

The 'learning movement' (the fifth column of Table 1) refers to dominant patterns and directions of physical, discursive and cognitive motion in historically different organizational frameworks of work. Peripheral participation refers to novices moving gradually toward a perceived competent centre of an activity or community of practice (Lave and Wenger 1991). Focal involvement and linear and vertical improvement refer to intense closure around a shared problematic object, often organizationally chan-nelled into a movement of ascending or progressing along a predetermined linear or vertical pipeline of specialized expertise.

Expansive swarming engagement and multi-directional pulsation refer to star-like patterns of movement where the participants disperse outward to pursue their various trails and to expand the scope of the mycorrhizae but also return and come together in various ways to contribute to the forging of the runaway object. The notion of swarm-ing is borrowed from the study of distributed collaboration patterns among social insects, such as ants and bees (Bonabeau *et al.* 1999). Models from the insect worlds are simulated to build systems of artificial intelligence. Interestingly enough, mycorrhizae behave in ways somewhat similar to the social insects: when one of the filaments con-tacts a food supply, the entire fungal colony mobilizes and reallocates resources to exploit the new food. Unfortunately, popular applications of the swarming notion in studies or organizations and innovations (Gloor 2006) have thus far added little to the basic idea.

Expansive swarming is not just hectic active movement. It has multiple rhythms of improvization and persistence that correspond to the dual dynamics of swift situational concerted action and pursuit of a repeatedly reconfigured long-term perspective in knotworking. Improvization has attracted the attention of organizational researchers seeking models for swift trust and weakly scripted but well focused collaborative prob-lem solving in jazz and other forms of improvized collective performance. Persistence refers to patient dwelling in the object over long periods of time, alternating between intense action and more detached observation or even partial withdrawal. It includes pausing, backing up, regrouping and finding detours or new openings in the face of obstacles. Interestingly, Whorf's (1956) classic description of 'preparation' in Hopi culture displays some crucial features of persistence:

> A characteristic of Hopi behavior is the emphasis on preparation. This includes announcing and getting ready for events well beforehand, elaborate precautions to

insure persistence of desired conditions, and stress on good will as the preparer of right results . . . To the Hopi, for whom time is not motion but a 'getting later' of everything that has ever been done, unvarying repetition is not wasted but accumulated. It is storing up an invisible change that holds over into later events.

(Whorf 1956: 148–51)

The concepts of this framework are far from finished and stabilized. They are first approximations, meant to open up a field for further debate, theoretical work and experimentation in activity fields with complex runaway objects, seeking to build collaboration in knot-like ways, beyond the models of stable and well bounded institutions and teams.

Breaking away into mycorrhizae activities

The most obvious examples of mycorrhizae-like activities at the moment are the open source communities in software development and the peer-to-peer (P2P) networks in cultural production and exchange:

> What do music file exchanges like KaZaA and Gnutella, collaborative news networks like Slashdot and Kuro5hin and open source operating systems like Linux have in common? They are all forms of digital culture that are networked in technology, are P2P in organization and are collaborative in principle. Although they may seem to be on the fringes of the digital scene, their impact on existing cultural practices may well turn out to be disproportionate to their apparent position; indeed, their implications for how we define certain practices, including the practice of citizenship, and how we participate in cultural production are potentially transformative. These systems might be seen as part of a larger participatory turn whereby the users generate the content, evident in such diverse activities as fan fiction production, computer gaming and club culture. Although the notion of 'participatory culture' is not without its complexities, even at its simplest level of meaning, the concept signals a blurring of the boundaries between the categories of production and consumption and a subversion of established hierarchies of cultural value and authority.
>
> (Uricchio 2004: 86; see also Vaidhyanathan 2004;
> Subramanian and Goodman 2005)

The other important area where mycorrhizae-like organizing has become manifest is in grass-roots political activism:

> On the one hand, grassroots activists have developed highly advanced forms of computer-mediated alternative and tactical media, including Indymedia, culture jamming, hacktivism, and electronic civil disobedience. These practices have facilitated the emergence of globally coordinated transnational counterpublics while providing creative mechanisms for flexibly intervening within dominant communication circuits. On the other hand, activists have appropriated the Internet into their everyday routines, largely through e-mail lists and Web sites, favoring the rise of highly flexible and decentralized network forms. At the same time, the network has also emerged as a broader cultural ideal, as digital technologies generate new

political values and vocabularies, which are often directly inscribed into organizational and technological network architectures, suggesting a powerful dialectic among technology, norm, and form, mediated by human practice. Finally, activists are building a new digital media culture through the practice of informational utopias, involving experimentation with new technologies and the projection of utopian ideals regarding open participation and horizontal collaboration onto emerging forms of networked space.

(Juris 2005: 204–5; see also Hardt and Negri 2005)

Alternative utopias have the tendency of evaporating or being integrated into existing forms of production and power. Uricchio (2004: 89) points out that 'corporations are increasingly aware of the power of participatory culture and are incorporating elements of P2P culture in their own marketing'. Weber (2004: 234) adds that 'as open source software becomes increasingly mainstream in corporate applications, people have started companies to customize and service the software, and these companies have to make money, follow corporate law, and otherwise interface with conventional economic and legal systems'. This brings up the difficult dilemma of *livelihood:* 'it is not at all clear how communities and networks will provide for their members' (Uricchio 2004: 89). The dilemma may take the form: sell out or starve.

Another dilemma in the present literature is the relationship between the new organizational forms and *technology*. The analyses mentioned above tacitly or openly tend to make the emergence and existence of mycorrhizae-like organizational patterns entirely dependent on, even generated by, digital technologies. Steven Weber's discussion of possibilities of open source models in primary care medicine is an instructive example of the two dilemmas:

> Consider, for example, the structure of medical knowledge in a common family practice type setting, which is interestingly parallel to the structure of knowledge for in-house software development. My doctor in Berkeley has a hard problem to solve. I present myself to her with an atypical sinus infection, low-grade fever, aching muscles, and a family history of heart disease. The bad news is that I represent to her a highly customized configuration and a finely grained problem. The good news is that there almost certainly is a similarly configured patient presenting somewhere else at the same time. At the very least, other doctors are solving pieces of my problem in other settings . . . The second piece of bad news, though, is that she will find it extremely difficult to access that distributed knowledge and thus will most likely have to figure out my problem without much help. In fact, doctors have very cumbersome means of upgrading the common medical knowledge that they draw on to support their work . . .
>
> (Weber 2004: 268)

Weber argues that medical doctors would benefit enormously from a capacity to share their solutions online. He asks whether much of what has been considered tacit knowledge in medical practice may actually become representable digitally when bandwidth increases. He concludes that 'a positive answer would make certain aspects of medical practice an obvious place to experiment with open source style knowledge production' (Weber 2004: 269).

Weber's example implies that the *livelihood dilemma* may be approached by extending

open source models to domains of practice which already have a stable, well institutionalized economic basis, whether in the public or in the private sphere. An obvious
prerequisite is that there are pressing contradictions in the existing practices that may
be resolved by means of introducing the new models. Weber's example also implies that
all this will be possible when the technology allows it – when there is enough bandwidth
for smooth digitizing and sharing of previously tacit medical knowledge. This leaves us
prisoners of the *technology dilemma*. Over the past two decades, medical practitioners
have heard time and again the technological promises of unified and user-friendly
information systems that make the sharing and using of medical records a pleasure.
Promises of bandwidth revolution just don't cut the ice any more.

From the point of view of activity theory, Weber's example has a fundamental weakness. It is not based on a careful consideration of the *object* (e.g. Engeström and
Blackler 2005). In an open source software community such as Linux, the object is a
concrete product, an operating system that keeps evolving as the developers and users
contribute to its improvement. The object is at the same time distributed and unified:
everyone can have it and tinker with it on his or her desktop, but it is also one and the
same basic system for all. The object is at the same time a product and a project: it does
useful work for users, yet it is unfinished, full of challenges and continuously developed
further. And it is truly a runaway object: it is a source of pride in that it is conquering
the world by being better and cheaper than its commercial competitors. These features
give the object unusual holding power.

What would be the characteristics of the object of shared knowledge production in
medicine? Perhaps the best available answer comes from the community called the
Synaptic Leap (http://thesynapticleap.org/?q=). It is an open source biomedical
research community that describes its object as follows:

> Diseases found exclusively in tropical regions predominantly afflict poor people in
> developing countries. The typical profit-driven pharmaceutical economic model
> fails with these diseases because there is simply no money to be made. However, the
> very fact that there's no profit incentive to research these diseases makes them
> perfect candidates for open source style research; there's no profit incentive to keep
> secrets either. Our pilot research communities focusing on tropical diseases are:
> Malaria, schistosomiasis, tuberculosis.

It is too early to judge to what extent the Synaptic Leap will actually be able to produce
new solutions to tropical diseases. However, as Benkler (2006: 121) observes, its success
is not dependent on medical researchers' benevolence only:

> The capital cost of effective economic action in the industrial economy shunted
> sharing to its economic peripheries ... The emerging restructuring of capital
> investment in digital networks – in particular, the phenomenon of user-capitalized
> computation and communications capabilities – are at least partly reversing that
> effect.

When this technological and economic opportunity is combined with a powerful runaway object, such as tropical diseases, something radically new may indeed emerge.
However, as the metaphor of mycorrhizae reminds us, this is happening in a field of
symbiotic forms. Most of the researchers involved in the Synaptic Leap will continue

working in their traditional research institutions while they simultaneously contribute to the open source effort. This opens up an interesting landscape of learning to negotiate and balance multiple parallel loyalties, both mutually enriching and hostile to one another.

Key questions to consider

1 In what ways does activity theory help to problematize the concept of communities of practice?
2 What are the implications of the open source community's way of working for the concept of communities of practice?
3 How might Lave and Wenger's concept be expanded to embrace the complexity of work activity and types of organization found in knowledge-intensive sectors of the economy?

References

Adler, P. S. and Heckscher, C. (2006) 'Towards a collaborative community', in C. Heckscher and P. S. Adler (eds) *The Firm as a Collaborative Community: Reconstructing Trust in the Knowledge Economy*, Oxford: Oxford University Press.

Ainley, P. and Rainbird, H. (eds) (1999) *Apprenticeship: Towards a New Paradigm of Learning*, London: Kogan Page.

Allen, M. F. (1991) *The Ecology of Mycorrhizae*, Cambridge: Cambridge University Press.

Altshuler, A. and Luberoff, D. (2003) *Mega-projects: The Changing Politics of Urban Public Investment*, Washington, DC: Brookings Institution.

Benkler, Y. (2006) *The Wealth of Networks: How Social Production transforms Markets and Freedom*, New Haven, CT: Yale University Press.

Bonabeau, E., Dorigo, M. and Theraulaz, G. (1999) *Swarm Intelligence: From Natural to Artificial Systems*, New York: Oxford University Press.

Borden, I. (2001) *Skateboarding, Space and the City: Architecture, the Body and Performative Critique*, New York: Berg.

Ciborra, C. (2002) *The Labyrinths of Information: Challenging the Wisdom of Systems*, Oxford: Oxford University Press.

Cussins, A. (1992) 'Content, embodiment and objectivity: the theory of cognitive trails', *Mind*, 101: 651–88.

Davydov, V. V. and Zinchenko, V. P. (1981) 'The principle of development in psychology', *Soviet Psychology*, 20 (1): 22–46.

Davydov, V. V., Slobodchikov, V. I. and Tsukerman, G. A. (2003) 'The elementary school student as an agent of learning activity', *Journal of Russian and East European Psychology*, 41 (5): 63–76.

Deleuze, G. and Guattari, F. (1987) *A Thousand Plateaus: Capitalism and Schizophrenia*, Minneapolis, MN: University of Minnesota Press.

DiBona, C., Ockman, S. and Stone, M. (eds) (1999) *Open Sources: Voices from the Open Source Revolution*, Sebastopol, CA: O'Reilly.

Engeström, Y. (1987) *Learning by Expanding: An Activity-theoretical Approach to Developmental Research*, Helsinki: Orienta-Konsultit.

Engeström, Y. (2005) 'Knotworking to create collaborative intentionality capital in fluid organizational fields', in M. M. Beyerlein, S. T. Beyerlein and F. A. Kennedy (eds) *Collaborative Capital: Creating Intangible Value*, Amsterdam: Elsevier.

Engeström, Y. (in press) 'Enriching the theory of expansive learning: lessons from journeys toward co-configuration', *Mind, Culture, and Activity*, 12.

Engeström, Y. and Blackler, F. (2005) 'On the life of the object', *Organization*, 12: 307–30.

Engeström, Y., Engeström, R. and Vähäaho, T. (1999) 'When the centre does not hold: the importance of knotworking', in Hedegaard, M., Chaiklin S. and Jensen, U. J. (eds), *Activity Theory and Social Practice: Cultural–Historical Approaches*, Aarhus: Aarhus University Press.

Feller, J., Fitzgerald, B., Hissam, S. A. and Lakhani, K. R. (eds) (2005) *Perspectives on Free and Open Source Software*, Cambridge, MA: MIT Press.

Flyvbjerg, B., Bruzelius, N. and Rothengatter, W. (2003) *Megaprojects and Risk: An Anatomy of Ambition*, Cambridge: Cambridge University Press.

Giddens, A. (1991) *The Consequences of Modernity*, Cambridge: Polity Press.

Giddens, A. (2000) *Runaway world: How Globalization is Reshaping our Lives*, London: BrunnerRoutledge.

Gloor, P. A. (2006) *Swarm Creativity: Competitive Advantage through Collaborative Innovation Networks*, Oxford: Oxford University Press.

Hardt, M. and Negri, A. (2005) *Multitude: War and Democracy in the Age of Empire*, London: Hamish Hamilton.

Juris, J. S. (2005) 'The new digital media and activist networking within anti-corporate globalization movements', *Annals of the American Academy of Political and Social Science*, 597: 189–208.

Knorr-Cetina, K. (2003) 'From pipes to scopes: the flow architecture of financial markets', *Distinktion*, 7: 7–23.

Lave, J. and Wenger, E. (1991) *Situated Learning: Legitimate Peripheral Participation*, Cambridge: Cambridge University Press.

Law, J. (ed.) (1991) *A Sociology of Monsters: Essays on Power, Technology, and Domination*, London: Routledge.

Lee, G. K. and Cole, R. E. (2003) 'From a firm-based to a community-based model of knowledge creation: the case of the Linux kernel development', *Organization Science*, 14: 633–49.

Obmascik, M. (2004) *The Big Year: A Tale of Man, Nature, and Fowl Obsession*, New York: Free Press.

Prahalad, C. K. and Ramaswamy, V. (2004) *The Future of Competition: Co-creating Unique Value with Customers*, Boston, MA: Harvard Business School Press.

Rafael, V. L. (2003) 'The cell phone and the crowd: messianic politics in the contemporary Philippines', *Public Culture*, 15: 399–425.

Rheingold, H. (2002) *Smart Mobs: The Next Social Revolution*, Cambridge: Perseus.

Rorabaugh, W. J. (1986) *The Craft Apprentice: From Franklin to the Machine Age in America*, Oxford: Oxford University Press.

Sharma, A. K. and Johri, B. N. (eds) (2002) *Arbuscular Mycorrhizae: Interactions in Plants, Rhizosphere and Soils*, Enfield: Science Publishers.

Subramanian, R. and Goodman, B. D. (eds) (2005) *Peer to Peer Computing: The Evolution of a Disruptive Technology*, Hershey, PA: Idea Publishing Group.

Uricchio, W. (2004) 'Beyond the great divide: collaborative networks and the challenge to dominant conceptions of creative industries', *International Journal of Cultural Studies*, 7: 79–90.

Vaidhyanathan, S. (2004) *The Anarchist in the Library: How the Clash between Freedom and Control is Hacking the Real World and Crashing the System*, New York: Basic Books.

Vickers, M. H. (2001) *Work and Unseen Chronic Illness: Silent Voices*, London: Routledge.

Victor, B., and Boynton, A. C. (1998) *Invented Here: Maximizing your Organization's Internal Growth and Profitability*, Boston, MA: Harvard Business School Press.

von Hippel, E. (2005) *Democratizing Innovation*, Cambridge, MA: MIT Press.

Weber, S. (2004) *The Success of Open Source*, Cambridge, MA: Harvard University Press.

Wenger, E. (1998) *Communities of Practice: Learning, Meaning and Identity*, Cambridge: Cambridge University Press.

Wenger, E., McDermott, R. and Snyder, W. (2002) *Cultivating Communities of Practice: A Guide to Managing Knowledge*, Boston, MA: Harvard Business School Press.

Whorf, B. L. (1956) *Language, Thought, and Reality: Selected Writings of Benjamin Lee Whorf*, Cambridge, MA: MIT Press.

5   Including the missing subject

Placing the personal within the community

Stephen Billett

Key themes in this chapter

- The social and relational character of learning through participation in the social (community) of practice
- The role of individual agency in the concept of situated learning
- The relational interdependence between the social world of working life and individuals as workers
- Use of 'stories' to illuminate the interplay between the 'personal' and the relational in social participation

The concept of community of practice, particularly as originally articulated by Lave and Wenger (1991), provided a timely and useful salve to accounts of learning from cognitive psychology that were still predominant at the time of its publication. These accounts privileged individuals' cognitive processes and contribution to learning and proposed that human performance arose largely as a product of the clever manipulation by individuals of their cognitive structures (Ericsson and Smith 1991). In many ways the slim monograph, *Situated Learning*, highlighted and became a rallying point for those seeking alternatives to the cognitive account. Its publication occurred when the demonstrated inadequacies of cognitive theories were causing adherents of these theories to look elsewhere to understand learning and human cognition.

In the following decade, and to this moment, in response to continued dissatisfaction with cognitive accounts that viewed humans as cognitive systems, there has been an increased emphasis on the contributions of social practices and situational factors to individuals' cognition and learning. This included the need for individuals to engage with and secure the capacities required for performance in culturally derived practices, such as those for work and for study in educational institutions. In particular, a strong interest in learning arising from engagement with the immediate and situated social experience emerged. Central to this interest and a motif for its enactment has been the concept of 'communities of practice' (Lave and Wenger 1991), albeit far more often more popularly endorsed than critically appraised for its emphasis of the contributions of the immediate social experience. With any movement, some adherents press their case strongly and comprehensively, often seeking to enthusiastically redress premises that they wish to overturn or transform. Yet, in moves away from human cognition being seen as a process occurring largely within the individual, the particular attributes that individuals bring to cognitive processes (i.e. the person and the personal) have become de-emphasized and, in some cases, overlooked. Moreover, discussions about the socio-geneses of knowledge and learning often fail to engage the individual, even in its socially personal form that arises through ontogeny or life history.

In essence, the subject is often missing or lacking in its representations within contemporary theorizing, particularly those that privilege the contributions of the immediate situation in which individuals think, act and learn. Indeed, with a move away from learning focused upon individual cognitive processes, the 'individual' has seemingly become an unfashionable and tainted term. This is unfortunate and uninformed. Here the individual is rendered socially idiosyncratic, peculiar and perhaps unique through their engagement and negotiation with the social world. The personal arises from the social (Harre 1995). This proposition is plausible because of the on-going nature of individuals' particular negotiations with situated manifestations of socially derived knowledge that they encounter:

> personality becomes socially guided and individually constructed in the course of human life. People are born as potential persons, the process of becoming actual persons takes place through individual transformations of social experience.
>
> (Harre 1995: 373)

Indeed, there is perhaps nothing more social than the personally specific legacies that arise from individuals' engagement with the social world throughout their life histories or ontogenies (Billett 2003). The learning that comprises this legacy is inevitably personal because of, first, individuals' particular sets of experiences that will be necessarily peculiar to an individual. Second, as neither the contributions of the social world nor those of the individual alone are potent or sufficient enough to secure either asocial or socially subjugated legacies, the individual necessarily needs to engage agentically and selectively to secure ontological security (Giddens 1991) or equilibrium (i.e. to make sense of what they experience and respond to it). Thirdly, the negotiations between the individual and social are shaped by their agency, which includes personal interests, focuses and energies. Humans are subject to emotion, inconsistency in responses, exhaustion and inept responses that are not adequately accounted for in either cognitive or social constructivist accounts. Fourth, these negotiations are mediated by individuals' construals and constructions that are shaped by their personal histories. In these ways, the socially derived, but personal, legacies arise through histories of experience, that is, those that come earlier or pre-mediate experiences inevitably play a role in individuals' cognition and, therefore, their learning (Billett 2003). This includes how they negotiate with the contributions of immediate situated social experience.

Whilst the popular portrayal of *Situated Learning* (Lave and Wenger 1991) focuses on the community or situated contributions to learning, this chapter identifies an important role for the person within social practice: their engagement and their learning. In particular, it proposes that the relations between persons and the community of practice are relational. In doing so, they suggest that, rather than the individual being posterior to the social practice in which they engage, the relationship is agentic on both sides. That is, while the social situation can press its case through its norms and practice, these are mediated by the individuals' agency in the form of what others describe in terms of individuals' subjectivity, intentionality and interest.

This chapter seeks to rehearse and synthesize a set of ideas to promote the central role of the personal in considerations of human cognition (thinking, acting and learning) within social theorizing about learning, in ways consonant with what is advanced in *Situated Learning*. This case has at its heart elaboration of the central role of the subject in mediating the social experience and situated manifestations that individuals negotiate with in their everyday lives. It proposes an interdependence between social and personal factors. Moreover, it is argued that this interdependence is relational, intertwined in some instances yet disengaged in others. Instances from the work lives of contemporary workers are used to detail and illustrate the case. In all, the chapter seeks to reinstate the personal within social practice as being essential for both individuals' learning and the remaking of the social or community practice.

In making this case the chapter is structured as follows. Firstly, an account of Lave and Wenger's contribution to a consideration of both the personal and relational is elaborated, through the lens of my own theoretical interest in personal trajectories. This section includes a personal perspective of their contributions to my theorizing. This is because, as Bloomer *et al.* (2004) have argued, one's life history or ontogeny shapes the flow, focus and direction of individuals' theorizing about learning. However, such an approach is quite consistent with what Lave and Wenger (1991) proposed in terms of the personal engaging with the social. This is elaborated through a discussion of how learning needs to be understood as relational interdependence between the social world of working life and individuals as workers, with a particularly potent mediating role being exercised in these negotiations by the individual.

The personal and the relational

Lave and Wenger (1991) examined the relations between situated experience and individuals' learning. As noted earlier, by far its most well known legacy was to introduce the concept of 'community of practice' as a means of understanding the situational contribution to cognition and, in particular, the role of participation in social practices to individuals' learning. This concept has been widely used and, hence, deserves the timely critique offered within this collected volume. As has occurred with other ideas, the concept of community of practice has been widely adopted, celebrated and often uncritically appraised and referred to in ways inconsistent with the authors' intents. However, in fairness to those who seized upon its potential to address issues of individual learning and organizational development, one of the authors elaborated the concept of community practice in a highly instrumental way in a subsequent publication (Wenger, 1998). Multiple schemes for communities of practice were offered in this publication to achieve these goals. Indeed, Wenger claimed in a talk in Boston, USA, in 2003 that the concept of the 'community practice is now a global phenomenon, its reach has extended even as far as Australia' (Wenger 2003).

The original publication set out more modestly to propose a view of learning that incorporated the contribution of the immediate social experience to individuals' learning. It was widely read (even in Australia). However, it was the focus on the situation and the conceptualization of a community of practice as something through which learning within a social practice might occur that became the central focus of its impact, and this still continues. At the very time of writing this chapter my university is creating a number of 'communities of practice' that are directed towards achieving its strategic goals. These 'communities' have been nominated by the university executive and endorsed through its policy process. At a meeting of a committee in which I am a member, the chair advised the committee that we are now a community of practice.

In some ways, the impact of the original publication was not surprising. The book followed on from Brown *et al.*'s seminal paper (1989) on situated cognition, and then Collins *et al.*'s (1989) chapter on cognitive apprenticeships, which, like the Lave and Wenger book, provided conceptual platforms to appraise the contribution of social situations, partners, practice and artefacts to human cognition. This was followed by other texts on distributed cognition, that is, distributed across socially situated systems (see, for example, Resnick *et al.* 1991; Resnick *et al.* 1997). These publications were timely and welcomed. They came when many in the field of learning were realizing that theories within cognitive psychology were inadequate in understanding human learning as something shaped not only by individuals' capacities to secure, effectively organize and deploy their knowledge structures but also by the social world beyond individuals. Consequently, theoretical positions that emphasized individual contributions, but failed to adequately account for and acknowledge the contributions of the social world to human cognition were rightly seen to be incomplete. Since the time of the publication of these seminal pieces much, if not most, theorizing about learning has come to emphasize the immediate social contribution to cognition, that is, the contributions of the physically located and socially immediate situations in which individuals think and act. In this way, social contributions are seen as being those expressed and engaged with in a particular physical location (that is, the immediate social circumstances that project a particular kind of social suggestion, such as schools, workplaces, universities) in which the individuals engage with others and with socially derived norms and practices and artefacts (Resnick *et al.* 1991; Salomon 1997). Such views were helpful in understanding, for instance, workplaces as learning environments, with the concept of community practice being embraced as a means to understand that learning.

It was in such an environment that theorists and practitioners welcomed the concept of community of practice as a premise to understand how learning occurs through individuals' engagement with social partners and institutions. This sat comfortably within theories emphasizing the social contributions to learning. Indeed, advocates of situated social contributions to human cognition suggested that individuals are mere placeholders or components within distributed systems of cognition (Hutchins 1991; Pea 1993), and other popular theories (for example, activity systems) seem to de-emphasize or deny human agency, subjectivity and the contribution that arises through human construal and construction of what social world suggests to individuals (Engeström 1993). Certainly, some of that enthusiasm for this highly situated conception of learning has waned over time. Yet this may be a result of communities of practice becoming widely adopted and being presented as an instrumental approach to managing individuals' learning and professional development, and in ways aligned to meeting governmental and employer goals. Less emphasis has been given to critiquing the conceptual integrity of the concept of community practice.

Like others in the field (for example, Cobb 1998), while valuing the quality of much of its argument, ultimately the concept of community practice became less helpful for me to understand how people learn through work and in workplaces. A concern arose from the contributions of the individual being de-emphasized in the kind of theorizing that was arising through broad acceptance of the situated basis of cognition (Somerville and Abrahamsson 2003). In particular, the privileging of the immediate social experience (for example, the particular situation in which individuals act) seemed to be in contrast to what the data from my studies in workplaces were revealing, about the importance of how individuals elect to engage with what was afforded them by workplace settings (Billett 1993, 1994, 2001a). Hence, although initially engaging with concepts such as communities of practice and activity systems to understand the situational contributions of workplaces, my theoretical trajectory was motivated by the need to understand the relations between the social practices and individuals. This included the means by which individuals elect to participate in workplace settings and construct their understanding through that participation. This commenced with a paper arguing that both the individual and social contributions should be reconciled (Billett 1996). Later I found the concept of co-participation at work (Billett 2001a, 2002, 2004), helpful. Co-participation comprises dualities between the affordances of the workplace, on the one hand, and individuals' engagement, on the other, and was used to understand these relations and their implications for learning. These ideas were and are being elaborated in current conceptualizations of learning as arising through a relational interdependence between individual and social world (Billett 2003, 2006a). Here also the contribution of brute fact (Searle 1995) in the form of maturation processes, time, and so on, is seen to be central to a comprehensive account of ontogeny or life history.

Importantly, data from workplaces of different kinds, over time, consistently emphasized the importance of dualities that comprise both contributions or affordances of the workplace and the bases by which individuals elect to engage with what is afforded them and the relationships between them. That is, the agency of both the social and individual being enacted relationally in the immediate social experience of engagement in workplaces. Consequently, since 1995, much of my work is to understand how the personal, as constructed through socially derived and shaped individual histories or ontogenies, shapes human development and societal change.

The current emphasis on socially situated experience also masks another significant social legacy: the uniquely socially shaped nature of the person and personal. This arises and evolves through ongoing negotiations between the individual and the social throughout individuals' life histories or ontogenies and serves to mediate subsequent immediate experiences. These negotiations are on-going and construed and resolved in ways that are inevitably personally particular, and potentially unique (Billett 2006a). Moreover, these negotiations between the personal and the social are central to key questions within the social sciences. What is it that brings about personal and societal change: social structures, individual agency or some combination of two? It seems that as individuals engage in thinking and acting they themselves are not only learning but also engaging in the process of remaking and, possibly, transforming culturally derived practices (Billett 2006b). In essence, through understanding how the negotiated contributions of both the personal and the social world shape human cognition, another form of development arises: change to society and social structures.

So it seems important to move beyond accounting only for the contributions of the physical and situational factors to include those accounting for how learning occurs in inclusion of the role that individuals play in construing, interpreting, engaging with what was being suggested by social world. Along the way, situated cognition deserved to be defended against claims that it presented individuals' participation in social practice as being inevitably benign. Lave (1999) has stated that this was not her intention. There is much in the original book (Lave and Wenger 1991) to support her assertion, as well as her standing as an individual who is unlikely ever to see social practices, such as workplaces, as being benign, nor is such a position consistent with her disciplinary base of critical anthropology. So, like other but popularly held, but erroneous, views, such as

Piaget not considering the social (always an odd claim, for someone who was one of the first professors of sociology) and Vygotsky's 'zone of proximal development' being mainly about the agency of the social partner and not the learner, there was a sense that the concept of community practice as advanced in *Situated Learning* is being misrepresented.

In addition, the focus on communities of practice and its misrepresentation may well have served to mask other and important contributions made in Lave and Wenger's book. Central to these is its discussion about the relations between the personal and social. Within *Situated Learning* are arguments and presentations that are highly consistent with a theoretical position that engages the personal within a social frame. The book introduces the concepts of participation, interdependence and relational bases that now resonate strongly with my current theorizing. It was only in preparing this chapter that I re-engaged and became reacquainted with this slim volume and became aware of these emphases. This re-engagement occurred at a time and with a set of interests that were quite distinct from my first engagement with the book, and through the exercise of quite different conceptual lenses and interests. All this supports the central contention that the interaction between the social and the personal is relational. As a doctoral student in the early 1990s seeking to understand the contribution of workplace experiences to individuals' cognition, this text had an authority and pertinence to my theorizing that was of a particularly potent kind, and its conceptualization of communities of practice was helpful to capture the objective entity that comprised the workplace and its affordances, as were activity systems. Now what the book affords me and how I engage with it are quite different. So there are relational bases to my engagement with this social artefact.

I now find that this text is in many ways highly consistent with and supportive of my conceptual trajectory. Through this re-engagement I am now questioning whether that earlier reading provided me with important concepts at that time which have only more recently shaped much of my current conceptual trajectory. These may not have been at the forefront of my theorizing at that time, but nevertheless have some kind of legacy that prompted my subsequent trajectory. Consequently, it seems only appropriate to engage with this text to elaborate its contributions to the on-going, but recently revitalized, deliberations about relations between the individual and social.

Social and cognition

As noted, and in contrast to other widely adopted theories which emphasize the social contributions to cognition, Lave and Wenger (1991) proposed a central place for the individual or personal in their theorizing. In critiquing the cognitive perspective, they suggested that 'painting a picture of the person as primarily cognitive tends to provide non-personal view of knowledge, skills, tasks activities and learning' (Lave and Wenger 1991: 52). Yet they also offered the following caution:

> In contrast, to insist on starting with social practice, or taking participation to be the crucial process, and including the social world as the core of the analysis only seems to eclipse the person.

> (1991: 52)

Instead they emphasized the need for a consideration of both the person and relations between the personal and the social in understanding learning through participation in social practice: 'the person defines as well as is defined by these relations' (1991: 53). This consideration of the person is quite distinct from that offered through other contemporaneous accounts. For instance, Cole and Engeström (1997), in discussing concepts of activity systems within distributed cognition, give only limited consideration to the person. Here, in the only section of the chapter which refers to the person, they see the personal in terms of individuals' brains and write that 'one must keep in mind that knowledge and forms of thought are not uniformly distributed in the brain . . . ' (Cole and Engeström 1997: 12). Elsewhere, Engeström (1999) in a chapter entitled 'Activity theory and individual and social transformation', emphasizes historicism and fails to make mention of or effectively position the individual within the conceptual scheme despite the individual featuring in the chapter title. A consideration of individuals' contributions remains quite underdeveloped. The only reference to the personal arises from the author's reflections. However, the conceptual importance of these personal reflections does not seem to have carried over into the chapter's theoretical position.

In contrast to the relational position that Lave and Wenger (1991) propose, Engeström's (1999) presentation sees the individual as embedded within an activity system, rather than offering a basis by which they might participate with different degrees of engagement, and perhaps virtually none. Instead the individual is embedded as being one of a number of elements. The consciousness which may underpin the bases for, direction of and intentionality of engagement within social practice is reduced to that of being an element with set and preordained relations between objects and mediating artefacts. However, while some will argue that these associations are relational, there seems little room for the agency of individuals in construing and constructing the various contributions which they might engage with when participating in social practice such as paid work. Importantly, there seems to be little space for the individual to actively be selective in terms of engagement with or rebuttal of these elements, within this presentation.

Of course, these accounts were founded in particular theoretical premises whose interests and starting points are with the social and collective, not the individual. However, such a de-emphasis of the individual is not stipulated within social theorizing. Some sociological theorists openly acknowledge a key role for the individual. Berger and Luckman (1967), for instance, in their seminal work on the social construction of knowledge, are careful to point out that individuals engage in the social universe in quite distinct ways. This engagement is different in intensity and completeness. Giddens (1984), in his theory of structuration, suggests that there is reciprocity between the individual and the social in the transformation of self and society. The cultural psychologist Valsiner (2000) refers to the unique sense making and construal of social experiences which comprise individuals' cognitive experiences. Moreover, others suggest that the relationship between the individual and the social world is not one of individuals merely negotiating with social suggestion (i.e. its norms, values, practices), but what individuals decide is worthy of their engagement (Goodnow 1990), learn to be dissuaded by and dis-identify with what is being suggested (Hodges, 1998), and even a requirement to rebuff and ignore much of what is being socially suggested to the individual (Valsiner 2000). What drives and guides this negotiation, and either its acceptance or rejection by individuals, seems to be analogous to what Piaget (1968) advanced as the psychological processes of individuals' desire to maintain equilibrium,

Van Lehn's (1989) concept of maintaining viability, and Giddens's (1991) notions of individuals striving to realize ontological security. There is, therefore, a human need to understand, comprehend and make sense of what is being experienced. This is done by construing, constructing and engaging with what is experienced in ways shaped by factors associated with the personal in both individual and social constructivist theories of knowledge and emphasizing humans' active and selective role in making meaning and constructing knowledge. So it seems problematic to attempt to advance a theory of learning, even ones founded in a situational basis for cognition, that does not position human capacities, consciousness and subjectivity as a central concern. To do so would be to deny human consciousness and individual subjectivity (i.e. their cognitive experience), and their roles in human cognition, and learning.

Relations and interdependence in learning through and for work

The inadequacies of having a predominant focus on the immediate social and physical situation became apparent in my own studies of individuals' engagement in and learning through work and in workplaces. Differences in perceptions of the value placed on particular kinds of contributions to learning through work were identified in early studies of workers' learning in coal mines (Billett 1993) and in a secondary production plant (Billett 1994). Here, while identifying particular sets of contributions to these workers' learning and the factors constraining or inhibiting that learning, clear differences emerged in what kind of contributions were valued by individuals when learning through the same kinds of work activities and interactions. Similar, but more detailed, accounts of individuals' construals of workplace contributions were identified in a study of hairdressers' participation and learning in hairdressing salons. Essentially, this study demonstrated that, beyond the contributions of the situational manifestation of the practice of hairdressing, it was the hairdressers' personal histories that shaped how they engaged with the workplace, its norms and practices, including preferences for hairdressing procedures (Billett 2003). In these public and easily surveyable workplace settings, in which managers and supervisors could monitor the activities of hairdressing staff, hairdressers, including novices, exercised distinct preferences for hairdressing procedures and provided personally founded conceptions of hairdressing principles and practices. So, despite working in a workplace setting that had set practices (i.e. 'what we do here is . . . ') and means of monitoring and exercising those practices, these hairdressers were able to shape decision making about how they styled their clients' hair based on their personal preferences for practice. Moreover, these hairdressers' selection of which hairdressing salon to engage in was not arbitrary. Instead it was shaped by the particular intentions or imperatives that were personal in origin, even if not yet fulfilled.

From this study it was concluded that to understand learning activities situated in a particular workplace necessarily requires a consideration not just of situational factors but also of those individuals who act, participate and learn through their participation in those settings (Fenwick 1998; Somerville 2002). Personal factors include those associated with individuals' conceptions, agency, intentionality, energy and interest in participating and learning through the workplace (Billett *et al.* 2005; Fenwick 2002; Somerville 2002). Similarly Fuller and Unwin (2003) found that relations between apprentices and experienced trade workers are becoming reciprocal and relational. Young apprentices brought particular contributions to the apprenticeship process in the form of understandings about technology that the experienced trade workers lacked. So the traditional posterior relations between the experienced trade worker and apprentice were overturned by the changing requirements of work performance. Knowledge of electronic technology militated against the existing knowledge of the trade workers and buoyed the standing and contribution of the apprentices.

The relational nature of participation was also evidenced in the hairdressing salons through the ways in which different actors (e.g. managers, owners, experienced hairdressers, novices) were invited to participate and in what ways they elected to take up that invitation to participate (Billett 2003). Hence there is interdependence between the personal and social contributions being enacted through participation in work. In some circumstances the invitation is highly engaging, in others quite easy to ignore. This was even a factor for the engagement of more peripheral participants – clients – as well as for hairdressers. In one hairdressing salon there was a particularly dominant male owner who was also a very competent hairdresser as well as being relatively exotic within the community in which the salon was located. Some of the salon's clients seemed to enjoy having their presence acknowledged by this hairdresser. Their eyes would seek his, and he would elect how and when to acknowledge their presence in his salon. Yet to other clients his acknowledgement was of no interest. The particular qualities of this hairdresser, that some found so engaging, were, therefore, less so or not at all engaging for others. The types of negotiations that occurred between the salon's clients and the salon were shaped by these relations.

Moreover, the presence and impact of the male hairdresser had particular consequences for how hairdressing was practised in the salon. He had a set of practices to which his employees had to comply strictly. This included the need to work in silence and not to initiate conversations with clients ('no yappers'). Such a requirement added to the complexity of work activities, because another rule was that the most experienced hairdresser available had to work on the most demanding hairdressing task of any client in the salon. Therefore there was considerable movement, with hairdressers taking over clients from one another. In order to conduct their work the hairdressers developed a set of hand signals and gestures to indicate work instructions to one another. In this way there was a particularly potent and immediate social suggestion shaping workplace activities and in interactions in this salon. However, despite this strong social pressure and means of monitoring, there remained the evidence of the hairdressers making their decisions about hairdressing procedures based on their personal preferences within the range of treatments that were permissible within the salon. Indeed, across all of the hairdressers in all four salons, there was evidence of the bases for their decision making about practice and their conceptual constructs of hairdressing were shaped by personal experience and histories (Billett 2003).

The evidence captured through observation and interview about the exercise of social suggestions in terms of work practices, norms and values, and their projection through the actions of owners and managers, was complicated by other evidence from interviews, concept maps and responses to a set of uniform workplace problems. What was suggested was that situational factors provided a particular manifestation of the practice of hairdressing. These were quite distinct across the different hairdressing salons (Billett 2001b). However, beyond these affordances were the personal bases by which individuals construed and constructed what they experienced in the particular work situation. For some, these were the first hairdressing salons in which they had worked, whilst other hairdressers had had experience in a diverse range of hairdressing salons.

For each the particular motivations and interests associated with their hairdressing work extended to ways in which they managed the hairdressing task. In each workplace, therefore, there were quite personal bases to engage with what was afforded, to construe and construct from those affordances and elect in what ways to engage in identifying, offering and enacting particular hairdressing treatments. Hence there were relational bases between the contributions of the social and individual, which were enacted in a relational way.

These workplaces, therefore, stand as environments in which cognition and learning need be understood through the psychological processes comprising engagement between situational contributions. This may well reflect cultural practices and other social factors, and individual conceptions and agency which are personally socially derived. Moreover, it is perhaps through individuals seeking to make sense of what they know and what they want to achieve that comprises the inter-psychological negotiation. Beyond the pressure of the immediate social circumstance are the agency, intentionality and subjectivity of the learner.

In more recent studies this issue of relations between the personal and the workplace situation has continued to be a source of significance in understanding individuals' learning through work and their working life. In particular, this enquiry is directed towards understanding what directs individuals' lifelong learning efforts. For instance, in a study of five workers' learning throughout their work life (Billett and Pavlova 2005), the role of individuals in constructing and securing what they wish to achieve through their working life was clearly identifiable as comprising an interdependence between the workplace afforded them and how they elected to participate in it. The dependence upon a work environment, that can assist individuals to 'be themselves' at work, was evident in this study. The single mother who was employed in a fruit and vegetable wholesale market required this environment to help her create an identity outside her home. Beyond providing remuneration to support her family, the workplace permitted her an environment in which she could be something other than a care giver to her children. Similarly, the motor mechanic required the dealership to enable him to practise his craft, but also to realise some personal ambitions about being a supervisor and client manager through fulfilling his desire to assist people whose vehicles had mechanical problems. Then there was the manager of the public sector organization that was providing him with well paid and secure work, which, in turn, addressed his need to provide for his family, security for his future through the provision of superannuation, and allow him to make up for having engaged only in low-paid work early in his working life. For the electronics engineer, the corporation that employed him as an engineer granted him the professional status that he had worked to secure since arriving in Australia as a migrant from Russia. It had been a long journey and he had to develop a level of English language that would allow him to practise his electronics skills. There was also the retired footballer who had been granted the opportunity to develop a career in insurance brokerage by a company which had taken him on after his retirement from life as a professional sportsman. For each of these workers there was a degree of dependence upon the workplace to achieve their goals.

Yet that dependence was also relational and shaped by these individuals' desire to be themselves. They were able to negotiate and achieve their goals through their work. For instance, the woman in the fruit market was able to negotiate a way of working and a particular interest that permitted her to achieve some of her personal goals about being well regarded in the workplace and having an identity outside of home. Conversely, the electronics engineer was able to exercise agency. In particular, his expertise in rail transport was prized in a transport company seeking to expand in that area. Yet he had expectations about his self that led him to become increasingly frustrated as he felt that his contribution was being under-recognized and under-utilized. For the manager of the public sector organization, however, such concerns about workplace recognition were not as important, not as personally confronting, because of his focus on interests outside the workplace. These instances of relational engagement for the individuals' purposes were matched by the requirement of the workplaces for the contributions of the employees to secure their goals. Above all, it was the relational ways in which the pressure of the workplace and the agency of the individuals came together that emphasized the need to understand both in a consideration of learning through work and throughout working life.

Conclusion

It has been proposed here that the key and likely lasting legacy of Lave and Wenger (1991) is not through its elaboration and advocacy of the concept of communities of practice. Instead the lasting legacy of the book is likely to be associated with its prescient work about the relationship between the personal and immediate social experience in learning through participation. Building upon these contributions, it is possible to propose that inter-psychological processes need to be seen far more as those between the immediate social experience and personally social experience of individuals. In this way the social contributions to learning are extended beyond those provided by the immediate or situated experience to include those that are enacted through a history of personally founded negotiations between the individual and the social world that arise throughout unique ontogenies. Moreover, rather than a process founded on securing high levels of intersubjectivity or shared meaning, the prospects for common meaning are likely to be more remote and perhaps reserved only for experiences that are openly observable. Even then, while a phenomenon may have some common meaning, its construal by individuals will be shaped by particular sets of values, subjectivities and the discourses to which they have access.

It would be indeed heartening if these contributions, what they mean for education, for prospects for learning, and importantly their focus on the individuals who are to be subject to curriculum and pedagogy, could be as widely engaged with as those of the concept of community of practice. Then, perhaps, the discussion about the relations between individuals and the social world might be enriched and the resources available and prospects for provision such as education, professional development and learning through work might be best directed.

Key questions to consider

1   What are the implications of the role of individual agency for the creation and sustainability of communities of practice?
2   What factors might impede or facilitate the exertion of individual agency within communities of practice in contemporary workplaces?
3   Is it to the advantage or disadvantage of communities of practice for individuals to exert their agency?

4   What implications does this chapter have for the providers of education and training and for careers advisers?

References

Berger, P. L. and Luckman, T. (1967) *The Social Construction of Reality*, Harmondsworth: Penguin Books.

Billett, S. (1993) 'Authenticity and a culture of workpractice', *Australian and New Zealand Journal of Vocational Education Research*, 2 (1): 1–29.

Billett, S. (1994) 'Situated learning: a workplace experience', *Australian Journal of Adult and Community Education*, 34 (2): 112–30.

Billett, S. (1996) 'Situated learning: bridging sociocultural and cognitive theorising', *Learning and Instruction*, 6 (3): 263–80.

Billett, S. (2001a) 'Coparticipation at work: affordance and engagement', in T. Fenwick (ed.) *Sociocultural Perspectives on Learning through Work* XCII, San Francisco: Jossey Bass/Wiley.

Billett, S. (2001b) 'Knowing in practice: re-conceptualising vocational expertise', *Learning and Instruction*, 11 (6): 431–52.

Billett, S. (2002) 'Workplace pedagogic practices: co-participation and learning', *British Journal of Educational Studies*, 50 (4): 457–81.

Billett, S. (2003) 'Sociogeneses, activity and ontogeny', *Culture and Psychology*, 9 (2): 133–69.

Billett, S. (2004) 'Co-participation at work: learning through work and throughout working lives', *Studies in the Education of Adults*, 36 (2): 190–205.

Billett, S. (2006a) 'Relational interdependence between social and individual agency in work and working life', *Mind, Culture and Activity*, 13 (1): 53–69.

Billett, S. (2006b) *Work, Change and Workers*, Dordrecht: Springer.

Billett, S., and Pavlova, M. (2005) 'Learning through working life: self and individuals' agentic action', *International Journal of Lifelong Education*, 24 (3): 195–211.

Billett, S., Smith, R., and Barker, M. (2005) 'Understanding work, learning and the remaking of cultural practices', *Studies in Continuing Education*, 27 (3): 219–37.

Bloomer, M., Hodkinson, P. and Billet, S. (2004) 'The significance of ontogeny and habitus in constructing theories of learning', *Studies in Continuing Education*, 26 (1): 19–43.

Brown, J. S., Collins, A. and Duguid, P. (1989) 'Situated cognition and the culture of learning', *Educational Researcher*, 18 (1): 32–4.

Cobb, P. (1998) 'Learning from distributed theories of intelligence', *Mind, Culture, and Activity*, 5 (3): 187–204.

Cole, M., and Engeström, Y. (1997) 'A cultural-historical approach to distributed cognition', in Salomon, G. (ed.) *Distributed Cognitions: Psychological and Educational Considerations*, Cambridge: Cambridge University Press.

Collins, A., Brown, J. S. and Newman, S. E. (1989) 'Cognitive apprenticeship: teaching the crafts of reading, writing and mathematics', in Resnick, L. B. (ed.) *Knowledge, Learning and Instruction: Essays in Honour of Robert Glaser*, Hillsdale, NJ: Erlbaum.

Engeström, Y. (1993) 'Development studies of work as a testbench of activity theory: the case of primary care medical practice', in Chaiklin, S. and Lave, J. (eds) *Understanding Practice: Perspectives on Activity and Context*, Cambridge: Cambridge University Press.

Engeström, Y. (1999) 'Activity theory and individual and social transformations', in Engeström, Y., Miettinen, R. and Punamaki, R. L. (eds) *Perspectives on Activity Theory*, Cambridge: Cambridge University Press.

Ericsson, K. A. and Smith, J. (1991) *Towards a General Theory of Expertise*, Cambridge: Cambridge University Press.

Fenwick, T. (1998) 'Women's development of self in the workplace', *International Journal of Lifelong Learning*, 17 (3): 199–217.

Fenwick, T. (2002) 'Lady, Inc.: women learning, negotiating subjectivity in entrepeneurial discourses', *International Journal of Lifelong Education*, 21 (2): 162–77.

Fuller, A. and Unwin, A. (2003) 'Fostering workplace learning: looking through the lens of apprenticeships', *European Educational Research Journal*, 2 (1), 41–55.

Giddens, A. (1984) *The Constitution of Society*, Cambridge: Polity Press.

Giddens, A. (1991) *Modernity and Self-identity: Self and Society in the late Modern Age*, Stanford, CA: Stanford University Press.

Goodnow, J. J. (1990) 'The socialisation of cognition: what's involved?' in Stigler, J. W., Shweder, R. A. and Herdt, G. (eds) *Cultural Psychology*, Cambridge: Cambridge University Press.

Harre, R. (1995) 'The necessity of personhood as embedded being', *Theory and Psychology*, 5: 369–73.

Hodges, D. C. (1998) 'Participation as dis-identification with/in a community of practice', *Mind, Culture and Activity*, 5 (4): 272–90.

Hodkinson, P., Billett, S. and Bloomer, M. (2004) 'The significance of ontogeny and habitus in constructing theories of learning', *Studies in Continuing Education*, 26 (1): 19–43.

Hutchins, E. (1991) 'The social organization of distributed cognition', in Resnick, L. B., Levine, J. M. and Teasley, S. D. (eds) *Perspectives on Socially Shared Cognition*, Washington, DC: American Psychological Association.

Lave, J. (1999) Unpublished personal communication, University of California, Berkeley, 24 March.

Lave, J., and Wenger, E. (1991) *Situated Learning: Legitimate Peripheral Participation*, Cambridge: Cambridge University Press.

Pea, R. D. (1993) 'Practices of distributed intelligence and designs for education', in G. Salomon (ed.) *Distributed Cognitions*, New York: Cambridge University Press.

Piaget, J. (1968) *Structuralism*, trans. C. Maschler, London: Routledge.

Resnick, L. B., Levine, J. M. and Teasley, S. D. (eds) (1991) *Perspectives on Socially Shared Cognition*, Washington, DC: American Psychological Association.

Resnick, L. B., Pontecorvo, C., Säljö, R. and Burge, B. (1997) 'Introduction', in Resnick, L. B., Pontecorvo, C., Säljö, R. and Burge, B. (eds), *Discourse, Tools and Reasoning: Essays on Situated Cognition*, Berlin: Springer.

Salomon, G. (1997) *Distributed Cognitions: Psychological and Educational Considerations*, Cambridge: Cambridge University Press.

Searle, J. R. (1995) *The Construction of Social Reality*, London: Penguin.

Somerville, M. (2002) 'Changing Masculine Work Cultures', paper presented at the 'Envisioning Practice – Implementing Change' conference, Gold Coast.

Somerville, M., and Abrahamsson, L. (2003) 'Trainers and learners constructing a community of practice: masculine work cultures and learning safety in the mining industry', *Studies in the Education of Adults*, 35 (1): 19–34.

Valsiner, J. (2000) *Culture and Human Development*, London: Sage.

Van Lehn, V. (1989) 'Towards a theory of impasse-driven learning', in H. Mandl and A. Lesgold (eds) *Learning Issues for Intelligent Tutoring Systems*, New York: Springer.

Wenger, E. (1998) *Communities of Practice: Learning, Meaning, and Identity*, Cambridge: Cambridge University Press.

Wenger, E. (2003) Breakfast keynote to the Practice-oriented Education conference 'Building an Inclusive Model for Integrating Learning and Work', Northeastern University, Boston, MA, 10–12 April.

6 Cultivating network analysis

Rethinking the concept of 'community' within 'communities of practice'

Nick Jewson

Key themes in this chapter

- Assumptions about 'community' embedded in the notion of communities of practice
- Contrasting sociological theories of 'community' and their implications
- The application of network concepts to the analysis of communities of practice
- Social differentiation and communities of practice

The concept of community is central to theories of 'legitimate peripheral participation', 'situated learning' and, most of all, 'communities of practice'. The term appears twice in the second sentence – four times in the first paragraph – of Lave and Wenger's classic text (1991: 29). It is even more prominent in Wenger (1998) and Wenger *et al.* (2002). However, unlike 'practice', the concept of community remains relatively under-developed in their works. As a result, unquestioned theoretical assumptions are incorporated into their analysis that both create a range of conceptual difficulties and exclude other perspectives that are more fruitful. This chapter will argue that the notion of communities of practice has, implicitly and uncritically, drawn on one particular theoretical tradition in the study of communities – that which focuses on the symbolic construction of imagined collective entities. It is further suggested that an alternative approach – theories of social networks – offers a better way of addressing some of the common criticisms that have been levelled at the idea of communities of practice.

The next section offers an evaluation of the notion of communities of practice, outlining some common criticisms. The chapter goes on to explore theoretical assumptions about community embedded in Lave and Wenger (1991) and, in particular, Wenger (1998). It then sketches an alternative approach, based on theories of social networks. There follows a short section on the contribution of actor-network theory. The final substantive section explores the societal context of communities of practice through the lens of network theories. The chapter closes with a brief conclusion.

Strengths and weaknesses

The idea of communities of practice has made a huge impact on the understanding of learning processes. It played a leading role in shifting metaphors of learning, from the passive acquisition of knowledge to active participation in practices that generate identities and meanings (Felstead *et al.* 2005; Fuller *et al.* 2005). Lave and Wenger (1991) and Wenger (1998) highlighted the social context of practical activities, lived experiences and emergent identifications. They situated learning within and through active engagement in processes of negotiation, belonging and transition within particular social situations.

The concept of communities of practice has come a long way since its inception, not least as indicated by the subtitle of Wenger *et al.* (2002), 'a guide to managing knowledge' (see Hughes in this volume). This chapter, however, focuses on the earlier texts of Lave and Wenger (1991) and, most extensively, Wenger (1998). The latter, in particular, represents the most developed attempt to generate a serious academic exposition of the concept of communities of practice. As has been noted elsewhere (Barton and Tusting, 2005: 6), although Wenger's (1998) book is very well written, and wide-ranging in its use of sociological and psychological theories, it is also strangely frustrating. Its concepts are sometimes slippery and elusive. It invokes caveats that do not appear to reflect the general direction of the argument. Nevertheless, for students of communities of practice Wenger (1998) remains an essential and powerful point of reference.

This chapter does not seek to detract from the contribution of Lave and Wenger (1991) and Wenger (1998). Rather, it seeks to develop some key themes in their work through a critical examination of assumptions embedded in their model. However, the first step is to identify some of the main weaknesses in the conceptualization of communities of practice identified by critics and commentators (see, for example, Barton and Tusting 2005; Contu and Willmott 2003; Fox 2000; Fuller and Unwin 2004; Fuller *et al.* 2005; Hodkinson 2004; Hodkinson and Hodkinson 2003; Rainbird *et al.* 2004; Swan *et al.* 2002). The list that follows is not comprehensive (see also Fuller elsewhere in this volume), but it highlights some of the more prominent issues that can be addressed by incorporating network theories of social relationships into the analysis.

Critics have suggested that the concept of communities of practice fails to provide sufficient explanation or examination of:

1   Processes of disagreement, conflict and struggle, other than as tensions between newcomers and old-timers.
2   Processes of exclusion, discrimination and oppression.
3   Sources of innovation, the emphasis being on the transmission of existing practices.
4   The full range of learning trajectories, the emphasis being solely on the absorption of newcomers into positions of authority.
5   The social and spatial boundaries of communities of practice, resulting in inflation of the concept to include more and more types of social situations.
6   Power differentials and struggles within and between communities of practice.
7   Broader historical and cultural contexts of communities of practice.

It is the contention of this chapter that these problems can be addressed, and to some degree remedied, through an examination of the unquestioned assumptions about community embedded in Lave and Wenger (1991) and Wenger (1998).

The concept of 'community'

It has sometimes been suggested that the term 'community' is a particularly confused and unhelpful term within social science, bedevilled by a multitude of fuzzy meanings (for useful general overviews, see Crow and Allan 1994; Delanty 2003). In fact the conceptual uncertainties surrounding the term are no greater than those attached to many other sociological concepts, such as class, ethnicity and gender. However, in everyday language 'community' is used very loosely and often in ways that strongly imply value judgements. Popular usage generally connotes harmony, co-operation, unity and altruistic care for others. It is informed by nostalgic perceptions of a lost era – when social bonds were supposedly more local, simple, warm and face-to-face – as well as by a yearning to recreate this 'golden age'. Versions of such ideas have been marshalled within conservative, liberal and radical ideologies, although it is particularly associated with reactionary conservatism. They have been, and still are, regularly invoked in debates about social policy (see for example, Etzioni 1997; Frazier 1999; Putnam 2000).

As a result, the term 'community' leads a hectic and promiscuous life as sociological concept, popular mythology and social policy principle. The potential for contamination of the first usage by the second and third is considerable, as frequently noted in the sociological literature. Hence those who invoke the concept in rigorous academic analysis need to be explicit and precise about what they mean and, indeed, to consider whether it is helpful at all for their purposes. This Wenger (1998) and Lave and Wenger (1991) fail to do. Wenger is aware of the moral and ideological value judgements embedded in some uses of the term 'community' (1998: 76) but does not reflect on the wisdom of employing a concept that, in his own words, has overwhelmingly 'positive' associations.

Within sociological theory there are several different approaches to the formal definition and analysis of community ties. Prominent are those which represent community as: special territory or sacred place, elective interest group, symbolically constructed sense of belonging and configuration of social network bonds. Neither Lave and Wenger (1991) nor Wenger (1998) discusses theories of community, nor do they position themselves within these contrasting approaches. Uncritically they draw most extensively on the notion of community as a symbolically constructed sense of belonging. Thus a particular way of thinking about community is incorporated into their work without overt reflection or critique.

It should be noted at this point that Wenger (1998) argues that communities of practice are *sui generis* and cannot be understood by reducing them to their component parts of 'community' and 'practice'. He asserts that they are 'a special type of community' and that 'the term community of practice should be viewed as a unit' (1998: 72). Thus he seeks to distinguish communities of practice from other types of social configuration, such as residential neighbourhoods, teams, networks or groups. Furthermore, at one point he defines community as '*a way of talking* about the social configurations in which our enterprises are defined as worth pursuing and our participation is recognizable as competence' (1998: 5, emphasis added). 'Meaning', 'practice' and 'identity' are similarly defined as ways of talking. However, the direction of Wenger's argument is not towards discourse and linguistic analysis. Instead he portrays learning as the emergence of identity. Identity refers to a developing sense of belonging to a community of practice defined by the distinctive social characteristics of 'mutual engagement', 'joint enterprise' and 'shared repertoire' (1998: 72–85). 'Mutual engagement' refers to involvement in a multiplicity of actions, the meanings of which are negotiated among members. 'Joint enterprise' is characterized by involvement in a common endeavour, comprising collective processes of negotiated practical action, common accountability and mutual engagement. 'Shared repertoire' comprises 'routines, words, tools, ways of doing things, stories, gestures, symbols, genres, actions, or concepts' (1998: 83) developed and deployed over time.

Identity is, in many ways, the key concept in Wenger's analysis. He conceives identity as a 'pivot between the social and the individual' which 'avoids a simplistic individual–society dichotomy without doing away with the distinction' (1998: 145). Wenger's notion of community is wrapped around his exposition of identity: 'Building an identity consists of negotiating the meanings of our experience of membership in social communities' (1998: 145). Identity entails 'viewing the very definition of individuality as something that is part of the practices of specific communities' (1998: 146) and 'the formation of a community of practice is also the negotiation of identities' (1998: 149). Elsewhere he argues that identity is social because 'it is produced as a lived experience of participation in specific communities' (1998: 151). Membership of a community of practice 'translates into an identity as a form of competence' (1998: 153). Thus Wenger's formulation highlights negotiated and shared experiences of generating and participating in worlds of meaning within particular kinds of social groups. He argues, such meanings become 'reified', that is, perceived by members as objects with a force and power of their own, even though they are, in reality, imagined social constructions of the group (1998: 57–61).

This approach is redolent of the analysis of community ties developed most systematically in the work of Cohen (1982, 1985, 1986). Cohen argues that communities are essentially imagined entities (Anderson 1991), created around shared cultural meanings and collective identities, forged in and through symbols and rituals. Symbols are conceived as highly condensed systems of communication of values, beliefs and feelings. They enable diverse people to express a common allegiance because symbols are imprecise, ambiguous, ineffable and intuitive. Cohen's work is, thus, characterized by a relational perspective, but one in which community is derived from perceived cultural differences between 'us' and 'them', symbolically expressed in reified notions of 'the other'. Thus, Cohen's analysis of the command and influence of symbols has many similarities with Wenger's account of reification.

This approach has much to commend it but also suffers from certain limitations. It tends to neglect the potential for violence, conflict, discrimination and persecution inherent in the formation of relationships between insiders and outsiders, 'own' and 'other'. Boundaries are conceived in symbolic and cultural terms, specifically eschewing structural interpretations of difference. In highlighting the social construction of symbolic boundaries between insiders and outsiders there is relatively little analysis of boundaries within the group. The exclusive nature of communities is emphasized in a way which is more redolent of clan-based, tribal and remote rural societies than contemporary urban industrial ways of life. Research increasingly suggests that the latter are characterized by complex and fluid participation in a multiple range of more or less voluntary, overlapping, segmented ties. Moreover, it is difficult to envisage how empirical research within this tradition can proceed other than by means of qualitative ethnographic methodologies.

What are the implications of this conception of community for the analysis of communities of practice? Wenger recognizes that participation in communities of practice may take the form of conflict, competition and rivalry rather than consensus, co-operation and mutual respect (e.g. 1998: 56, 77). However, although he acknowledges these possibilities, he does not incorporate into his theory *conceptual* mechanisms for analysing or interpreting them. In Wenger's analysis, conflict and power struggles are *contingent* events, not processes inherent in and constituent of configurations of social interdependences. He is aware of the issue but his conceptualization of community does not offer him tools to analyse their origins, forms or effects. The only systemic source of tension identified is that between newcomers and 'old-timers'; i.e. generational struggles. Similarly, the exclusionary and reactionary potential of communities of practice to oppose change and innovation is acknowledged but not explained (see Wenger *et al.* 2002: 139). It is noted (e.g. Lave and Wenger 1991: 76; Wenger *et al.* 2002: 140–50) but attributed to 'human frailties' (Wenger *et al.* 2002: 140) rather than structural characteristics of social relationships. Wenger cautions against over-romanticizing communities of practice or assuming they are necessarily 'benevolent' (1998: 132) but nevertheless assumes a degree of innovation and creativity in their activities that contrasts with the dead hand of bureaucracy. Whilst warning of possible 'harmful effects' (1998: 85), he does not account for the source and strength of these effects, or by whom and on what grounds they are to be judged harmful.

An alternative approach: network analysis

Unlike symbolic theories of community, network analysis focuses on the configuration of interdependent relationships between members (an excellent introduction is provided by Scott 2000). Network theories examine relationships, bonds and interdependences between people, groups and institutions. Opportunities and constraints are conceived as characteristics of these networks of linkages, not as the attributes of individual agents or free-floating cultural belief systems. Network theories, then, investigate 'the *structure* of social action' (Scott 2000: 4, emphasis in the original).

The concept of power is integral to network models of social relations. Power is conceived as an attribute or quality of network connections themselves, not as a separate force, capacity or thing commanded by individuals. Since network ties are a product of *inter*dependences between people, power is always a two-way street. Although the balance of power within networks is typically unequal and favours some participants, all have a degree of influence on others. Thus network perspectives highlight that slaves have power over masters, children over adults, novices over old-timers (see, for example, Owen-Pugh in this volume). The power of members is a product of their shifting positions within networks. Power is not an attribute of individuals or objects. It is as a result of the organization of people and things in networks of relations that some can dominate more effectively than others. Network analysis does not presuppose either peace and harmony or conflict and struggle between network members. Rather it seeks to reflect the Janus-faced balance of opposing pressures within social relations. Network connections may well entail contest or conflict *at the same time* as they entail co-operation and co-ordination. Networks are frequently held together by cross-cutting ties of collaboration and struggle, rather than by agreed symbolic orders, moral values and unitary identifications.

Network analysis may focus on a particular individual – 'ego-centric networks' – or a whole group – 'socio-centric networks'. Networks can be represented as matrices, tables, graphs and diagrams. Qualitative data are a very valuable source of information about the way networks function and are experienced but network analysis is also conducive to quantitative analysis, using a range of sophisticated mathematical techniques and concepts. Network concepts, thus, bridge the divide between qualitative and quantitative methodologies (see Felstead *et al.* 2005).

In addition to its distinctive general theoretical perspective, network analysis offers a range of useful specific concepts.

Stars and bridges

The extent to which an individual, or cluster of individuals, controls information, resources and influence depends on their strategic location within the overall network of ties. A simple way of investigating such strategic powers is to construct a map of the links between members, as measured by indices such as frequency of contact, friendship choices or financial links. It is common to find that some members have many and frequent links ('stars'), others few ('isolates'). Stars may well occupy positions of power and leadership, derived from their location in the network. However, isolates are not necessarily without influence. Those on the periphery of a network may have attenuated connections with the centres of decision making but nevertheless exercise great importance as the primary point of contact with outsiders and members of other networks (for example, receptionists, porters and concierges). Their network position may confer status (as representatives of the whole network) and power (as gatekeepers). The powers, attitudes and identities of members are, thus, interpreted as functions of their relational position within networks. Moreover, differences in the identifications and learning trajectories of members are conceived as inevitable aspects of the differentiation of network structures.

The significance of a pathway within a network also depends on its location within the total configuration of relationships. So, for example, it is not uncommon to find that some bonds link together a number of clusters of dense relationships within a network, such as several different communities of practice within a firm. Individuals who control these links – known as 'bridges' – may be relatively isolated within each network but develop highly prized skills in mediating between diverse groups and generating partnerships, acting as diplomats, negotiators or go-betweens. Such individuals may also be important sources of innovation, since their structural position enables them to transmit and translate ideas from one context into another. These qualities reflect their *position* in the network of relations. They are *relational* effects rather than simply personal psychological characteristics or normative values.

Centralized and decentralized networks

The degree of centralization of a network, as a whole, should not be confused with the degree of centrality of any particular point or individual within it. Centralization refers to the overall pattern of network integration. Visual representations of centralized networks portray them as web-shaped, with all connections leading to a few key points. Decentralized networks, in contrast, are lattice-shaped and polycentric. Centralized and decentralized networks present contrasting structural constraints and opportunities, reflected in patterns of power and influence, compliance and struggle, innovation and resistance.

Highly centralized networks are more likely to be characterized by unitary codes of behaviour and thought, hierarchies of prestige and authority, and norms of deference to established authority. Communications between points on the network are likely to pass along a few standardized channels that are readily subject to central policing. Hence they facilitate panoptical surveillance and monitoring of subordinates by seniors or their agents. In contrast, decentralized networks have many local clusters but contain few positions of global centrality. Communications travel independently between regions of the network through multiple and diverse channels that are too dispersed to be easily regulated. As a result, heresy abounds and apostates flourish. There is an open clash of opinions, perceptions and perspectives that cannot be easily censored or sanctioned by central authority figures. A thousand flowers bloom but there is less sense of completeness, singularity and harmony than in centralized networks.

It should be clear that situated learning has quite different implications in highly centralized and decentralized networks, generating different beliefs, values, identities and ways of life. The difference is not between strong communities and weak communities but between different structures of communal relationships. Furthermore, the impact of centralization and decentralization is mediated by the size of the network. Thus, for example, the sensibilities of members of centralized networks who experience immediate, face-to-face and direct contact with points of authority are likely to be different from those in centralized networks where centres of authority are remote, opaque and operated by intermediary agents. Similarly, decentralized networks may be characterized by direct exchanges of views between participants or indirect conduits of communication.

Clusters and cliques

It is common to find that some of the pathways within networks form clusters or cliques. Networks may comprise a series of clusters, or even clusters nested within clusters. Some networks may be neither centralized nor decentralized but rather composed of a series of cliques or clusters, each of which is relatively centralized but none of which dominates the network as a whole. Here bridging points and connections that link the clusters may be particularly powerful and influential.

The formation of cliques and clusters has obvious implications for learning, since they shape the flows and editing of information, the exercise of power and authority, and the paths through which influence is exercised at a distance. Cluster members may believe they have more in common with one another than with other network members. Stereotypes may influence the way members of clusters behave towards one another and their perceptions of outsiders. Clusters may support subcultures that express variant forms of dominant norms and values. However, once again these are network effects.

Network density

'Density' is another important concept in network analysis. Density refers to the completeness of a network, or 'the extent to which all possible relations are present' (Scott 2000: 32). A high-density network is one in which a high proportion of members are *directly* connected to one another. In contrast, a low-density network is one in which many points are not directly connected but are linked *indirectly* through second, third or 'nth' parties. Obviously, for a network to exist there have to be some direct ties but in low-density networks a high proportion of members are connected through intermediaries. In high-density networks, then, members are in contact with one another independently of any particular member. Low-density networks, in contrast, are those in which many associates of individual members are not in contact with, or possibly not even aware of, others.

This is a simplified version of a complex notion, but enough has been said to point towards the significance of network density. High-density networks exert powerful pressures on individual members to orient their attitudes, behaviour and emotions outwards towards the group. Group surveillance is intense. Collective belonging and fitting in with the group are the key source of identity. A successful life is deemed to be one in which an individual lives up to the standards imposed by pre-existing normative codes that characterize the group. Where network density is low, identification processes tend to be more individualistic and individuated. Membership is more likely to be a product of choice. Emphasis is placed on personal achievements, inner states of consciousness and emotional ties with individuals. Success entails forging personal lifestyles rather than conforming to group expectations.

It should be strongly emphasized here that the point at issue is not that of the presence and absence of network ties but rather of the form or configuration of such ties. Thus both high and low-density networks may entail situated learning processes characterized by participation, emergent identification and legitimate peripheral practice. Both may support what Wenger (1998) calls 'mutual engagement', 'joint enterprise' and 'shared repertoires'. However, members of high and low-density networks are likely to develop different socio-psychological sensibilities and identities.

It may be tempting to identify communities of practice solely with high-density networks. However, it is precisely these types of networks that are often inward-looking, defensive and resistant to change (see, for example, Wallman's 1986 comparison of the London boroughs of Battersea and Bow). Moreover, so-called 'weak ties' of low-density networks appear often to be a crucial resource in negotiating new and unfamiliar situations. Innovative, confident and dynamic communities of practice, then, may be characterized by relatively low-density social bonds. Furthermore, developments in the overall organization of advanced industrial societies (discussed below) are tending to undermine the conditions which facilitate the emergence and maintenance of high-density networks. Research suggests that increasing numbers of people maintain extensive personal networks of relations with family, friends and co-workers but that these are low-density ties with limited direct cross-contact between participants (see, for example, Wellman and Berkowitz 1988; Delanty 2003).

Network boundaries

Wenger (1998) devotes a whole chapter to boundaries and, indeed, comes close to using network models to illustrate his arguments; for example in the use of diagrams to describe types of cross-boundary *encounters* within communities of practice (1998: 113). However, he does not use network models to identify the configurations of social *relationships* that *constitute* communities of practice. His notion of the 'edge' or 'periphery' of a community of practice is a metaphor rather than a concrete relational concept. Hence the encounters described by Wenger are fortuitous, uncontextualized and contingent, whereas network models identify the relational constraints and imperatives that shape, drive and limit social interactions. Thus, for example, Wenger identifies the important roles played by brokers who span boundaries, involving 'translation, coordination and alignment between perspectives' (1998: 109). He recognizes the uncertainties and tensions often experienced by brokers who are members of more than one community of practice (1998: 109–10) and develops useful notions for describing their strategies (1998: 114–18). He does not, however, examine the overall patterns of network connectedness that determine the possibility, or otherwise, of any particular member exercising a brokerage, or bridging, role.

While the notion of boundaries is underdeveloped within theories of communities of practice, it is a central concept within network theory. Boundaries within and between networks are conceptualized in terms of breaks in the interconnections between members, as well as in terms of relative ease or difficulty with which individuals can change their positions within the network. Concepts such as centrality, centralization, cliques, clusters, bridges and density offer a distinctive perspective on boundaries within and between social networks. Furthermore, network analysis allows us to investigate the extent to which boundaries are porous or permeable. Some networks have many open ports of entry and exit whilst others have few doors that are heavily policed.

Lave and Wenger (1991) and Wenger (1998) offer few insights into the internal boundaries and divisions of communities of practice, other than their observations about interactions between newcomers and old-timers. The range of concepts offered by network analysis paints a far more complex picture. Network theory enables us to theorize not only boundaries around communities of practice, conceived as 'group' boundaries by Douglas (1970) in her memorable work, but also boundaries within, designated by Douglas as 'grid' boundaries. Douglas draws out the contrasting sensibilities associated with different combinations of group and grid boundaries. Thus, for example, she argues that a combination of strong group and weak grid boundaries is likely to generate a defensive, intense and embattled mentality, such as that of a cult or sect. In contrast, strong group combined with strong grid facilitates the emergence of a sense of perceived order, hierarchy and stability, associated with church-like organizations. The crucial point here is that boundary dispositions defined by network connections generate strikingly different ethical beliefs, material world views, modes of behaviour and patterns of learning. Network analysis points to the many different relational forms that may comprise communities of practice.

Learning trajectories

Wenger's discussion of forms of participation (1998: 165–87) touches on differences in learning trajectories but remains within a conceptual framework focused on individuals rather than the systemic determination of trajectory possibilities. Lave and Wenger (1991: 94) suggest that their empirical case study materials demonstrate that 'the authority of masters and their involvement in apprenticeship varies dramatically across communities of practice'. They go on to argue for a 'decentred' view of the master–apprenticeship relationship, on the grounds that 'mastery resides not in the master but in the organization of the community of practice of which the master is a part'. These interesting comments underline the need for a relational analysis of different types and forms of learning trajectories within communities of practice. However, Lave and Wenger (1991) and Wenger (1998) focus largely on the entry of newcomers and the transition from rookie to old-timer. Their conceptualization of community does not provide them with the intellectual tools necessary systematically to analyse the *organization* of communities of practice.

Different types of network offer different possibilities for learning trajectories. Network theory identifies a wide range of roles, positions, statuses and functions beyond those of rookie, novice and old-timer. For example, trajectories of development may take members towards different old-timer statuses, as bridges, stars, isolates, mediators or gatekeepers. Old-timers themselves may shift between these positions as their careers develop down different routes and over time. In all cases, movement and trajectories will be shaped by the strategic power exercised by individuals over others through their network position. Moreover, the overall form of the network will determine which *positions* are available within the community of practice at any particular time. Thus, for example, centralized and decentralized networks offer different possibilities; the role of mediator may be present in some network configurations but not others. Hence trajectories may be examined in terms of the constraints and affordances influencing the various egocentric biographies of individual members but also the sociocentric forces shaping the overall disposition of roles, statuses and identities. Learning trajectories are a function of network configuration.

Actor-network theory

The language of network theory, not to mention commonplace visual representations of networks as points and lines, might appear to encourage a reified view of social relations as fixed, unchanging and static 'things'. In contrast, Lave and Wenger (1991) and Wenger (1998) portray social relations as negotiated, emergent and performed products of collaborative participation in action. Hence it might be thought that network models run counter to the underlying premises of communities of practice. However, Actor-Network Theory (ANT) specifically eschews the trap of reification (Law 1986; Law and Hassard 1999; Callon 1986; Fox 2000; Swan *et al.* 2002; Mutch 2003).

Actor-network theory emphasizes *processes* of social network formation, the *vulnerability* of network alliances and connections, the requirement to *reproduce* and *maintain* networks on a continuous basis, and the resultant inherent tendency to *change*. ANT speaks of social order*ing* and social organiz*ing*, rather than social order and social organization, so as to emphasize the contingent, emergent nature of network ties. On this view, different combinations and alliances of network participants are constantly struggling to mobilize, create and sustain networks of relationships. Individuals and clusters of individuals seek to achieve their objectives through the formation of networks with others, but typically are confronted by other alliances trying to assemble and repair networks directed towards their own objectives. The capacity to control or direct the world *through* network connections is therefore always contingent and usually contested.

From this perspective, people, animals and objects all acquire significance and meaning because of their positioning within networked relationships. Non-human objects extend, broaden or deepen the controls that members exercise over others and the material world through network ties. Such texts and devices impose disciplines on network members who use them. They are, in a very real sense, a *part of* the network. Hence, ANT conceives networks as containing people *and* things. Thus, ANT enables us to incorporate Wenger's notion of 'shared repertoire' into a network context.

ANT offers a perspective on the formation of identities and the meaning of learning that incorporates power differentials and struggles for control. ANT argues those who dominate networks are in a position to develop mythologies, narratives and stories that characterize and justify their actions. To exercise power is to be in a position to generate and disseminate stories that prevail at the expense of the accounts of others, within and outside the network. Dominant members seek to extend networks, and hence their reach and influence, by recruiting new participants who have internalized their hege-monic tales. The more powerful convince others to behave in agreed ways through this 'translation process'. Their powers are derived from their dominance over the processes by which networks are reproduced.

Communities of practice and societal context

Wenger (1998: 79) notes that communities of practice are 'not self-contained entities' but are located in wider historical, cultural and institutional contexts 'with specific resources and constraints'. He observes that:

> Communities of practice cannot be considered in isolation from the rest of the world, or understood independently of other practices. Their various enterprises are closely interconnected. Their members and their artefacts are not just theirs alone. Their histories are not just internal; they are histories of articulation with the rest of the world.
>
> (Wenger 1998: 103)

However, Lave and Wenger (1991) and Wenger (1998) do not offer ways of analysing or explaining societal context. Its importance is stated but no analytical purchase offered on its form, extent or direction. Moreover, the five case studies presented in Lave and Wenger (1991: 59–88) span massively different types of societies without comment on their contrasting contexts. However, network analysis, in the form of theories of social differentiation, offers important clues.

It is a commonplace of sociological theory that the rise of 'modernity' has generated societies characterized by high levels of structural differentiation. There is a general tendency, as societies increase in scale, scope and complexity, for social bonds to become more specialized, clearly differentiated and hedged by formal boundaries. Specialized institutions and networks emerge engaged in specific, delineated, segregated and limited activities. The scope of activities organized within any particular institution or network becomes more circumscribed. As a result, in general, individuals become involved in a wider range of types of social networks, each with a narrower remit. Thus, as societies become more structurally differentiated, the communities of practice to which individuals belong multiply in number and become more specialized. Legitimate peripheral participation and situated learning are profoundly shaped by these structural features of the development of network connections.

Societies with relatively low levels of structural differentiation – such as those inhabited by Yucatec midwives and Vai and Gola tailors, featured in Lave and Wenger (1991) – are typically dominated by ties of kinship, clan and village. They are character-ized by an absence of multiple communities of practice and a paucity of opportunities to move between them. Participation, belonging and mutual engagement are lifelong, one-off and indelible commitments. Alternative joint enterprises are few. Shared reper-toires are jealously guarded secrets, not available as sources of innovation via net-worked bridges of translation. Relationships are typically multiplex, as each person is bound to others by ties which embrace multiple social activities and functions. This makes for high levels of network density and intense forms of surveillance and discip-line. Communities of practice bind their members closely, develop a strong sense of collective identity, raise high barriers to entry and exit from the group, and demand exclusive participation. Moreover, they operate in institutional contexts where they can offer multiple goods and services to members and in which the formal legal parameters of their licence and mandate are diffuse or obscure. As a result, although their activities may be geographically localized, their involvement in the lives of their members is large.

In societies with high levels of structural differentiation, members participate in many relatively insulated social contexts, each focused around limited and specialized activities and commitments. Even the most highly charged social bonds span only a part of the lived experience of any individual. Social life involves the negotiation of a biography that traverses these different networks and situations. Network densities are weaker and opportunities for social and geographical mobility enormously increased. As a result, people develop low-density 'personal communities' (Wellman 1979; Wellman and Berkowitz 1988) in which they maintain many social ties, possibly over considerable distances, but in which members are indirectly connected. There is far less material, psychological and social investment in any one community of practice. Rather than becoming more and more embedded within a single community of practice across a lifetime, identity may well lie in successfully traversing many communities of practice without becoming immured in any one. Indeed members of communities of practice may define their participation as that of a consumer, participating by choice, on a temporary basis, as long as their interests are served.

In these circumstances a cosmopolitan socio-psychological disposition emerges, in which identity becomes attached to generic transferable skills rather than particularized local knowledge. Structural differentiation of social networks promotes reflexivity in individuals as a result of their diverse experiences of the contrasting knowledge and skills base of many communities of practice. Innovation is generated by the diverse experiences and dispositions that new members bring to the community of practice as well as cross referencing between members (Swan *et al.* 2002; Mutch 2003; Fuller *et al.* 2005). The distinction between 'expansive' and 'restrictive' learning environments (Fuller and Unwin 2004) can be conceptualized as that between societal situations that promote multiple cross-cutting network ties (such as low-density networks with extensive bridges and 'weak' ties) and those that inhibit serendipitous cross-contacts within and between communities of practice.

Wenger is aware of some of these possibilities. He declares, 'we can participate in multiple communities of practice at once' (1998: 105). As a consequence, he argues, we are constantly 'passing boundaries – catching, as we peek into foreign chambers, glimpses of other realities and meanings; touching, as we pass by outlandish arrangements, objects of distant values; learning, as we coordinate our actions across boundaries, to live with decisions we have not made' (1998: 165). However, Wenger does not offer conceptual tools to theorize the social conditions of these sensibilities. As a result, he cannot analyse the extent to which such experiences are unequally distributed among the members of contemporary societies.

Industrialized, urbanized societies are indeed characterized by high levels of overall structural differentiation, but within these societies some people lead more differentiated lives than others. Class, gender, ethnicity and age shape the network configurations of various categories of citizens in sharply contrasting ways. For example, picking up on two of the case studies in Lave and Wenger (1991), it might be anticipated that the social networks of US Navy quartermasters are more centralized, dense and delineated than those of junior meat cutters in supermarkets. Thus, although all networks and network connections in highly differentiated societies stand in marked contrast to those of relatively undifferentiated societies, within structurally differentiated societies we may expect communities of practice to vary between social groups according to the particular configuration of network connections of their members.

It may well be that the high-flying managers to whom much of the managerialist literature on communities of practice is directed are among those most likely to experience low-density social networks and personal communities, and, hence, least likely to commit themselves within one community of practice. Ironically, those most strongly engaged within a single community of practice may arguably be said to be those manual workers in heavy industry who have highly developed occupational identities, ingrained semi-autonomous work practices and long-standing local residential patterns. However, this dwindling section of the work force – referred to by sociologists as the 'traditional' or 'proletarian' working class – is often disparaged as conservative, luddite and old-fashioned. The so-called down side of communities of practice often seems to refer to the defensive practices of disadvantaged but entrenched groups of workers (see Myers 2005 on Sellafield workers).

Conclusion

Network analysis yields an impressive array of conceptual tools. It offers a way of developing the concept of communities of practice that addresses many of the criticisms that have been aimed at the concept. Network theory makes it possible to turn the generalities of 'mutual engagement', 'joint enterprise' and 'shared repertoire' into specific measurable indices. Network theory opens up the possibility of distinguishing a much richer panoply of roles, positions and functions within communities of practice – beyond those of rookie, novice and old-timer – and hence a wider range of learning trajectories of individuals. Network theory enables us to distinguish different types of communities of practice, each with its own distinctive disposition of relationships, offering contrasting 'learning territories' (Fuller and Unwin 2004: 141). Network models do not merely allow for the possibility of conflict, inequality and power struggles, as do Lave and Wenger (1991) and Wenger (1998), but rather analyse the sources and outcomes of such processes. Similarly, network theories shed light on the social conditions that facilitate both innovation and conservatism. Network theories enable us to locate communities of practice within their wider societal contexts in ways which link up with other learning theories, such as the distinction between expansive and restrictive learning environments (Fuller and Unwin 2004). Network theories offer ways of conceptualizing boundaries that avoid conflating communities of practice. All this can be achieved without importing into the analysis the ideological baggage associated with the term 'community'. Wenger is at pains to distance communities of practice from mere networks: 'The term is not a synonym for group, team, or network' (1998: 74). However, it is the contention of this chapter that network theories enable us to specify and analyse structural aspects of small group relationships, rather than simply describe them, and build greater complexity into our theories without losing analytical purchase.

Key questions to consider

1   What ethical, moral and ideological assumptions are embedded in the popular use of the term 'community'?

2   What are the implications of different theorizations of 'community' for our understanding of 'communities of practice'?
3   Are communities *necessarily* harmonious and altruistic, or *necessarily* antagonistic and exclusive?
4   How do communities of practice in urban industrial societies differ from those in rural agricultural societies?
5   What characteristics do communities of practice have in common, and in what ways do they differ from one another?

References

Anderson, B. (1991) *Imagined Communities: Reflections on the Origins and Spread of Nationalism*, London: Verso.

Barton, D. and Tusting, K. (eds) (2005) *Beyond Communities of Practice: Language, Power and Social Context*, Cambridge: Cambridge University Press.

Callon, M. (1986) 'Some elements of a sociology of translation: domestication of the scallops and the fishermen of Saint Brieuc Bay', in Law, J. (ed.) *Power, Action and Belief: A new Sociology of Knowledge?* Sociological Review Monograph 32, London: Routledge.

Cohen, A. (1982) *Belonging: Identity and Social Organization in British Rural Cultures*, Manchester: Manchester University Press.

Cohen, A. (1985) *The Symbolic Construction of Community*, London: Tavistock.

Cohen, A. (ed.) (1986) *Symbolising Boundaries: Identity and Diversity in British Cultures*, Manchester: Manchester University Press.

Contu, A. and Willmott, H. (2003) 'Re-embedding situatedness: the importance of power relations in learning theory', *Organization Science*, 14 (3): 283–96.

Crow, G. and Allan, G. (1994) *Community Life: An Introduction to Local Social Relations*, Hemel Hempstead: Harvester Wheatsheaf.

Delanty, G. (2003) *Community*, London: Routledge.

Douglas, M. (1970) *Natural Symbols: Explorations in Cosmology*, London: Barrie & Rockliffe.

Etzioni, A. (1997) *The New Golden Rule: Community and Morality in a Democratic Society*, London: Profile Books.

Felstead, A., Fuller, A., Unwin, L., Ashton, D., Butler, P. and Lee, T. (2005) 'Surveying the scene: learning metaphors, survey design and the workplace context', *Journal of Education and Work*, 18 (4): 359–83.

Fox, S. (2000) 'Communities of practice, Foucault and actor-network theory', *Journal of Management Studies*, 37 (6): 853–67.

Frazier, E. (1999) *The Problem of Communitarian Politics: Unity and Conflict*, Oxford: Oxford University Press.

Fuller, A. and Unwin, L. (2004) 'Expansive learning environments: integrating organizational and personal development', in Rainbird, H., Fuller, A. and Munro, A. (eds), *Workplace Learning in Context*, London: Routledge.

Fuller, A., Hodkinson, H., Hodkinson, P. and Unwin, L. (2005) 'Learning as peripheral participation in communities of practice: a reassessment of key concepts in workplace learning', *British Educational Research Journal*, 31 (1): 49–68.

Hodkinson, P. (2004) 'Research as a form of work: expertise, community and methodological objectivity', *British Educational Research Journal*, 35 (1): 107–19.

Hodkinson, P. and Hodkinson, H. (2003) 'Individuals, communities of practice and the policy context: schoolteachers' learning in their workplace', *Studies in Continuing Education*, 25 (1): 3–21.

Lave, J. and Wenger, E. (1991) *Situated Learning: Legitimate Peripheral Participation*, Cambridge: Cambridge University Press.

Law, J. (1986) 'On the methods of long-distance control: vessels, navigation and the Portugese route to India', in Law, J. (ed.) *Power, Action and Belief: A new Sociology of Knowledge?* Sociological Review Monograph 32, London: Routledge.

Law, J. and Hassard, J. (eds) (1999) *Actor Network Theory and After*, Oxford: Blackwell.

Mutch, A. (2003) 'Communities of practice and habitus: a critique', *Organisation*, 24 (3): 383–401.

Myers, G. (2005) 'Communities of practice, risk and Sellafield', in Barton, D. and Tusting, K. (eds) *Beyond Communities of Practice: Language, Power and Social Context*, Cambridge: Cambridge University Press.

Putnam, R. D. (2000) *Bowling Alone: The Collapse and Revival of American Community*, New York: Simon & Schuster.

Rainbird, H., Munro, A. and Holly, L. (2004) 'The employment relationship and workplace learning', in Rainbird, H., Fuller, A. and Munro, A. (eds) *Workplace Learning Context*, London: Routledge.

Scott, J. (2000) *Social Network Analysis: A Handbook*, 2nd edn, London: Sage.

Swan, J., Scarbrough, H. and Robertson, M. (2002) 'The construction of "communities of practice" in the management of innovation', *Management Learning*, 33 (4): 477–96.

Wallman, S. (1986) 'Ethnicity and the boundary process in context', in Rex, J. and Mason, D. (eds), *Theories of Race and Ethnic Relations*, Cambridge: Cambridge University Press.

Wellman, B. (1979) 'The community question', *American Journal of Sociology*, 84: 1201–31.

Wellman, B. and Berkowitz, S. D. (eds) (1988) *Social Structures: A Network Approach*, Cambridge: Cambridge University Press.

Wenger, E. (1998) *Communities of Practice: Learning, Meaning and Identity*, Cambridge: Cambridge University Press.

Wenger, E., McDermott, R. and Snyder, W. M. (2002) *Cultivating Communities of Practice: A Guide to Managing Knowledge*, Boston, MA: Harvard Business School Press.

7 Theorizing sport as a community of practice

The coach–athlete relationship in British professional basketball

Valerie Owen-Pugh

Key themes in this chapter

- Power inequalities in British professional basketball
- The emotional dimensions of coach/athlete (old-timer/newcomer) relationships
- Social influences on the working of practice communities
- Assessment-driven development trajectories
- Legitimate peripheral participation in the development of elite athletic skill

Lave and Wenger (1991) have emphasized the value of learning through forms of practice-based apprenticeship. They offer a decentred view of human agency in which skill and knowledge emerge, not from the deliberate intentions of particular individuals, but through the co-engagement of the practice community as a whole. Viewed from this perspective, assessment-driven forms of instruction become inappropriate for promoting personally meaningful forms of learning. It is the role of the practice master (or 'old-timer') as a legitimator, rather than teacher, of practice that furthers the development of an apprentice's (or 'newcomer's') chosen career. In this scenario, the overwhelming majority of community members become masters of practice (although see also Wenger 1998: 154).

However, there are many forms of apprenticeship in which the status of master is reserved for an 'elite' group of learners, who have demonstrated through competitive forms of assessment that their skills are superior to those of their peers. In such cases the success of those who attain mastery can be ensured only by the failure of those who do not. Lave and Wenger's views of these contested development pathways appear to be conflicting and ambiguous. Their early work recognizes the role played by apprenticeship in delivering high levels of skill in disciplines such as 'medicine, law, the academy, professional sports, and the arts' (Lave and Wenger 1991: 63). However, it portrays assessment-driven learning as antithetical to the common good and a root cause of learner alienation and resistance. There seem to be at least three respects in which competitive pathways, in which only a minority can attain mastery, pose a challenge to Lave and Wenger's thinking. First, there would seem to be many circumstances in which personally meaningful learning can emerge from competitive relations, of which sport (at recreational as well as elite levels) is a case in point. Second, it would seem likely that practice communities offering competitive pathways would also need to offer newcomers suitably designed forms of instruction, underpinned by training pedagogy, to enable them to meet assessment standards. Third, there seems to be a need to acknowledge the potential complexity of old-timer/newcomer relations, in which masters of practice (as teachers and instructors) might work simultaneously both to empower their apprentices through the building of skill and to disempower them through obliging them to face assessment and potential failure.

This chapter will explore these issues by comparing Lave and Wenger's model with two alternative forms of theory. The first of these is the individualistic 'transmission' model that underpins conventional forms of teaching pedagogy, and was so heavily critiqued in their early work. The second is the 'process' theory of social development offered by Norbert Elias (e.g. Elias 1978, 2000). This discussion will compare the differing ways in which these theories conceptualize elite apprenticeship. It will use sport as an illustration, contextualizing Lave and Wenger's old-timers and newcomers as the coaches and athletes working at the professional end of British basketball. There are several advantages in focusing on British basketball. Like all sports, it offers a setting for learning in which competition plays an integral role in skills development and high-quality instruction is acknowledged to be critical to the achievement of successful performance outcomes. Like many sports, basketball offers a development context in which the commodifying pressures critiqued by Lave and Wenger (1991) are impacting on individuals' learning pathways and career opportunities. More unusually, it offers an example of a marginalized sport that is highly dependent on the use of migrant labour, two contextual features that place additional hurdles in the way of British player development (Maguire 1988; Owen-Pugh 2003, 2006).

The discussion will begin by introducing British basketball as a setting for player development. It will then explore the old timer/novice relationship, emphasizing the interdependence of coach and athlete. Next the chapter will compare the individualistic perspective of sports science with Lave and Wenger's 'situated' approach. This will be followed by an introduction to the theory of Norbert Elias, applied to an understanding of elite apprenticeship. Finally, the strengths and weaknesses of each theory will be compared and summarized.

British basketball as a setting for skills development

The game of basketball is a little over a century old, having been invented at Springfield College, Massachusetts, in 1891. Its development as a British sport commenced in 1936 with the formation of an English governing body, the Amateur Basketball Association. An independent professional league, the British Basketball League (BBL), was launched in 1987 by entrepreneur club owners. While the amateur game is now played throughout the UK, its professional arm is most strongly represented in England, where the majority of the BBL's 11 franchised clubs are located. At the time of writing, there are 112 senior men's and 43 senior women's teams in competition nationwide, with many more teams in competition in British junior and youth leagues, 'local' leagues and school and college leagues. While match attendance is low by comparison with traditional British game sports (BBL statistics for 1998–99 recorded a modest seasonal attendance of 1,049,000), there are signs of growing popularity. It is seen as a family game, free of the sleazy reputation often associated with its American counterpart, and highly popular as a participation sport among British youth. The number of Britons playing competitively overseas is also impressively high. During the 2002–03 season at least 40 British passport holders were playing in the North American college league (the NCAA) and at least 70 playing professionally outside the UK.

However, despite its increasing popularity, the sport still struggles to obtain government funding, commercial sponsorship and media coverage. One consequence, as Maguire (1988) notes, has been to make clubs at the professional end of the game vulnerable to merger, relocation and dissolution, contributing to a high level of 'turn-over' in league and divisional listings. In turn this has led to the casualization of employment opportunities, characterized by single-season contracts and salaries that are low by European standards. Moreover, the preference of professional clubs for employing migrant North American players to fill their prime 'starting five' places obliges many indigenous athletes to accept roles as bench players, accepting considerably less court time and, therefore, less career development. These features of the game create a highly uncertain learning environment for aspiring elite players. However, there are also other barriers to development that seem to be caused not so much by commercializing pressures as by the British game's status as a minority sport. For example, talented youth players are rarely offered opportunities for elite competition, obliging them to negotiate scholarships to North American colleges as a gateway to the NCAA competition circuit. Another is the nationwide fragmentation of development opportunities, caused by the geographical clustering of clubs in the English Midlands and southern counties. It seems that the development of both the sport and its athletes is an uncertain process, dependent on the working out of many enabling and constraining social pressures. These provide an ever-present backdrop to the working partnership between the athlete and coach. It is to this partnership that discussion now turns.

The coach–athlete relationship

The role of the elite sports coach is complex. Whether paid for their services or not, coaches may be expected to act not only as instructors, but also as motivators, leaders, gatekeepers and line managers. The extent to which these functions form part of any single job description will depend on the sport in question, its state of commercial development, the athlete's level of ability, and the coach's own level of career development. In British basketball, even among elite clubs, team coaches may not be paid directly for their services and may possess multiple organizational functions (for example, as club owners or players). However, they may be able to call on the support of one or two part-time assistants. They will invariably be ex-players, probably at elite competition level, and will almost certainly have had considerable experience of youth coaching. Their skills will have been acquired not only through attendance on formal training programmes but through a lifetime's experience of the game. In many respects, therefore, their position and role appear to be closely analogous to those of Lave and Wenger's 'old-timers'.

Coaches shoulder instructional responsibilities that often require them to work in a very intimate way with athletes while, at the same time, maintaining an appropriate professional distance (Jaques and Brackenridge 1999; Poczwardowski *et al.* 2002; Jowett 2003). Critically, they must ensure that athletes build effective performance skills through: developing and maintaining peak levels of physical fitness; engaging regularly in practice to build strength, stamina, agility and precision; and working to correct their technique in the light of feedback on performance. This work is informed by detailed and very precise forms of measurement and enacted through target setting. For example, in basketball, a player's performance is most commonly summarized through his/her match statistics. These comprise 19 measures in all, recording, not only allocated court time and shots attempted and made, but other contributions to game outcomes (such as foul counts, 'assists', 'rebounds', 'steals' and 'turnovers'). These measures are used to inform training strategies and record progress. Coaches must also work to build athletes' competitive strategies. In basketball this requires players to work as a team and to be thoroughly familiar with 'offensive' and 'defensive' forms of play. It is also important for coaches to build athletes' skills of emotional control, not only to ensure that they 'keep a cool head' and maintain concentration, but also to 'raise their game' and improve their performance overall.

However, the coach's role goes beyond the incremental building of skill and knowledge, since getting the best out of athletes entails entering them in competition against appropriately challenging opposition. This requires coaches also to act as selectors. In basketball, coaches must build teams from the most appropriate combinations of players and, during matches, also allocate the most suitable players to seconds of court time. This inevitably obliges them to exclude some athletes from development opportunities. Coaches of elite athletes may also have to weigh their obligations to athletes against their professional obligations to interest groups such as club and national managements, commercial sponsors, players' agents and the media, all of whom are likely to prioritize team success over athletic development. Effectively, therefore, their roles as instructors and team leaders can become compromised by promoting their own career advancement. Moreover, the selection decisions of coaches are often said to favour particular social groups. In British basketball, for example, indigenous players frequently complain of selection biases favouring North American migrants (Owen-Pugh 2006).

For their part, athletes committed to high performance must be prepared to make complex personal adjustments as they develop their skills. They must be willing continually to renegotiate their access to development opportunities through playing in competition matches and trying out for teams, risking failure and marginalization in the process. They must also be willing to conform to the vision of their coach and to the physical and mental training regime appropriate for their chosen sport. As a result, they may need to allow their coaches to make decisions not only about when and how they train and rest, but also about their diet, weight, living accommodation and body shape. While athletes must work to win competitions, they must also face the possibility that they may lose. In game sports, they must also learn to weigh their personal interests against those of their team. Like their coaches, athletes in commercialized forms of sport may be obliged to shoulder potentially conflictive obligations to commercial interest groups, such as sponsors and agents, the media and their 'public'. They may also have to adapt to the stresses of a migrant lifestyle. These conflicting social pressures can lead many young athletes to under-perform and even to abandon high performance sport altogether (Kerr and Goss 1997; Poczwardowski *et al.* 2002). Those who stay the course and achieve elite status may eventually earn themselves some freedom from constraint by choosing to represent the clubs, and indeed the countries, of their choice (Stokvis 2000; Maguire 1988). Here the conventional power asymmetry between athlete and coach can become reversed, allowing the athletes, rather than their coaches, to call the shots. For example, one top-level English football coach is quoted as saying, 'I learnt not to fall out with the players, because if you do, they won't play for you' (Jones *et al.* 2003: 221).

We can see, therefore, that an elite athlete and coach bring to their working relationship, not only a shared commitment to performance excellence, but conflicting commitments to many other parties, as well as to the development of their personal professional careers. The position is complicated further by their need to be, and to remain, subjectively compatible with one another. For example, research suggests that effective coach–athlete dyads need to agree about their goals and expectations, share similar working styles and be able to meet one another's affective needs through mutual displays of respect, trust, loyalty and empathy (Poczwardowski *et al.* 2002; Potrac *et al.* 2002; Jowett 2003). To remain successful in the long term, the partnership therefore needs to be able to reconcile many forms of social pressure. The complexity of these pressures increases the likelihood that even close and effective partnerships will break down. Where partnerships are not easy to dissolve, perhaps for contractual reasons, breakdowns can result in professional boundaries becoming crossed in personally damaging ways, even occasionally leading to forms of abuse. More commonly, however, the parties may find subversive solutions, for example athletes might deliberately underperform and coaches might deliberately drop high-performing athletes from teams (Stokvis 2000; Walton 2001; Jaques and Brackenridge 1999; Jowett 2003; Poczwardowski *et al.* 2002). Such breakdowns can come about even when coaches and athletes appear to be working well together. For example, Jowett (2003) shows how mutual Olympic success altered the emotional dynamics between a coach and an athlete in ways that damaged their subsequent working relationship and led to impaired future performance.

It would seem, therefore, that the development of elite athletic skill is not dependent simply on a coach's *individual* qualities as an instructor and motivator and an athlete's *personal* talent and willingness to commit to excellence. Arguably, it is better understood as a *relational* process dependent on the working out of complex forms of interdependence between novices, improvers and old-timers. Such interdependences must be understood to include not only the contracted obligations of the two parties but their compatibility at emotional levels and their mutual abilities to resolve a network of local and global social constraints. From this perspective, learning outcomes become unpredictable, frequently socially divisive and also personally damaging for both parties. This raises the question of how such complex and contested learning pathways may best be theorized.

The 'transmission model' of the development of athletic skills

Sports training pedagogies conventionally conform to a 'transmission' model underpinned by cognitive and behaviourist theoretical assumptions. From this perspective, the coach takes a central role in directing training, and graded forms of training and competition are used to build high-performance behaviours (such as an athlete's competition performance), cognitions (an athlete's 'inner' game) and affective states (an athlete's ability to control and exploit emotion). The development of skill is understood to be an individualized process, in which learning is located within the body and mind of the athlete. This can be understood as a systemic perspective in which the athlete works to correct performance in the light of feedback from coaches and ancillary staff. Taking this analogy a step further, it is possible to view an athlete's underperformance as systemic failure, needing to be rectified by the coach through forms of corrective action such as modifications to diet, exercise regimes and coaching schedules, or referrals to ancillary specialists such as physiotherapists and sports psychologists.

The transmission model offers proven principles to inform the design of training programmes. It makes possible verifiable measures of developmental progress, and it offers a workable strategy for identifying and correcting problems. Nevertheless, as a resource for *analysing* elite athletic development it possesses a number of limitations. Its cognitive-behavioural assumptions tend to reduce individual athletes to the role of information processors. Its individualistic assumptions offer little acknowledgement of the ways in which athletes' identities come to be shaped by the constraining and enabling influences of their social worlds. Also, in placing its primary focus on thought and behaviour, it has difficulty theorizing the emotional states that are so critical in high-performance sport, such as 'flow' (Czikszentmihalyi 1990; Pates *et al.* 2002) and its collective equivalent, 'emotional contagion' (Hatfield *et al.* 1994). While the transmission model is certainly useful as a means of informing training pedagogy, it offers only a partial account of the athlete as a whole person and has difficulty acknowledging some significant influences on performance outcomes. Lave and Wenger (1991) made similar criticisms with reference to classroom-based teaching. However as we will see, their theory also encounters difficulties in acknowledging the complexities of the coach–athlete relationship.

'Communities of practice' and the development of athletic skills

Memberships of individual British basketball clubs are continually in a state of flux, reflecting the seasonal meeting and parting of players, coaches, managers, support staff and spectators. In this respect they differ from the communities of practice described by Lave and Wenger (1991), which tended to possess memberships that were established and comparatively unchanging. Nevertheless, these clubs can be viewed as partners in a global community, in which relationships forged in a local neighbourhood can be maintained 'on the road' and 'on the net' as supporters meet up with friends and contacts at away games or keep in touch with their progress through internet sites. In this 'distributed' sense, they have much in common with Lave and Wenger's early field studies, offering newcomers of all persuasions – whether recreational participants, elite performers, spectators or volunteers – a route to valued identities of mastery, and providing opportunities for co-participation in personally meaningful practices. They therefore play host to many forms of 'legitimate peripheral participation'.

Moreover, the game is clearly characterized by the forms of generational and economic struggle given so much prominence in Lave and Wenger's early work. Its generational struggles are played out most uncompromisingly in team selection, as 'rookie' players are recruited and 'veterans' find themselves deselected as their strength, speed and agility begin to fail. Tensions between continuity and change are also evident in a wider sense, as the sport's supporters and promoters find themselves on opposite sides in disputes over match rules and changes to player eligibility regulations. Its economic dilemmas are also easy to see, shaped by dual processes of marginalization and commercialization, and reflected in debates over the viability of individual clubs, the availability of media partnerships and the use of migrant players. All these are issues hotly debated by British supporters (Maguire 1988; Owen-Pugh 2003).

Clearly, therefore, Lave and Wenger's model is a useful resource for exploring the relational and cultural dimensions of learning. It views individuals holistically. In contrast to the transmission model, it acknowledges the learner's search for an idealized identity as a master of practice. By conceptualizing learning as the collective negotiation of meaning, it makes it possible to acknowledge individuals' subjective interpretations of their social worlds; including, potentially, their emotional evaluations of self and other. It offers a means of acknowledging the disputed identities that are so common in sport, such as rivalries between clubs and teams and (in the case of a marginalized sport like British basketball) disputes over the national ownership of sporting forms.

However, in a number of critical respects, this theory fails to offer a sufficient account of athletic development. First, Lave and Wenger (1991) arguably underestimate the value of formal instruction. None of their field studies offers an example of formal teaching. Rather, they imply that the provision of legitimacy, combined with culturally specific forms of practice 'curriculum', should be sufficient to enable peer groups, near-peers and 'journeyfolk' to learn together in collegiate and creative ways. In contrast, and in common with all sports clubs, British basketball clubs promote a philosophy in which the provision of effective coaching is valued highly. Indeed, as the 'voice of the club', coaches command considerable respect within their community.

Second, the value that Lave and Wenger place on co-operative forms of working, and their linking of assessment-driven learning to commodifying processes, is not entirely convincing when applied to sports settings, where competition is valued for its own sake and has historical roots that pre-date the rise of capitalism. Despite the pressures of commercialization, the overwhelming majority of registered British basketball clubs still adopt an amateur, recreational ethos. The sport's UK governing bodies still promote the values of recreational competition, in which individuals compete with one another for the pleasure of self-fulfilment rather than monetary reward. While its contested learning pathways must undoubtedly move some learners in the direction of failure, and potential alienation, they clearly offer meaningful and valued identities to many others.

Third, by focusing on learning at the level of the community of practice, Lave and Wenger effectively prevent themselves from exploring the relational dimensions of learner subjectivities and the ways in which this may impact on the development of mastery. This prevents them from offering an adequate theory of emotion and obliges them to theorize individuals' searches for mastery without offering any means of acknowledging the complex affective states triggered by comparative evaluations of self and other, such as self-satisfaction, elation, anxiety, depression and shame. It also denies them an opportunity to explore the unexpected outcomes of learning, such as an athlete's underperformance or the failure of a previously successful coaching relationship.

Fourth, Lave and Wenger offer only limited means of exploring the insider–outsider struggles that are so characteristic of sports settings. In British basketball these struggles include disputes between amateur and professional lobbies over the 'ownership' of the game, and rivalries between indigenous and migrant players and coaches, in addition to the rivalries between clubs and teams that characterize all sports communities. While Lave and Wenger acknowledge that communities of practice can come into conflict, their theory focuses on the learning that takes place within and neglects the disputes that take place at their boundaries. Moreover, despite their emphasis on legitimizing processes, they fail to explore the ways in which communities of practice can work to expel or marginalize newcomers. This poses significant problems for theorizing learning in assessment-driven settings, where failure and marginalization are common learning outcomes.

This brings us to Eliasian theory which, as we will see, may offer a more effective theoretical means of exploring such matters. Since it is not possible to offer a detailed account of Elias's theory here, readers with little prior knowledge of his work may like to refer to Mennell's (1992) introduction. The present summary of Elias's ideas will touch briefly on just two aspects of his work, namely his theorizing of power and subjectivity.

'Figurational theory' and the development of athletic skills

The organizing principle on which Elias's theory is based is the 'figuration' (Elias 1978), a concept used to describe the ways in which individuals become bound to one another through their social interdependence. Effectively, figurations are networks of constraining and enabling forces that shape individuals' actions and the meanings they ascribe to them. Individuals are portrayed as working to advance their interests as a means of ensuring their personal well-being, often referred to in Eliasian writing as the 'pursuit of power opportunities'. Consequently, figurations should not be viewed as static structures but, rather, as dynamic processes in which the power asymmetries between individuals create tensions that drive social development and both enabling and constraining individuals' future courses of action. Although Elias's ideas have not previously been applied to collective forms of skills development, they have similarities to Lave and Wenger's cultural-historical perspective. However, Elias's theory offers a considerably more versatile account of social development, and therefore of learning. Where Lave and Wenger refer to the reproduction of communities, Elias offers an account of social development at global, local and interpersonal levels. Moreover, Eliasian theory also allows us considerably more purchase on both the power relations of learning and the subjective experiences of learners.

First, we will consider power. Since Elias saw power as a structural characteristic of all human relationships, it follows that we must view learning trajectories as politicized. For example, we can assume that such trajectories have the potential to convey power advantages on the learner, and we must recognize that, to ensure their well-being, all communities of learners, including communities of practice, will seek to find ways of controlling the rate and extent to which newcomers are allowed access to community-owned bodies of skill and meaning. Lave and Wenger make an analogous point when they refer to the 'continuity–displacement contradiction'. However, Eliasian theory recognizes that, since they emerge from the 'interweaving of countless individual interests and intentions' (Elias 2000: 312), the outcomes of figurational processes can never be predicted with certainty and, indeed, are often unintended consequences that are undesired by all parties to the process. If we apply this notion to learning trajectories, we are obliged to recognize that, even in formal instructional relationships, figurational processes can work themselves out in ways that serve to constrain, rather than enable, learning.

This is a conflictive portrayal of learning that clearly departs from Lave and Wenger's account of learner empowerment. However, as an explanatory position it potentially offers many advantages. It offers a means of theorizing the historical emergence of assessment-driven trajectories. It also becomes possible to theorize the role and power of the instructor. An Eliasian analysis would see sports coaches as offering two critical services to communities of practice. On the one hand, they offer athletes a critical ally in their pursuit of mastery; on the other, they function as agents of social control, limiting access to mastery to those deemed to be most worthy. Elias's theory also offers a means of exploring the conflictive dimensions of sports communities, such as the struggles that take place over new sporting forms, disputes between governing bodies, and rivalries between amateur and professional lobbies and migrant and indigenous players (Maguire 1988). Applied to the coach–athlete relationship, it allows us to explore the working of the dyad at both interpersonal and societal levels. From an Eliasian perspective, power asymmetries are viewed as dynamic and variable *inter*dependences. Consequently, it comes as no surprise that, despite the power accruing to the coach's role, high-performing athletes can often gain considerable control over the ways in which the parties work together. Elias's theory also offers a means of linking the form and direction of coach–athlete co-engagement with wider social processes. Here Elias reminds us that, since social development is always constrained by culture and history, the ways in which social pressures impact on the coach–athlete dyad will vary from one form of sport to another. Stokvis (2000) makes this point in relation to globalizing processes, noting that the disruptive influence of commercializing pressures is inevitably greater on media-friendly sports, where the sponsorship offered by the media giants has a significant effect on development outcomes.

We can now consider the Eliasian account of subjectivity. In Eliasian theory this is explored from a cultural-historical perspective, as 'social habitus', understood as the bodies of cultural meaning that are passed down over generations and serve to guide individuals' everyday living and working practices. In contrast to both the transmission and the community of practice models, emotion is accorded a central place in Eliasian theory. Consequently, habitus is understood to have both 'detached' (rational/cognitive) and 'involved' (emotional/affective) dimensions. While these two dimensions of habitus are assumed to coexist, Elias argued that, subject to figurational pressures, the balance between them can undergo historical changes. For example, Eliasian writers recognize the emergence of 'disciplined' workplace subjectivities in industrialized countries. These require people to make careful subjective appraisals of others' intentions as well as to reflect on their own actions and how they might be understood by others. Consequently, Eliasians argue, the societal norms of such countries have tended to favour the development of detached, rather than involved, subjectivities. These ideas are explored in detail by Elias in his theory of the 'civilizing process' (Elias 2000), and they have implications for the development of athletic skill. For example, Eliasian writers interpret the highly controlled forms of aggression found in modern game sports as evidence of the 'controlled decontrolling' of behaviour, in which the workings of societal and community norms have led athletes to acquire a highly sophisticated ability to fine-tune their emotions.

Given its centrality to their theory, it is important to consider how Elias would interpret Lave and Wenger's 'identity of mastery'. From an Eliasian perspective, there are both direct and indirect benefits to be gained by individuals working towards mastery of practice. On the one hand, once they have achieved mastery, their power is directly enhanced; for example, as we have seen, elite basketball players can acquire significant career bargaining opportunities. On the other hand, as masters of practice, individuals gain opportunities to forge valuable alliances with community power holders. Thus, in British basketball, high-performing athletes are popular with club owners and sponsors and can draw on their popularity at times of crisis. Such alliances can allow an underperforming player to retain his place on a team's 'starting five' even when his match statistics do not appear to warrant it (Owen-Pugh 2006).

We also need to consider how Elias interprets the normalizing processes of communities of practice; that is, the ways in which they uphold their espoused values and behavioural standards. Lave and Wenger explored these processes through their analysis of legitimate peripheral participation, stressing its empowering rather than its disempowering, qualities. An Eliasian analysis would take a very different line. Figurational analysis highlights the need for community power holders (such as Lave and Wenger's old-timers) both to uphold community norms, as a means of maintaining their personal power opportunities, and also their reluctance to admit newcomers unless they see definite advantages in doing so. This dynamic is recognized by Lave and Wenger in their 'continuity–displacement contradiction'. However, an Eliasian analysis would lay far greater stress on the capacity of members of communities of practice to manage learning trajectories to exclude and marginalize unwanted members. This phenomenon is discussed by Elias in his theory of 'established–outsider relations' (Elias and Scotson 1994), which describes how communities work to uphold the vested interests of their power holders, police the practice of their members and exclude 'outsiders' through the use of discursive strategies, such as polarized 'praise' and 'blame' gossip. We can often see these distancing strategies in sport, contextualized as struggles between vested interest groups over sporting values, norms and practices. They can also influence coach–athlete partnerships. For example, at the professional end of the game, British basketball players often find themselves marginalized as they struggle with North American migrants over access to court time (Owen-Pugh 2006). In this case, though geographically 'outsiders', the North American players have acquired social power through their alliances with club owners, sponsors and coaches that allows them to dominate the sport's development opportunities at the expense of indigenous players. Unlike Lave and Wenger's model, then, Elias's theory acknowledges the ways in which macro social forces, such as sports migration, can shape the actions and subjectivities of athletes and coaches, and consequently the ways in which they work together.

Summary and conclusions

This chapter evaluated Lave and Wenger's (1991) account of situated learning by making reference to the development of elite athletes in British basketball, a community of practice in which graded competition opportunities underpin the development of athletes at both recreational and professional levels. It has argued that the successful development of players is ensured not only by their personal motivation to achieve, and their collegiate relationships within peer groups, but by the quality of their working relationship with their coach. This relationship is characterized by a complex network of constraints at personal and subjective, as well as formal and contractual, levels. The dilemmas these create for both parties are exacerbated by commercializing processes, which increasingly encourage athletes and coaches to prioritize their personal career opportunities over their shared professional interests. Consequently, coach–athlete relationships, and the learning that emerges from them, should be viewed as dynamic and shaped by emergent conflicts of interest.

This discussion compared Lave and Wenger's model with two alternative approaches to theorizing the development of elite skills; namely, the systemic or 'transmission' perspective commonly used in sports science and Elias's theory of social development. Despite the success of the transmission model in informing training pedagogy, it offers only a limited means of acknowledging social and emotional influences on learning. It reduces the role of the coach to control and communication functions. This theory also has difficulty accounting for apparently 'illogical' development outcomes, such as underperformance of athletes and breakdown of coach–athlete partnerships.

In contrast, Lave and Wenger (1991) offer an account of learning that stresses collective empowerment within a community of practice that offers novices a route to mastery through legitimate peripheral participation. Unlike the transmission model, it locates learning in its cultural and historical context, and acknowledges that learning outcomes can be influenced by struggles over the ownership and appropriation of practice. However, this chapter has highlighted four critical limitations of Lave and Wenger's theory (1991). First, while they acknowledge the legitimizing roles played by a community's masters of practice, their model underestimates the importance of formal instruction. Second, they fail to theorize assessment-driven learning, in which individuals may compete with one another, not only for monetary reward but also for self-fulfilment. Although the competitive pathways found in sports skill development must undoubtedly lead to the alienation of many learners, they offer valued identities to many others, including amateur participants as well as professional athletes. Their ethical condemnation of contested learning trajectories therefore appears to be simplistic. Third, their model does not explore the ways in which learning is shaped by the subjective stances and relational positioning of individuals, and so cannot account for the breakdown of previously successful partnerships. Like the transmission model, their theory cannot account for the unexpected outcomes of learning. Fourth, they offer only a limited means of exploring the social divisions associated with learning, such as established–outsider rivalries and the ways in which communities of practice may work to marginalize newcomers.

In Elias's work we find a theoretical framework that appears sympathetic to Lave and Wenger's model. Both these forms of theory portray learning as culturally located and recognize individuals' quest for mastery. Both acknowledge that social struggles, including the struggles inherent in assessment-driven learning, may lead to alienation rather than mastery. However, Eliasian theory has the advantage of being able to acknowledge individual as well as collective forms of agency, and so make connections between global social processes and individuals' conscious subjectivities. While it recognizes the problems posed to learners by commodifying processes, it makes no value judgements about the influence of capitalism. Rather, it sees learner alienation as a response to perceived marginalization. From an Eliasian perspective, athletes' willingness to submit themselves to assessment-driven development is the outcome of figurational processes that give subjective salience to the power opportunities offered by sport. For example, the global media focus on football encourages many young people to see that game as a route to mastery. An Eliasian interpretation would also suggest that, as their commitment to elite performance deepens, athletes will become increasingly constrained by their search for mastery; elite sports careers can be stressful and therefore come at a price. Even so, many may gain power and relative freedom from constraint once they achieve mastery. Moreover, unlike the community of practice model, Eliasian theory offers a means of exploring the coach's role and its underpinning pedagogy, seeing these as a means not only of instructing newcomers but also of promoting the power opportunities of the community of practice as a whole.

Each of these three forms of theory makes a contribution to an overall understanding of coach–athlete relationships in British basketball. The transmission model offers insights into the working of individual bodies and minds that make it possible to design effective forms of training and intervention. Lave and Wenger provide a better understanding of the need to legitimize individuals' learning by offering them an attainable identity of mastery. In Elias's theory we find acknowledgement that figurational processes can work both to constrain and to enable the development of elite forms of skill. However, the conflicts between these theories should also be recognized. Critically, the community of practice model arguably understates the importance of the instructional relationship, which is given such prominence in the transmission model. It also lacks the means to explore the conflictive and subjective dimensions of learning. Here, Elias's model offers considerable advantages. It provides a better understanding of why many individuals submit themselves to the rigours of assessment-driven learning trajectories. Furthermore, it recognizes that the capacity to exclude and marginalize is inherent in all learning settings and learning trajectories, including Lave and Wenger's collegiate communities of practice.

Key questions to consider

1   To what extent and in what ways do we need to acknowledge the emotional dimensions of learning trajectories?
2   Does Elias's theory of social development complement, augment or supersede Lave and Wenger's model of the community of practice?
3   How are the forms of co-engagement in communities of practice shaped by power inequalities between newcomers and old-timers?
4   How useful is the concept of legitimate peripheral participation for theorizing the development of elite sports skill?
5   To what extent is learning in communities of practice shaped by social relations beyond their boundaries?

References

Czikszentmihalyi, M. (1990) *Flow: the Psychology of Optimal Experience*, New York: Harper & Row.

Elias, N. (1978) *What is Sociology?* trans. S. Mennell and G. Morrissey, first published in German 1970, New York: Columbia University Press.

Elias, N. (2000) *The Civilizing Process*, trans. E. Jephcott, first published 1939, rev. edn, Oxford: Blackwell.

Elias, N. and Scotson, J. (1994) *The Established and the Outsiders*, first published 1965, rev. edn, London: Sage.

Hatfield, E., Caciopo, J. T. and Rapson, R. L. (1994) *Emotional Contagion*, Cambridge: Cambridge University Press.

Jaques, R. and Brackenridge, C. (1999) 'Child abuse and the sports medicine consultation', *British Journal of Sports Medicine*, 33: 229–30.

Jones, R. L., Armour, K. M. and Potrac, P. (2003) 'Constructing expert knowledge: a case study of a top-level professional soccer coach', *Sport, Education and Society*, 8 (2): 213–29.

Jowett, S. (2003) 'When the "honeymoon" is over: a case study of a coach–athlete dyad in crisis', *Sport Psychologist*, 17: 444–60.

Kerr, G. A. and Goss, J. D. (1997) 'Personal control in elite gymnasts: the relationships between locus of control, self-esteem and trait anxiety', *Journal of Sport Behavior*, 20 (1): 69–82.

Lave, J. and Wenger, E. (1991) *Situated Learning: Legitimate Peripheral Participation*, Cambridge: Cambridge University Press.

Maguire, J. (1988) 'The commercialisation of English elite basketball, 1972–1988: a figurational perspective', *International Review for Sociology of Sport*, 2 (4): 305–23.

Mennell, S. (1992) *Norbert Elias: An Introduction*, first published 1989, rev. edn, Dublin: University College Dublin Press.

Owen-Pugh, V. A. (2003) 'The elite British Basketball Club as a "Community of Practice": situating Lave and Wenger's Model of Learning within Elias' Theory of the Group', Working Paper 40, Leicester: Centre for Labour Market Studies, University of Leicester.

Owen-Pugh, V. A. (2006) 'Exploring the development opportunities open to British basketball players in the post-Bosman era: a figurational analysis of the working relationship between professional coaches and players', mimeo, Leicester: Centre for Labour Market Studies, University of Leicester.

Pates, J., Cummings, A. and Maynard, I. (2002) 'The effects of hypnosis on flow states and three-point shooting performance in basketball players', *Sport Psychologist* 16: 34–47.

Poczwardowski, A., Barott, J. E. and Henschen, K. P. (2002) 'The athlete and coach: their relationship and its meaning. Results of an interpretative study', *International Journal of Sport Psychology* 33: 116–40.

Potrac, P., Jones, R. and Armour, K. (2002) '"It's all about getting respect": the coaching behaviors of an expert English soccer coach', *Sport, Education and Society*, 7 (7): 183–202.

Stokvis, R. (2000) 'Globalization, commercialization and individualization: conflicts and changes in elite athletics', *Culture, Sport, Society*, 3 (1): 22–34.

Walton, T. (2001) 'The Sprewell/Carlesimo episode: unacceptable violence or unacceptable victim?' *Sociology of Sport Journal*, 18 (3): 345–57.

Wenger, E. (1998) *Communities of Practice: Learning, Meaning and Identity*, Cambridge: Cambridge University Press.

8 The transition to work and adulthood

Becoming adults via communities of practice

John Goodwin

Key themes in this chapter

- The utility of the communities of practice concept for exploring transitions to adulthood
- How the communities of practice model might be extended through using the work of Norbert Elias
- The relationship between occupational socialization and adult socialization
- The links between social development and psychological development in transitions from novice to old-timer

The role of work in the transition to adulthood is not a new concern, with many authors suggesting a clear link between work and the processes of becoming an adult (Banks *et al.* 1992; Pilcher 1995). For example, Pilcher (1995) describes the transition to work as marking a period in young people's lives where they are defined 'in terms of what they no longer are (children) and what they nearly are (adults)' (Pilcher 1995: 58). These debates have recently been extended by authors exploring the role of formal and informal workplace learning in the formation of worker identities (Lawy 2006). Central to some of these approaches is the theoretical framework of Lave and Wenger (1991), with authors utilizing the concepts of 'legitimate peripheral participation' and 'communities of practice' (Lave and Wenger 1991; Wenger 1998). These concepts have been applied to a range of learning contexts including work-based learning and apprenticeships, education and training frameworks and organizational learning (see Fuller 1996; Cornford and Gunn 1998; Driver 2002). There have also been numerous discussions considering the theoretical coherence of Lave and Wenger's approach (Hodkinson and Hodkinson 2003; Owen-Pugh 2003; Fuller and Unwin 2004). These highlight that, whilst Lave and Wenger's approach marks an important step forward in understanding learning at work, their theorizing requires extension in order to accommodate certain limitations. Such limitations include Lave and Wenger's undeveloped considerations of power (Owen-Pugh 2003; Fuller and Unwin 2004), fantasy elements (Owen-Pugh 2003), the importance of formal learning, the value of previous experience, and learning beyond the achievement of full community membership (Fuller and Unwin 2003a, 2004).

An additional aspect of Lave and Wenger's work that remains largely unexplored, and which could be further developed, is the contribution that the concepts of 'legitimate peripheral participation' and 'communities of practice' can make to an understanding of the development from childhood to adulthood via the transition to work.

Indeed, Lave and Wenger's model of the transformation of novices into old-timers could be used to signify a broader transition from childhood to becoming a full adult member of a community at work and elsewhere. Lave and Wenger (1991) allude to this process suggesting 'we might equally have turned to studies of socialization; children, after all, are quintessentially legitimate peripheral participants in adult social worlds' (Lave and Wenger 1991: 32). Wenger (1998: 277) also recognizes the significance that working with adults has on the formation of young worker identities:

> it is desirable to increase opportunities for relationships with adults just being adults, while downplaying the institutional aspects of their role as educators. What students need in developing their own identities is contact with a variety of adults who are willing to invite them into their adulthood.
>
> (Wenger 1998: 277)

However, if we are to extend Lave and Wenger's analysis in this direction we also need to understand the process of learning the norms and behaviours of an 'adult community' as well as the process of occupational socialization that Lave and Wenger describe. If the transition to adulthood is to be effective, young workers need to acquire adult behavioural standards and occupational skills to move beyond their status as legitimate peripheral participants in the workplace. Without acquiring the norms and behaviours of the adult workers around them, young workers cannot fully participate in adult working life. One analytical possibility, in this connection, is to utilize Norbert Elias's (largely unknown) writings on the transitions to work and adulthood (see Elias 1961).

Linking Lave and Wenger with Elias

A number of authors have recognized the benefits of using Elias to extend Lave and Wenger's theorizing (see Gherardi 1999; Owen-Pugh 2003; Goodwin and O'Connor 2005), indeed, the two approaches have important parallels when considering the transition to adulthood. First, Lave and Wenger's (1991) starting point is very similar to Elias's, as both question the *homo clausus* or closed personality view of human beings, emphasizing instead the relational character of identity and 'the social'. For both Elias and Lave and Wenger 'who we are' is not the product of an internal cognitive process but instead emerges out of 'participation in an activity system about which participants share understandings concerning what they are doing and what that means in their lives and for their communities' (Lave and Wenger 1991: 98).

Second, Lave and Wenger (1991) and Elias (1961) highlight the peripheral status of young workers at the beginning of their careers. For Elias, when young people go to work they have to make broader adjustments to situations and to roles which are new and the implications of which were 'often imperfectly understood by them and by the adults concerned, and for which they are in many cases not too well prepared' (Young Worker Project 1962a: 2). This transition, Elias suggests, is a difficult process, since the norms, the behaviour and the attitudes of adults at work differ considerably from those of adults with whom young people are familiar. Elias argues that this in turn is due to the limited amount of contact between young people and adults outside of family, friends and teachers. It is here that the work of Elias could make a useful addition to the theorizing of Lave and Wenger in that Elias articulates a very clear separation between young people and the adults who surround them. In many ways, this offers a means of extending Lave and Wenger's notion of legitimate peripheral participation. From the minutes of the meetings relating to the 'Adjustment of Young Workers to Work Situations and Adult Roles' Elias argues that:

> a complex society such as ours requires customarily a prolonged period of indirect preparation and training for adult life. By indirect I mean from the age of 5 to 14, 15 or 16, the . . . children of our society are trained for their adult tasks in special institutions which we call schools, where they learn . . . knowledge about the adult world past, present and future not by direct contact with it, but largely from books. Their actual knowledge of the adult world . . . [is] relatively limited.
>
> (Young Worker Project 1962b: 2)

Because of this separation of adults and young people, before entering work adolescents have a highly selective and unrealistic perception of the adult world and of their life in it. The encounter with reality demands a reorganization of their perception. For Elias, this is a painful process for at least two different reasons. First, because every strongly enforced reorganization of perceptions is painful. Second, to all intents and purposes the 'social reality' to which the youngsters have to get used is unsatisfactory and 'the gap between the adult reality as it turns out to be is very great indeed' (Elias 1961: 1). This has similarities with Lave and Wenger's approach, where legitimate peripheral participants do not perceive their peripherality before they enter the workplace, and only begin to understand their separateness from the older established workers around them once at work and trying to adjust. However, the key conceptual contribution of Elias here is that it asks us centrally to consider the emotional impact of being a peripheral participant. Elias argues that the relative absence of direct relationships between children and adults other than their parents, the differences between the fantasies of future adult roles and the actual reality of adult life, may lead to this experience being characterized by feelings of 'shock'. For example, a young person might, before entering employment, have a fantasy-laden perception of work as overwhelmingly a positive experience – one which is unlikely to impact upon them in a negative manner. In such a fantasy, a young person might not yet perceive the reality of adult working life as being one without long school holidays, short working days and extended 'break times'. The reality of work is different from that envisaged by the young person and, for Elias, the realization that nothing will ever be the same in terms of school holidays or the general loss of the 'freedoms' that accompany childhood lead the young person to experience a 'reality shock'.

Both Elias (2001) and Lave and Wenger (1991) emphasize the historical context of the present in which the 'shaping of an individual depends on the historical development of the social standard' (Elias 2001: 23) or, respectively, where learning involves the 'historical production, transformation and change of persons' (Lave and Wenger 1991: 50). Indeed, understanding the link between processes of change in social relations and processes of change in habitus is the central concern of much of Elias's work. It is worth noting here that, while the concept of habitus is more commonly associated with the work of Bourdieu, Elias's use of the term pre-dates Bourdieu's by some forty years. While there is not space here to undertake a full comparison of Elias's and Bourdieu's conceptualizations, it is significant that Bourdieu was aware of the work of Elias and, indeed, cited Elias's ideas relating to the development of social habitus in the introduction to his (Bourdieu's) text *Distinction: A Social Critique of the Judgement of Taste* (1984). A key difference between their conceptualizations of habitus, however, is that Bourdieu's working arguably retains a structuralist bias (see, for example, DeJong 2001) and, for the present discussion at least, Elias's formulation offers greater empirical utility, particularly in relation to the study of transitions to adulthood.

Elias conceptualized the transition to adulthood as centring on the interrelationship of *sociogenesis* (the processes of development and transformation in social relations) and *psychogenesis* (the processes of development and transformation in the personality structure that accompany such social changes) (van Krieken 1998; Goodwin and O'Connor 2002). For Elias, habitus is not innate but 'habituated' – a constituent part of an individual by learning through social experience, developing as part of an ongoing process beginning at birth and continuing through childhood and youth (van Krieken, 1998; Goodwin and O'Connor 2002). The interrelationship between sociogenesis *and* psychogenesis means that the transition to adulthood cannot take place in social isolation since the learning of adult behaviours is possible only thanks to interactions with adults. As such, the transition from school to work is a central process through which young people are habituated – through which they learn the norms, attitudes, and the new adult codes of behaviour. Again Lave and Wenger's notion of legitimate peripheral participation also overlaps, to some extent, with Elias's conceptualization of the interrelationship between sociogenesis and psychogenesis in describing how (to use Elias's terms) changes in a nexus of social relationships, a community of practice, link with changes in an individual's habitus. However, as Lave and Wenger are at pains to point out, such a change in habitus is not one of simply 'acquiring' workplace skills but is, instead, a broader transformatory process central to the transition to adult life. In a similar manner, Elias suggests that young workers need to make:

> adjustment to relationships with older workers, supervisors, etc., in factory and workshop . . . [such as] learning new codes of behaviour, problems of competition and co-operation, conforming and nonconforming . . . coping with tensions in social relations, etc.
>
> (Elias 1961: 1)

This transformatory process, according to Goodwin and O'Connor (2002), requires young people, on entering work, to have to begin communicating with adults who are not family members and, as such, work becomes a site through which young workers can begin fully to engage with the sociocultural practices of adulthood. Such practices include learning to behave responsibly as opposed to exhibiting childish behaviours such as 'time wasting' or 'messing about'. It could also mean learning to conform to specific workplace behaviours such as conforming to adult hours of work, including clocking in, reduced break times, limited vacation time. Adult behavioural standards also require young workers to learn to cope with workplace tensions and conflicts themselves rather than relying on family members or adult friends to resolve their problems. More broadly, in Eliasian terms, the transition from school to work requires young workers to develop the foresight and self-restraint of the adults around them. This means moving from childhood, in which individuals can express their feelings with a considerable degree of freedom, and largely without consequences, to adulthood, where individuals (largely unconsciously) regulate and control their own behaviours in line with the behavioural standards of the time.

Supplementing Lave and Wenger (1991) with the work of Norbert Elias perhaps provides a more complete conceptual framework for explaining how young people become both workers and adults via a process such as legitimate peripheral participation. Only by developing such workplace skills and learning adult norms and behaviours can the young people become full participants in the sociocultural practice of the community as adults and workers. In the next section, empirical data from Elias's 'Adjustment of Young Workers to Work Situations and Adult Roles' project is used to examine the transition to adulthood of 854 young adults in the 1960s in the city of Leicester. These data were collected between 1962 and 1964 from those who left school during the summer and at Christmas 1960 and 1962. The majority of the respondents were aged between sixteen and eighteen (see Goodwin and O'Connor 2002).

Becoming adults via communities of practice

It is impossible in a chapter such as this to cover all the aspects of adult behaviour that are learned during the transition to adulthood. The discussion will focus first on young workers' experiences of learning from other adults how to do the job. The discussion will then move on to consider how the young workers in the sample perceived adulthood and the learning of (and conforming to) appropriate adult behaviour. The data provide a useful insight into the actual experiences of young workers and highlight the separation or peripherality of the young people from the older workers around them. The data also highlight that the young workers, when entering work, began to get a better idea of what it meant to be an adult *vis-à-vis* appropriate standards of adult behaviour. Such themes reflect the central concerns of both Lave and Wenger (1991) and Elias (1961).

Learning to do the job from older workers

One of the main features of both Lave and Wenger's (1991) and Elias's work is the centrality of older adults in the transformation experience of the young. In Lave and Wenger's approach it is clear that older or more experienced workers were central to a novice's ability to be transformed from legitimate peripheral participants to old-timers. For Elias (1961), working with older people had the same transformatory effect, with older workers being central to the skill development process. For many young workers the transition from legitimate peripheral participants began as soon as they arrived at work, with some encountering formal inductions to the job or more usually through a process of informal learning. In Elias's (1961) study the young people were asked, 'When you started did anybody show you how to do the job, and in what way?' This question was intended to ascertain how the young workers had initially acquired the skills required to do the job. There were a range of responses to these questions, the majority of which suggested that someone had shown them how to do the work, even if it was a simple demonstration of the basics. The extent to which the young workers were trained for the job or inducted into the role varied from formal training courses to informal chats with friends. The following quotes illustrate these themes:

> When I started at the drawing office one of the chaps there showed me how to make the catalogues up. When I were downstairs the foreman showed me how the

job worked, y'know, what to do, and then two to three weeks later the men told me – just a general outline of what happens.

(Hosiery worker)

Yes, when you first go into the factory you go into a training school where there are instructors. In the offices there was a clerk doing the job I'm doing now. He showed me what to do and stayed with me for a fortnight and then if I had any queries I just went to him and asked him.

(Apprentice engineer)

Yes – show you what to do and you just carry on and they show you more and more each day until you're doing it on your own.

(Trainee mechanic)

I went to training school for a day and at the first shop I went to the manager and first hand showed me.

(Grocery assistant, aged fifteen)

Yes, there's a fair amount of instruction . . . [pause] There was another boy, he'd been there two or three years. I stayed with him for two or three weeks, then I went to another mechanic.

(Sewing machine mechanic, aged fifteen)

Yes, in a sense, but fifty per cent had to find out for myself. A lad there a bit tougher than me shown me the fill of the job . . . However, on this job you don't exactly get told, only have to press a button or pull a chain to fill the cake bags.

(Bakery assistant, aged fifteen)

However, there were those who felt they were just left to get on with it. For example, the young workers suggested that:

. . . no, not really. First of all says just wander round – asked people questions . . .

(Hosiery worker, aged fifteen)

Well, no, because when I first started there was this rather old-fashioned manager who was, as you often get with older managers, set in their ideas and they won't let anybody else change them. If I had any ideas I had to keep them to myself. I didn't get on with him very well but after that, especially having that experience of working on my own in the shop, it built me up.

(Salesman, aged fifteen)

No, you grope your way. To start with, it's a bit dodgy. But it works quite well.

(Lathe operator, aged seventeen)

However, in the main, regardless of whether the young workers were trained formally in a training school or informally on the job, a common feature is the centrality of older, more experienced workers in the young workers' learning process. The following quotes from the interview schedules illustrate these themes:

Taught you things no one else would.

(Trainee mechanic)

I like the people older than me better than those around my own age group. That applies only to workmates. I think they appreciate you more, give you more help and more chances to do the job.

(Apprentice painter and decorator)

Get on all right, pick up some useful hints, but on some things you just can't agree with them . . . They'll say that old paints are better than the new ones that come out. I disagree on that sort of thing. They think older things are better. I think new are better.

(Apprentice painter and decorator)

Working with other people. You watch them and think, 'I must do that.'

(Shop assistant)

However, although the majority said that they got on well with the older workers, and suggested that the older workers taught them the job, some raised issues of generational differences in terms of communication and understanding. Others recounted how older workers played tricks on them and bullied them. Some young workers suggested that:

When I was doing my training they used to be quite soft on you and then when you finish your training they get a bit harder, but they're all right otherwise.

(Mineworker)

You sometimes feel inferior to them but they make you feel like that more or less. Well, you know, they don't like to talk to you, except the lad that is over you and the instructor.

(Apprentice engineer)

The quotations outlined above highlight clearly the themes central to the works of Lave and Wenger and Elias. There is a consistent sense of young people having to engage with older workers during the transition process. The older workers appear to be central to developing the occupational skills of the young workers and, in the main, the young people acknowledge the importance of older workers as 'old-timers'. The young workers discussed above are clearly at the start of their careers and are evidently peripheral participants. However, the quotations also reveal some of the anxiety that Elias alluded to, with the young workers not feeling entirely comfortable with their relationships with older colleagues. These themes are developed further in the next section.

Learning and conforming to appropriate standards of adult behaviour

The young workers in Elias's study were asked questions about their relationships with the older workers in the organization and on their transition to adulthood, including 'What sort of things make a boy/girl become an adult?' and 'Do you think of yourself as an adult?' An analysis of these questions reveals the extent to which the young workers themselves thought they were becoming immersed in the socio-cultural practices of the adult group at work.

Based on their early working experiences, the young workers were very clear what characteristics were essential to acquire to become adults at work. Many in the sample thought that becoming an adult meant behaving more responsibly, 'learning to behave' and not 'messing around' as they had done at school. Based on their interactions with the adults around them, other more subtle features of adulthood also came to the fore such as 'responsibility', 'politeness' 'having pride, 'not being sloppy', 'not wasting time' and having 'respect' for the skilled workers around them. In the words of the young workers themselves:

> Not shouting and gallivanting about. When he settles down and just behaves like an adult.
>
> (Hosiery worker)

> There is a realization you've got to work for a living: you can't mess about like you did at school.
>
> (Clerk)

> At school you are sloppy – don't care about what you do. At work you've got to take responsibility for what you do. You've got to do it, and that's it.
>
> (Apprentice engineer)

> A sense of responsibility. Having to do things you don't really want to do. Being with adults all the time.
>
> (Typist)

> You have to be polite – talk like an adult and act like one.
>
> (Spinner)

As well as being able to identify appropriate adult behaviours, 574 of the 854 young workers interviewed felt that they had begun to acquire the behaviours of adulthood identified above. However, the young workers themselves clearly identify their transformation into adulthood as part of a learning process based on their interaction with older workers. For example, some of the young workers reflected that:

> When you start going out on your own, like, your own job, no one showing you how to do it, and you've got to take pride in yourself and your work. I suppose you feel more of an adult then.
>
> (Hosiery worker)

> Working with older people makes you think like them.
>
> (Wage clerk)

> I think if you are working with a man and he is showing you what to do . . . that's how you learn to be an adult.
>
> (Spinner's lad)

> Mixing with adults all the day, you see the way they behave and you copy them.
>
> (Cost clerk)

> Working with adults – you start acting like an adult. An adult doesn't run around, just takes his time doing his work.
>
> (Hosiery worker)

The young workers were asked to identify how they had changed. Many of the young workers simply stated that mixing with older workers had changed their behaviours and attitudes, making them more polite and respectful. More important, the young workers felt that working with older workers had made them grow up. Others indicated that they had become more adult, behaving more like adults than they had done previously. Again, the young workers were clear that these changes were as a direct result of interacting with older workers in their workplaces.

> I suppose I'm beginning to grow up – have responsibility of my work. And I think mixing with people of an older age group makes you change your ways.
>
> (Trainee typist)

> I've grown up a lot more, definitely, with working with older people.
>
> (Clerk)

> ... when you work with a hundred to two hundred blokes you see you're all the same and it's no good trying to be a bit uppity with the others, 'cos you soon get pulled down if you do.
>
> (Engineering draughtsman)

> I've grown up. You get a wider scope. Life is nothing until you go out to work. You are working with men. You learn a lot of things about how older people live – you're working with men instead of lads.
>
> (Toolmaker)

> You seem to grow up a lot quicker when you leave school and start work, and working with older people helps a lot as well. I suppose getting to know different people and getting to know what everyone is like. Widening your outlook.
>
> (Audio typist)

However, although the young workers had begun to identify adult behaviours, had realized that they were learning those behaviours from the adults around them and they were beginning to grow up, many in the sample still felt that they were still quite early on in this process of transformation and were still largely peripheral. Instead the young workers perceived themselves as still being in a transition stage where they were not yet adults but neither were they still children (see O'Connor and Goodwin 2005). Such an idea is prominent in the following responses to the question 'Are you an adult?'

> ... half and half, I suppose. I can't do so much work as the men, but I do more than the young ones.
>
> (Hosiery worker)

> Sometimes yes, sometimes no. Being at work you're an adult. But then you're not old enough to be an adult. People treat you as a lad or an apprentice, which means you're not an adult.
>
> (Hosiery worker)

Further still, for some of the young workers 'work' was still seen as part of an adult world of which they had little experience, and which they did not fully understand and that was both frightening and unfriendly.

It is one thing to identify the appropriate behavioural standards, as the young workers had in this study, but it is another thing to internalize them and develop the foresight required to behave like or as an adult. There are also clear and specific work-place behaviours that the young workers had to learn quickly. For example, in their childhood, and whilst still at school, the young workers had other adults to tell them when to do things, when to take a break and when to work. However, the transition to work marks another step in the transition to adulthood, as it is at work when young people begin to regulate and control their own behaviours.

To many of the young workers, having to regulate their own behaviour, take relatively short breaks and keep time also came as a bit of a shock. For example, in discussing break times and arriving at work the young workers commented that:

> They're a bit sharp in the morning. If you're two minutes over time you can lose half an hour's pay.
>
> (Craft apprentice)

> I keep strictly to time – some might be a couple of minutes late coming back after dinner, not more than that.
>
> (Apprentice fitter)

> Nobody stops for tea if we've got work to do. You're not allowed to.
>
> (Cost clerk)

> All keep strictly to 75 minutes dinner time, ten minutes morning and all about the same afternoon.
>
> (Boot and shoe worker)

Although the young workers do not like the earlier starts and the short breaks they soon begin to internalize what is required and to regulate their own behaviour in order to conform to the standards of their workplace. Consider the following:

> At first I weren't too pleased at getting up at six-thirty. I didn't like that much but I've got used to it.
>
> (Hosiery engineer)

> Once you're used to it you're used to it, and you keep like clockwork.
>
> (Apprentice carpenter)

Although these behaviours are learnt, the young workers also learn from the older workers around them when they can 'bend the rules' or take extra time, and often the young workers observed what was going on around them before they behaved differently from what was required:

> Boys only take longer breaks if men do. [The] boys stand up when the men stand up!
>
> (Apprentice panel beater)

From the extracts above we can clearly see that the transition to work involves much more than simply acquiring the skills to do the job. These young workers had to learn to behave completely differently, regulate their own behaviours, adopt the behaviours around them, develop the foresight required to 'keep time', and, it is argued here, all this is central to the legitimate peripheral participation process and the transition to 'old-timer' status.

Conclusion

The transition from school to work is a useful site to explore Lave and Wenger's conceptualizations of communities of practice and legitimate peripheral participation. One can clearly see, from the data above, young people making the transition from novices to old-timers via their interactions with the older workers around them. However, those interactions take two forms and ultimately lead to the learning of two 'types' of behaviour – the occupational behaviours and skills required to do the job and the behaviours appropriate to being an adult. It is perhaps the case that the latter has been absent from Lave and Wenger theorizing, with their over-concentration on occupational practice. However, the acquisition of adult behavioural standards is equally important in the transition from novice to old-timer, and it is arguably here where using Elias to supplement the work of Lave and Wenger offers the most.

One has to be mindful that the data presented here are from a historical data set reflecting the views and experiences of young workers some forty years ago. However, one of the strengths of historical data such as these is that they allow us to analyse this material in the light of contemporary debates. Such data may also provide a more accurate picture of respondents' thoughts and feelings at the time the research was carried out as a point of comparison with contemporary patterns. With this in mind, the findings presented here have considerable potential relevance to the existing 'moral panic' surrounding young people in contemporary Britain. For example, it has been suggested in the media that young people now do not know how to interact with adults who are not family members and that young adults do not appear to be able to demonstrate self-restraint or have the foresight to understand the consequences of their actions. These experiences may relate directly to the increasingly fragmented and complex character of the transition from school to work whereby it is often the case that young workers do not become members of communities of practice until their mid-twenties and, in consequence, do not learn the behavioural standards of adulthood as previous generations may have done. As such, a synthesis of the work of Lave and Wenger and Elias offers a means by which we can more adequately understand processes of legitimate peripheral participation within the present-day world.

Key questions to consider

1　To what extent do the concepts of sociogenesis and psychogenesis provide the conceptual basis for a reworking of 'legitimate peripheral participation'?
2　How might social processes 'outside' communities of practice inform what goes on 'within' them?
3　In what ways is the transition from school to work a learning process?
4　How might the experiences of workers documented in this chapter differ from those of their present-day counterparts?

References

Banks, M., Bates, I., Breakwell, G., Bynner, J., Emler, N., Jamieson, L. and Roberts, K. (1992) *Careers and Identities*, Milton Keynes: Open University Press.

Bourdieu, P. (1984) *Distinction: A Social Critique of the Judgement of Taste*, Cambridge, MA: Harvard University Press.

Cornford, I. and Gunn, D. (1998) 'Work-based learning of commercial cookery apprentices in the New South Wales hospitalities industry', *Journal of Vocational Education and Training*, 50 (4): 549–68.

DeJong, M. J. (2001) 'Elias and Bourdieu', *International Journal of Contemporary Sociology*, 38 (1): 64–86.

Driver, M. (2002) 'Learning and leadership in organisations: toward complementary communities of practice', *Management Learning*, 33 (1): 99–126.

Elias, N. (1961) Application for a grant for special research to DSIR, unpublished.

Elias, N. (2001) *The Society of Individuals*, New York: Continuum.

Fuller, A. (1996) 'Modern apprenticeship, process and learning: some emerging issues', *Journal of Vocational Education and Training*, 48 (3): 229–48.

Fuller, A. and Unwin, L. (1998) 'Reconceptualising apprenticeship: exploring the relationship between work and learning', *Journal of Vocational Education and Training*, 50 (2): 153–71.

Fuller, A. and Unwin, L. (2003a) 'Learning as apprentices in the contemporary UK workplace: creating and managing expansive and restrictive participation', *Journal of Education and Work*, 16 (4): 407–26.

Fuller, A. and Unwin, L. (2003b) 'Creating a modern apprenticeship: a critique of the UK's multi-sector, social inclusion approach', *Journal of Education and Work*, 16 (1): 5–25.

Fuller, A. and Unwin, L. (2004) 'Expansive learning environments: integrating personal and organisational development', in Rainbird, H., Fuller, A. and Munro, A. (eds) *Workplace Learning in Context*, London: Routledge.

Gherardi, S. (1999) 'Learning as problem-driven or learning in the face of mystery?' *Organization Studies*, 20 (1): 101–24.

Goodwin, J. and O'Connor, H. (2002) *Forty Years On: Norbert Elias and the Young Worker Project*, ESRC Young Worker Project, Research Paper 2, Leicester: CLMS, University of Leicester.

Goodwin, J. and O'Connor, H. (2003) 'The Role of Work in the Transition to Adulthood: Norbert Elias and the Young Worker Project', European Research Network on Transitions in Youth, University of Madeira, Funchal, 4–6 September.

Goodwin, J. and O'Connor, H. (2004) 'A Lifetime of Learning? The Experience of Learning during 40 Years at Work', European Conference on Educational Research, University of Crete, 22–25 September.

Goodwin, J. and O'Connor, H. (2005) *A Life Time of Learning? The Experiences of Learning During 40 years at Work*, ESRC Young Worker Project, Research Paper 7, Leicester: CLMS, University of Leicester.

Hodkinson, P. and Hodkinson, H. (2003) 'Rethinking Communities of Practice: A Case Study of Schoolteachers' Workplace Learning', paper presented to the third International Conference of Researching Work and Learning, 'Work and Lifelong Learning in Different Contexts', Tampere, Finland, 25–27 July.

Lave, J. and Wenger, E. (1991) *Situated Learning: Legitimate Peripheral Participation*, Cambridge: Cambridge University Press.

Lawy, R. (2006) 'Connective learning: young people's identity and knowledge-making in work and non-work contexts', *British Journal of Sociology of Education*, Vol. 27, No. 3, July 2006, pp. 325–340.

O'Connor, H. and Goodwin, J. (2005) 'Girls' perceptions of adulthood in the 1960s', in Pilcher,

J., Pole, C., and Williams, J. (eds) *Young People in Transition: Becoming Citizens?* London: Palgrave.

Owen-Pugh, V. (2003) *The Elite British Basketball Club as a 'Community of Practice': Situating Lave and Wenger's Model of Learning within Elias' Theory of the Group*, Working Paper 40, Centre for Labour Market Studies, University of Leicester.

Pilcher, J. (1995) *Age and Generation in Modern Britain*, Oxford: Oxford University Press.

van Krieken, R. V. (1998) *Norbert Elias*, London: Routledge.

Wenger, E. (1998) *Communities of Practice: Learning, Meaning and Identity*, Cambridge: Cambridge University Press.

Young Worker Project (1962a) Minutes of Second Meeting, 7 March 1962, Marbach: Deutsches Literaturarchiv (unpublished).

Young Worker Project (1962b) Minutes of Fifth Meeting, 18 April 1962, Marbach: Deutsches Literaturarchiv (unpublished).

Acknowledgements

This chapter is part of the project 'From Young Workers to Older Workers', ESRC (R000223653). Many thanks to Henrietta O'Connor, Susan Walker, Jason Hughes and Lorna Unwin for their comments and to the Norbert Elias Foundation for permission to quote from papers deposited at the Deutsches Literaturarchiv, Marbach, Germany.

9 English apprenticeship from past to present

The challenges and consequences of rampant 'community' diversity

Lorna Unwin

Key themes in this chapter

- Apprenticeship in historical context
- Critiques the concept of communities of practice in contemporary economies
- Comparison of Lave and Wenger's concept of apprenticeship with contemporary British experience
- Contests the acceptance of diversity as a positive characteristic of the apprenticeship model

The concept of 'apprenticeship' is central to Lave and Wenger's (1991) thesis on 'situated learning'. On page one of their seminal text, they note that 'Our initial intention in writing what has gradually evolved into this book was to rescue the idea of *apprenticeship*' (Lave and Wenger 1991: 29, original emphasis). This arose out of their concern that, in the 1980s, the term 'apprenticeship' was being used in their workplace, the Institute for Research on Learning at Palo Alto in California, 'as a token of solidarity and as a focus for discussions on the nature of learning' and as a 'synonym for situated learning' (Lave and Wenger 1991: 29–30). Indeed, despite Lave and Wenger's colleagues having no real certainty about the meaning of the term, it had become so pervasive in discussions about learning as to be 'in danger of becoming meaningless' (Lave and Wenger 1991: 30).

In the introduction of his own book, entitled *Communities of Practice*, Wenger (1998: 11) remembers how he and Lave wanted to 'articulate what it was about apprenticeship that seemed so compelling as a learning process'. By studying case studies of different varieties of apprenticeship, and by thinking through why the term apprenticeship was so often used in a metaphorical way by many people in all walks of life when they described a process of learning to become skilled (whether in a job-specific sense or, say, in playing a musical instrument), Lave and Wenger evolved their theory of legitimate peripheral participation. Apprenticeship gave them the key to the theory because it exemplifies the notion of a 'newcomer' embarking on a journey, supported by 'old-timers', towards 'the mastery of knowledge and skill' through participation in a community of practice (Lave and Wenger 1991: 29). At the same time, Lave and Wenger are at pains to stress that their use of the term 'apprenticeship' transcends stereotypical images of the medieval and feudal master–apprentice relationship and the exploitative use of apprenticeship by some employers in capitalist society. Wenger (1998: 11) also calls for a broader perspective, one that moves away from 'a master/student or mentor/mentee relationship to one of changing participation and identity transformation in a community of practice'.

This chapter explores the extent to which Lave and Wenger's discussion and application of the term 'apprenticeship' relate to accounts of the lived reality of apprenticeship experience in the distant past and in the contemporary labour market in Britain, a country that endured the world's first industrial revolution. In particular, it will examine the types of 'communities of practice' that British apprentices have found themselves in throughout history. The historical and cultural foundations of British vocational education and training have led to a different approach to apprenticeship in recent years from that found in many other European countries and in North America. This chapter will argue that, ironically, the use of the term 'apprenticeship' in the early part of the twenty-first century in Britain is as 'meaningless' as it had become for Lave and Wenger and their colleagues a quarter of a century ago. This is not because the term 'apprenticeship' is simply being used too loosely in common parlance but because successive governments since the late 1990s have chosen to use the term 'apprenticeship' to describe a series of government-funded youth training schemes, many of which bear the hallmarks of the disreputable apprenticeships that Lave and Wenger sought to move beyond.

The chapter is divided into four sections: the first section discusses the meaning of 'apprenticeship' in its historical context; the second examines the lived reality of contemporary government-funded apprenticeships in England; the third explores the problems that the contemporary British approach to apprenticeship causes for the concept of legitimate peripheral participation; the fourth offers some concluding remarks.

Apprenticeship and the labour process

If asked for their image of an 'apprentice', most people would probably conjure up a range of stereotypes, including the young man assisting the master stonemason in the building of one of Europe's great Gothic cathedrals, his equivalent several hundred years later learning to make exquisite furniture in the workshops of Thomas Chippendale, and their modern cousins being trained to be engineers in one of the twentieth century's car factories or chefs in a top London restaurant. The images might, though not necessarily, include young women training to be hairdressers or dressmakers, and some might extend to the major role apprentices played in the studios of the world's great artists, including Leonardo Da Vinci and Michelangelo. In many people's minds these apprentices would be part of a community exhibiting the characteristics which Lave and Wenger (1991) identified as constituting a 'community of practice': shared goals and values; the transmission of community-specific knowledge and skills from one generation to another; supportive practices to assist the transition from legitimate peripheral participation to full community member; and access for apprentices to the 'information, resources, and opportunities for participation' they need (Lave and Wenger 1991: 101).

Lave and Wenger's (1991) concept of a 'community of practice' arises from the five very different examples of apprenticeship which they present in the form of short vignettes: midwives, tailors, quartermasters, butchers and, by way of a distinctive alternative, alcoholics attending meetings of Alcoholics Anonymous. In doing so, they stress that apprenticeship has tended to be dismissed by educationalists as an outdated model of vocational education and training, particularly because of 'its sorry reputation in Western Europe' and its association with the exploitation of workers in the United

States in the 1920s and 1930s (Lave and Wenger 1991: 64). Yet, they argue, the form that apprenticeship takes reflects the fact that it is a socially situated model of learning and, hence, it may be exploitative, even cruel, or it may be 'benign, relatively egalitarian and nonexploitative in character', as in the cases they found in West Africa. This is one of the most important insights in Lave and Wenger's (1991) book, for it draws attention to the fact that any model of learning, including formal schooling, begins as an abstract concept and becomes shaped into many diverse forms by the political, social and economic climate it inhabits. In addition, and as Billett (in this volume) highlights, the behaviour and motivation of the individuals concerned (apprentices, 'old-timers', managers, supervisors) work with the actual context to shape conditions and types of social relations that create unique environments for learning. Schooling has not been summarily dismissed in the same way as apprenticeship as a model of learning, yet many schools could not be said to be exemplars of pedagogic practice and many adults speak passionately about how their school experiences left them with low self-esteem.

It cannot be denied, however, that apprenticeship in England, as in many other industrially advanced developed countries, has played a major role in the exploitation of young workers (including children) over many centuries. In her history of apprenticeship in England from 1600 to 1914 Joan Lane (1996: 219) draws on contemporaneous records (including diaries, memoirs, apprentice indenture papers, parish records and press cuttings) to chart this exploitation, which often included violent attacks on apprentices:

> Physical violence to apprentices was common in a majority of trades for spoiled work, disobedience or unruly behaviour and to many inarticulate men physical correction was the only punishment they knew how to give . . . and apprentices had few privileges or wages to be reduced as an alternative to corporal punishment.

The disciplining of apprentices formed part of the parent–child nature of the apprenticeship model itself, and it is still the case in some industries that the agreement between the employer and the apprentice (referred to in the past as the 'indenture') is also signed by the apprentice's parents or guardians in the case of apprentices under the age of 18. As late as the 1960s the relationship between apprentice and employer did not, necessarily, embody the caring and nurturing virtues suggested by Lave and Wenger as being important to self-sustaining communities. Recalling his apprenticeship in a factory making parts for a well known car manufacturer in the 1960s, this engineer vividly portrays the apprentice–employer relationship:

> You never spoke to the manager. He was a god, an absolute god. There were so many layers between him and you anyway that there would be no necessity for you ever to speak to him . . . They [the chargehands] weren't afraid to rule with a rod of iron in terms of language and so on. You'd get all sorts of earwigging. That was the way it was, but it was a regime driven by fear in those days, very much us and them.
> (Fuller and Unwin 2001: 22)

Whilst apprenticeship in the medieval period was certainly formulated on the basis that the apprentice was handed over by his parents and placed in the charge of the 'master' for a set period of time, a significant change took place in many continental European countries in the nineteenth century, when apprenticeship was embraced as part of the state-controlled vocational education system. In Britain, however, apprenticeship remained completely separate from the education system and was viewed as part of labour market training (Ryan 1998, 1999). This means that employers were, and remain so to this day in Britain, seen to be the most important stakeholder, whereas in many other European countries apprenticeships form part of a social partnership approach to vocational education that includes employers, education institutions, trade unions and government working together to ensure that the needs of the apprentice, the employer and the wider society are met (see Clarke and Herrmann 2004). Trade unions have always, until relatively recently, played a major role in British apprenticeships, but, unlike the European social partnership model, this has been an industrial relations function, with unions insisting on certain restrictions, such as that apprenticeships must be 'time-served' to protect the jobs of older workers (see Ryan 1999). Lave and Wenger (1991) reflect the concern of trade unions the world over about the inherent tension within the apprenticeship model in that the survival and reproduction of communities of practice depends on newcomers but, at the same time, their arrival threatens the role of old-timers. They note that 'the sustained participation of newcomers, becoming old-timers, must involve conflict between the forces that support processes of learning and those that work against them' (Lave and Wenger 1991: 57).

The dominant role of employers in the organization and management of British apprenticeship and the lack of sustained partnerships with education meant that different forms of apprenticeship training were allowed to flourish (see Ryan and Unwin 2001). Some apprentices were trained entirely on the job, whilst others spent periods of time attending colleges of further education or training schools run by large companies as well as receiving training in the workplace. Some apprentices studied for qualifications, others simply 'served their time'. In contrast, in continental Europe, the vocational education of apprentices was much more highly regulated and, hence, more uniform. In this respect Lave and Wenger's (1991) discussion of apprentice butchers in American supermarkets comes closer to the British tradition than their other case studies. When apprentices are regarded primarily as hired labourers in the same way as any other worker, then they are at the mercy of the employer in terms of how much access they may get to learning opportunities above and beyond their immediate work tasks. Lave and Wenger's (1991: 76) apprentice butchers are a 'cheap source of unskilled labour, put to work in ways that deny them access to activities in the arenas of mature practice'. As such Lave and Wenger (1991: 76) use the example of the butchers' apprenticeship to illustrate the way in which 'particular forms of apprenticeship can prevent rather than facilitate learning'.

In terms of the theory of situated learning, however, the fact that some apprentices have access to off-the-job education and training opportunities whilst others learn entirely in the workplace is not necessarily a problem. If access to the resources and people they need to gain mastery of the skills and knowledge embedded in the community of practice can be acquired entirely through the workplace, then apprentices will progress on their journey to become full participants. For the Yucatec midwives in Mexico, learning the skills and knowledge they need takes place as part of their daily routine. Lave and Wenger (1991: 68) note that, 'Teaching does not seem to be central either to the identities of master midwives or to learning.' In contrast, the Vai and Gola tailors in West Africa experience a highly structured apprenticeship in which a curriculum is delivered through sessions of formal instruction and immersion in the daily practice of making clothes. Both models of apprenticeship are acceptable to Lave and

Wenger because they take place within communities of practice that support the newcomer's journey to full participation and mastery.

It is significant that the apprentice butchers represent, for Lave and Wenger, an example of how apprentices can be part of a malfunctioning community of practice and, therefore, cannot be said to be experiencing apprenticeship in the truest sense. The significance lies in the fact that the butchers are the only case study among the five presented by Lave and Wenger that actually comes from a contemporary work setting in an advanced economy. Yet if, as they claim, the concepts of legitimate peripheral participation, community of practice and, indeed, apprenticeship have widespread applicability to the process of learning across both formal and informal settings, then they have to make sense in the context of dynamic workplaces in advanced economies. Lave and Wenger's case studies of apprenticeship all share a sense of continuity in terms of the skills and vocational knowledge that their communities need to share and develop. Yet, today, long-standing definitions and shared understandings of the meaning of the concept of 'skill' are being tested and reinterpreted across all sectors of the economy. As the service sectors have expanded, the language of skills has shifted from notions of manual activity to include terms such as 'transferable', 'interpersonal', 'soft' and 'generic', some of which embrace concepts such as personality, attributes, qualities and behaviours (see Payne 2000; Keep and Mayhew 1999). In addition, sectors such as retailing, hospitality, hairdressing, financial services and the media look for what Nickson *et al.* (2003: 185–6) call 'aesthetic labour':

> 'looking good' or 'sounding right' are the most overt manifestations of aesthetic labour. In essence, with aesthetic labour, employers are seeking employees who can portray the firm's image through their work, and at the same time appeal to the sense of the customer for those firms' commercial benefit.

The diverse nature of the work and labour process in advanced economies means that apprenticeship, if it is to survive, will have to find ways to adapt itself to the many and varied work 'communities', but the hard question is whether it can do so without sacrificing the characteristics that, Lave and Wenger argue, enable apprenticeship to take individuals on a journey from peripheral participation to full membership of effective communities of practice.

Contemporary English apprenticeship

This section of the chapter considers the meaning of Lave and Wenger's concepts of apprenticeship and communities of practice within the context of government-funded apprenticeship programmes in England. The focus on England, as opposed to Britain, is deliberate, as recently devolved government powers to Scotland, Wales and Northern Ireland are heralding the development of some distinct vocational education and training policies in those 'home nations'. It has to be said, however, that much of what follows still applies throughout Britain, largely, of course, because the British economy does not and never will respect the new government boundaries.

A government-funded apprenticeship is one of the pathways available to 16 to 25-year-olds in England. Government involvement in apprenticeship is, however, relatively recent. Britain has taken a voluntarist approach to labour market and training policies since the early industrial revolution of the eighteenth century (Green 1990). Until as late as 1964 British governments had not had any statutory involvement in the provision or regulation of industrial training. Despite a hundred years or so of concern that Britain was falling behind other industrialized nations in terms of the stock and quality of skills in its work force, it wasn't until 1963 and the introduction of the Industrial Training Act that government finally made a serious intervention in vocational education and training. The Act called for the establishment of a number of sectoral Industrial Training Boards (ITBs) whose role was to impose a training levy on employers in order to improve the quality and consistency of training programmes, including apprenticeship. Given the very long voluntarist tradition, however, the ITBs were faced with considerable resistance from employers and they struggled to achieve their goals. With regard to apprenticeship, the ITBs were faced with a particular problem, in that their terms of reference did not permit them to connect improvements in the quality of apprenticeship training to acceptance that apprentice pay rates might have to be reduced (see Marsden and Ryan 1991). In stark contrast to Germany, where there had long been a consensus among the social partners that apprentices would receive training allowances rather than the market wage for their sector in order that the appropriate funds could be invested in their training, pay rates for apprentices in the UK were negotiated between trade unions and employers separately from discussions about training provision (see Marsden and Ryan 1991; Sheldrake and Vickerstaff 1987). The ITBs were faced, therefore, with the dilemma that asking employers to invest more money in apprenticeship training would, necessarily, mean a reduction in the number of apprenticeship places. Given that the ITBs were not afforded extra funding to offset employers' higher training costs, the result was a reduction in apprenticeship numbers. The ITBs, particularly with regard to engineering, did have some impact on the quality of apprenticeship programmes (see Senker 1992), but Marsden and Ryan (1991) argue that an opportunity was missed in the mid-1960s to reconfigure UK apprenticeships along the lines of the German model of 'low pay, high quality, high volume'.

The decline in apprenticeship numbers triggered by the ITBs was further exacerbated in the 1970s as UK manufacturing was hit by the worldwide oil crisis. In response to a rapid rise in youth unemployment (and television pictures of young people rioting in the streets of some British cities) a series of youth work experience and training schemes was introduced by the then Conservative government under Margaret Thatcher, culminating in the Youth Training Scheme (YTS) in 1983 (see Unwin and Wellington 2001). The case for YTS had been made in a report, *A New Training Initiative*, from the Manpower Services Commission (MSC) in 1981 (MSC 1981). This was the first substantive attempt by the state to design, organize and fund an apprenticeship-style programme for 16 to 19-year-olds, though they were to be called 'trainees', as apprentices recruited in the age-old way directly by employers still existed. The importance of the introduction of YTS cannot be overestimated, as it has had a profound and lasting effect on the image, meaning and status of vocational education in general. First, YTS was a vehicle for creating new forms of training provision and management that continue today. As Finn (1987: 136) has argued:

> Conservative policy did not consist of a simple expansion of provision to meet the growing numbers of the young unemployed. It involved an active restructuring of the various institutions and agencies which controlled training programmes.

The restructuring that Finn refers to needs to be viewed in the context of the Conservative government's hostility to any attempt by the state to tell employers how to run their businesses. Whilst NTI called for substantial state funding for YTS the new scheme was to be delivered through agencies (many of them newly created commercial training organizations) which would handle all the bureaucratic and regulatory requirements of the scheme on behalf of employers, whose own role would be to provide work placements. This allowed many employers to accept youth trainees without having to take any responsibility for the substantive components of their training programme, a situation that was the complete opposite to the traditional concept of apprenticeship and, indeed, is deeply contrary to the concept of communities of practice as outlined by Lave and Wenger (1991).

Another important way in which YTS has had a lasting impact is that it failed to reverse the poor image it attained very early on in its life. This image portrayed YTS as (1) a scheme used by employers for cheap labour, (2) a pathway that was suitable only for young people who were incapable of gaining entry to full-time, post-compulsory education courses or to the labour market, and (3) a pathway that offered poor-quality training and support for trainees. There were, of course, many YTS trainees who had very good experiences in that they found placements with reputable employers committed to workforce development and employee progression. These experiences could not, however, overcome the very negative publicity that YTS attracted in the print and broadcast media, in schools and colleges, in the academic research community and among the general public. In consequence, government-funded youth training programmes came to be seen as pathways to avoid, and this haunts the contemporary apprenticeship programme.

In 1994 the then Conservative government introduced a publicly funded programme called Modern Apprenticeship (MA), open to 16 to 25-year-olds, as an attempt to increase the stock of intermediate skills (see Unwin and Wellington 2001). The use of the term 'apprenticeship' for the first time with regard to a government-funded training scheme was a deliberate attempt to distinguish the new programme from the existing and discredited training schemes. The government believed that the general public trusted the concept of apprenticeship, as, for them, it denoted quality training and employer commitment (Unwin and Wellington 2001). The term 'Modern' was also a deliberate attempt to show the government was trying to reinvent the apprenticeship model for the contemporary economy. This meant that: (1) apprenticeships would lead to a level 3 qualification in order to build stocks of intermediate skills; (2) apprenticeships would no longer be 'time-served' but would last as long as was necessary for apprentices to complete the prescribed qualifications,[1] (3) apprenticeships would be available in a much wider range of occupational sectors, and (4) apprenticeships should be open equally to women and ethnic minorities as well as white men. Whilst (1) and (2) have been achieved, and there are nearly as many female apprentices as male, the sectors are deeply segregated in terms of both gender and ethnicity (for more detail see Fuller *et al.* 2005).

In 2004, under the second term of the New Labour government, the term 'Modern' was dropped and the government-funded programme is now called 'Apprenticeships', as it embraces all youth training at both levels 2 and 3. In essence, then, the original attempt to use the term 'apprenticeship' to signal that the government (and the general public) knew that the existing training schemes were not of sufficient quality was abandoned. Fuller and Unwin (2003a) have argued that this decision reflects the third Blair government's struggle to balance its competitiveness and social inclusion agendas. On the one hand, there is a determination to increase skill levels, whilst, on the other, apprenticeship is seen as a pathway for young people who either cannot or choose not to stay in full-time education and then progress to university. In this regard, apprenticeship has travelled a long way from being a model of skill formation closely connected with the business needs of employers. In the case of the level 2 apprenticeships, for example, some apprentices do not have employed status and so are paid an Education Maintenance Allowance (funded by the government) by the training provider (college or private training company) which oversees their apprenticeship.

Apprenticeship frameworks are available in 92 occupational sectors, though the vast majority of apprentices are located within just 12 frameworks: engineering, construction, hairdressing, automotive manufacturing, business administration, hospitality, early years care and education, electro-technical, customer service, health and social care, retail, plumbing (see www.apprenticeships.org.uk).

Seven of the twelve most populated sectors cover the service industries, many of which would not have had a history of running apprenticeships prior to 1994. The service sectors recruit the vast majority of their apprentices on to the level 2 programme, unlike the more traditional apprenticeship sectors (such as engineering), where the focus is on level 3 skills. We can see, therefore, that the original aim of the apprenticeship programme introduced in 1994 to boost the UK's stock of intermediate skills has been abandoned (see Fuller and Unwin 2003a).

Costs are shared between the employer, who pays the apprentice's wages, and the state, which funds training towards the attainment of mandatory qualifications (NVQs, Technical Certificates and Key Skill units) and any other vocational awards which have been approved as part of the sectoral 'frameworks' which employers and training providers have to abide by. The funding mechanism for apprenticeship continues along the same lines established when YTS was introduced. As was discussed earlier, this gives a central role to training providers rather than employers. As a consequence, not enough is known about what happens to apprentices in the workplace, as it is very difficult for researchers to gain access to those employers who have apprentices owing to the gatekeeping role of the training providers (see Fuller and Unwin 2003a).

The struggle for a dual identity

The government-funded apprenticeship programmes exist within Britain's highly flexible labour market and, hence, any employer can recruit apprentices regardless of whether they have trained trainers or any experience of managing the type of substantive workforce development programmes associated with apprenticeship. Employers involved in apprenticeship are, of course, inspected to ensure they meet health and safety requirements but, beyond that, there is very little monitoring of their involvement. Training providers are inspected with regard to their provision of training and support for apprentices, and this again indicates the separation in the government's mind of training from employment. From the apprentice's point of view, they are required to trust the system and hope that they find a placement with an employer who is committed to the concept of an apprenticeship. This means creating conditions in the workplace whereby the apprentice's dual identity, as worker and learner, is protected. The problem for many apprentices is that their employers want them to move far too quickly to the position of being productive workers, and, hence, they are denied the opportunity to spend appropriate time as legitimate peripheral participants (see Fuller and Unwin 2003b).

Apprenticeship frameworks differ in terms of the specified qualifications to be achieved, and the amount (if any) of off-the-job training. In traditional sectors such as engineering, an apprentice would typically spend the first year in a college of further education learning the basic theoretical knowledge and practical skills to then move into the workplace in their second year. They would then spend one day per week attending the college and/or other off-the-job training workshops and four days a week on their employer's premises. Over a period of three to four years, they would acquire a range of nationally recognized qualifications. In direct contrast, an apprentice in the retail sector would receive virtually all their training on the employer's premises, apart from the odd day here and there to attend a specialist course on health and safety, or perhaps to acquire knowledge about new products. They might complete their apprenticeship in a few months.

Fuller and Unwin (2003b) have conceptualized the very different types of learning environments which UK apprentices encounter as an 'expansive–restrictive' continuum (see also Fuller in this volume). Apprentices who find themselves in organizations that create learning environments closer to the expansive end of the continuum will find their apprenticeship is underpinned by a number of key features not found in organizations closer to the restrictive end. These features include:

1 Embedding apprenticeship within the broader business plan of the organization.
2 Embedding apprenticeship within the broader workforce development plans of the organization.
3 Protecting the dual identity of the apprentice as learner and worker throughout the apprenticeship.
4 Providing opportunities to learn in different settings (on and off the job).
5 Ensuring qualifications are achieved within the period of the apprenticeship.

Given that some organizations, particularly small enterprises with less than ten employees, may find it difficult to provide an apprentice with the variety of learning opportunities available in a much larger workplace site, the government needs to find ways to deliver an 'expansive' apprenticeship programme for all young people. This would mean, therefore, a much stronger commitment to a core entitlement for each apprenticeship, around which the sectoral specific components would sit. Thus every apprentice would be entitled to spend one day a week (or in a block period) off the job engaging in vocational education, including time in a simulated working environment (e.g. a college restaurant or engineering workshop) to acquire skills not covered by their employer. This matters because, unlike the Yucatec midwives, apprentices in the contemporary British labour market have to survive in a dynamic and turbulent economy and compete with an ever-increasing number of university graduates whose qualifications are adding to a creeping credentialism (Brown and Hesketh 2004).

Conclusion

There are some splendid examples of 'expansive' apprenticeships in Britain in all sectors of the economy. The abiding problem, however, is that too many apprenticeships lie towards the restrictive end of the continuum, and too many are merely masquerading as apprenticeships when in reality they are no more than short-term work experience placements. The completion figures reveal that, even in the sectors with long traditions of running apprenticeships, just over 50 per cent of apprentices achieve the prescribed qualifications, and in some of the service sectors achievement rates are abysmal: for example, 16 per cent in health and social care, 31 per cent in hospitality.

There are a number of reasons for this poor performance: (1) employers can, without any penalty, remove young people from their apprenticeships before they have attained the prescribed qualifications and employ them as part of the normal work force; (2) some apprentices enter the programme with low levels of general education and struggle with the qualification requirements; (3) some providers offer a poor service and fail to monitor apprentice progress, and some local government agencies perform better than others in managing providers; (4) in some sectors the prescribed qualifications have minimal relevance to actual workplace activity.

This chapter has tried to explain how government-funded apprenticeship in Britain offers very different experiences in terms of learning, working and career prospects to the young people who enter the foundation or the advanced versions of the programme. In that sense, it is a highly flexible programme suited to the unregulated nature of the British labour market and a business environment where some employers concentrate on the short-term profit demands of their shareholders and others operate at the low-quality end of the product market (see Lloyd and Payne 2002; Keep and Mayhew 2001). Paradoxically, whilst Lave and Wenger celebrate the diversity of structure and approach in their examples of apprenticeship, the contemporary approach to apprenticeship in Britain has led to such diversity as to make the term 'apprenticeship' as meaningless as Lave and Wenger feared to be the case when they embarked on their ground-breaking study some 20 or so years ago.

Key questions to consider

1   To what extent are Lave and Wenger justified in arguing that the concept of apprenticeship can be broadened to encompass approaches as diverse as the Yucatec midwives and the US butchers?
2   Does the apprenticeship model have meaning in contemporary advanced economies?
3   Can the concept of communities of practice be generalized to such an extent that it can encompass all forms of workplace?
4   Is the concept of legitimate peripheral participation viable in sectors where labour turnover is rapid and where notions of skill and vocational knowledge are difficult to articulate?

Note

1   Historically, the length of apprenticeships was determined by the craft guilds, and then later by negotiation between employers and the trade unions. The concept of 'time served' related to the belief that apprentices needed time to mature, to become socialized into the occupation and to practise their skills.

References

Brown, P. and Hesketh, A. (2004) *The Mismanagement of Talent*, Oxford: Oxford University Press.

Clarke, L. and Herrmann, G. (2004) 'The institutionalisation of skill in Britain and Germany: examples from the construction sector', in Warhurst, C., Grugulis, I. and Keep, E. (eds) *The Skills that Matter*, London: Palgrave Macmillan.

Finn, D. (1987) *Training without Jobs: New Deals and Broken Promises*, London: Macmillan.

Fuller, A. and Unwin, L. (2001) *From Cordwainers to Customer Service: the changing Relationship between Apprentices, Employers and Communities in England*, SKOPE Monograph 3, Oxford: Universities of Oxford and Warwick.

Fuller, A. and Unwin, L. (2003a) 'Creating a "Modern Apprenticeship": a critique of the UK's multi-sector, social inclusion approach', *Journal of Education and Work*, 16 (1): 5–25.

Fuller, A. and Unwin, L. (2003b) 'Learning as apprentices in the contemporary UK workplace: creating and managing expansive and restrictive participation', *Journal of Education and Work*, 16 (4): 406–27.

Fuller, A., Beck, V. and Unwin, L. (2005) 'The gendered nature of apprenticeship: employers' and young people's perspectives', *Education and Training*, 47 (4–5): 298–311.

Green, A. (1990) *Education and State Formation*, Basingstoke: Macmillan.

Keep, E. and Mayhew, K. (1999) 'The assessment: knowledge, skills and competitiveness', *Oxford Review of Economic Policy*, 15 (1):1–15.

Keep, E. and Mayhew, K. (2001) *Globalisation, Models of Competitive Advantage and Skills*, SKOPE Working Paper 22, Universities of Oxford and Warwick, www.skope.ox.ac.uk.

Lane, J. (1996) *Apprenticeship in England*, London: UCL Press.

Lave, J. and Wenger, E. (1991) *Situated Learning: Legitimate Peripheral Participation*, Cambridge: Cambridge University Press.

Lloyd, C. and Payne, J. (2002) 'Developing a political economy of skill', *Journal of Education and Work*, 15 (4): 365–90.

Marsden, D. and Ryan, P. (1991) 'Initial training, labour market structure and public policy: intermediate skills in British and German industry', in Ryan, P. (ed.), *International Comparisons of Vocational Education and Training for Intermediate Skills*, London: Falmer Press.

MSC (1981) *A New Training Initiative: An Agenda for Action*, Sheffield: Manpower Services Commission.

Nickson, D., Warhurst, C., Cullen, A. M. and Watt, A. (2003) 'Bringing in the excluded? Aesthetic labour, skills and training in the "new" economy', *Journal of Education and Work*, 16 (2): 185–203.

Payne, J. (2000) 'The unbearable lightness of skill: the changing meaning of skill in UK policy discourses and some implications for education and training', *Journal of Education Policy*, 15 (3): 353–69.

Ryan, P. (1998) 'Is apprenticeship better? A review of the economic evidence', *Journal of Vocational Education and Training*, 50 (2): 289–322.

Ryan, P. (1999) 'The embedding of apprenticeship in industrial relations: British engineering, 1925–1965', in Ainley, P. and Rainbird, H. (eds) *Apprenticeship: Towards a New Paradigm of Learning*, London: Kogan Page.

Ryan, P. and Unwin, L. (2001) 'Apprenticeship in the British "training market"', *National Institute Economic Review*, 178: 99–114.

Senker, P. (1992) *Industrial Training in a Cold Climate: An Assessment of Britain's Training Policies*, Aldershot: Avebury Gower.

Sheldrake, J. and Vickerstaff, S. (1987) The *History of Industrial Training in Britain*, Aldershot: Avebury.

Unwin, L. and Wellington, J. (2001) *Young People's Experiences of Education, Training and Employment*, London: Kogan Page.

Wenger, E. (1998) *Communities of Practice*, Cambridge: Cambridge University Press.

10 Sexuality, gender and legitimate peripheral participation

An ethnographic study of a call centre

Matthew J. Brannan

Key themes in this chapter

- Legitimate peripheral participation
- Constellations of communities of practice
- Power inequalities in communities of practice
- The lived experience of novices
- Gendering of legitimate peripheral participation

This chapter explores empirically the process of legitimate peripheral participation within a workplace. It is drawn from an ethnographic investigation of AceCall, a large multi-client call centre located in the West Midlands, where I spent 13 months employed as a customer service representative (CSR). The demands placed upon CSRs are complex and often contradictory and this chapter seeks to document how growing participation in the community of practice, which constituted the call centre, provided opportunities for new CSRs to learn job requirements through active, but structured, involvement in the work of other CSRs. During the fieldwork for this research I participated fully in the daily routine of a CSR; taking full time employment in the research environment allowed me access to experience fully the process of becoming a competent full-time CSR. Furthermore I was able to discuss this transition with other members of staff and observe this process as other new members of staff joined the organization.

Ethnographic approaches to the study of the process of legitimate peripheral participation are particularly relevant, as they encourage sensitivity to the 'lived experience' of those who are being studied, in this case new CSRs, or 'newcomers', within the call centre. The research presented here forms part of a much broader investigation into all aspects of call centre life with specific reference to issues of workplace control and resistance (Brannan 2005a). The focus of this chapter is on the way in which new employees are systematically involved in the work process as a mode of training and development. The chapter draws upon material recorded in a fieldwork journal during the investigation, follow-up interviews and general observations, which were recorded whilst *in situ*. Follow-up interviews were conducted with a number of former team colleagues and call centre managers.

Despite a distinct move away from empirical anthropological and ethnographic considerations of the process of legitimate peripheral participation (which characterized the initial approach adopted by Lave and Wenger 1991: 30), in favour of a more overtly and consciously theoretical orientation, empirical studies retain the capacity to explore how those involved in such processes make sense of their situation and ascribe meaning to their experiences. It is in this spirit that this chapter explores, in an empirical context, how structured relations of power and gender combined to articulate the boundaries of participation for new employees, and, crucially, how the process of legitimate peripheral participation is differentiated along gender lines.

In drawing attention to the gendered differentiation of the process of legitimate peripheral participation, this chapter draws upon the growing literature on gender in organizations (see, for example, Adkins 1992). It is also argued that the job role undertaken by CSRs is becoming increasingly sexualized, and this theme is also reflected and examined through the lens of legitimate peripheral participation. The chapter is organized as follows. First, background details of the case study call centre are outlined and attention is drawn to the view that modern organizations consist of 'constellations' of communities of practice. Second, specific processes of legitimate peripheral participation that were observed during the fieldwork are documented and explored. Third, limitations to the process of legitimate peripheral participation at AceCall are discussed, before concluding comments are made.

AceCall as a constellation of communities of practice

AceCall is a large multi-client call centre in the West Midlands, which, over the duration of the fieldwork, grew from 250 to around 400 members of staff. AceCall is a division of AceCorp, a large multinational organization that specializes in the provision of international accountancy and consultancy services to other large-scale organizations. AceCall was established in the late 1980s to provide outsourced IT support for client organizations. It was integrated into AceCorp's consultancy policy, which at that time was advising organizations to outsource their non-core business functions to specialist providers. AceCall is recognized within the call centre industry as being particularly successful and, in large part, this success has been attributed to the way in which the organization has been able to develop a standardized approach to providing outsourced IT support to disparate organizations across many different industries. At the time of the fieldwork, for example, AceCall offered outsourced support to high-street banks, national rail providers, insurance companies, major international retailers and local government organizations. These clients, or in practical terms their employees, were considered to be AceCall's customers. Within AceCall each separate client would have a dedicated team of CSRs, led by a team leader, to provide support. The team structure is important in understanding the experience of work within AceCall, as the notion of specific teams was a key source of differentiation between various groups of workers within the call centre, to the extent that these might be analytically considered as distinct communities of practice in their own right.

In order to become an active member of any team within the Call Centre, all new recruits were required to complete a period of training, which would notionally last for around four weeks. The training consisted of two elements. First, structured technical training was provided centrally and aimed to ensure that all new recruits were given the generic technical skills needed to be able to understand and operate the various systems and procedures, such as the telephone system, the computer database and the correct call handling procedure. This training took place outside the call centre. It was conducted by a professional trainer and was attended by a pool of new recruits only. Very much separate from the normal activity of the call centre, reinforced by its location, this formal training lasted for around three days. It was referred to as 'basic training', a use of language which reflects an almost military approach to initial training. Second, once basic training had been completed, new CSRs were allocated to teams and more specific client training was provided in a decentralized fashion within the team structure. Whilst the basic training provided key skills, it was the informal, team-based training that was crucial to understanding how new members of staff became full participants, and hence is the focus of the remainder of this chapter. This informal training marked the first stage of integration between new members of staff and the call centre and was characterized by a process of increasing participation by new CSRs in the routine functions of the call centre.

CSRs were required to answer telephone calls from customers (employees of client organizations) who were experiencing computer problems. Calls were allocated by Automatic Call Distribution software that controlled the flow of work (see Bain and Taylor 2000; Callaghan and Thompson 2001; Taylor and Bain 1999). The CSRs would then be required to log the call by taking all relevant details of the problem and recording them on a computer database. Once this had been achieved, the CSRs could then end the initial interaction. The problem would then need to be resolved, and this was normally achieved by the CSRs contacting a third-party support organization to arrange for a solution to be worked on. The CSRs can, therefore, usefully be thought of as acting as an intermediary, collecting information about the initial problem and then arranging for a solution to be found. Once the problem had been logged with AceCall it was expected that the team of call centre workers would manage the problem until resolution. The CSRs therefore faced dual, and potentially contradictory, imperatives. They were required first to ensure that all calls were answered quickly and details taken accurately and, second, that problems were resolved as speedily as possible. The work process within the call centre was standardized, but slight variations existed between teams owing to specific client requirements. It was noticeable that the distinction between teams on the basis of clients remained robust. Moreover, in some cases, individual CSRs reported and demonstrated greater levels of attachment to clients than to AceCall. Within the course of their duties CSRs would, in their roles as intermediaries, become very familiar with client staff and also third-party support personnel. The concept of customer service within AceCall was espoused by the managers and team leaders, and the identification of individuals with clients was encouraged. In this respect call centre employees were clearly demarcated along team lines and such divisions were articulated to the extent that CSRs often, in discussion, identified themselves as working for the client rather than the call centre. This became particularly apparent to newcomers, and much of the dialogue – for example, surrounding the prioritization of goals and targets – sought to establish the primacy of the client in ensuring that their expectations were met. This was achieved, for example, by old-timers expressing pride in the degree to which a team faced tough standards and corresponding disgust at rival teams which faced less stringent targets.

The differentiation within AceCall between the various teams was, then, highly influenced by the teams' respective clients. However, for newcomers the identity of the client was important in terms of becoming familiar with the specific job requirements, or the nuanced nature of how the job should be performed. This represents a further variation on the ways in which customers may be co-opted to control workers (Sturdy *et al.* 2001). Old-timers, for example, were keen to highlight through demonstration the specific job requirements, and expected newcomers to learn these through imitation. Crucially, the differentiation between teams gave a particular emphasis to the learning of specific details and essentially effectively reinforced the idea of the team and its specific task through the exclusion and categorization of rival AceCall teams as 'other'.

AceCall demonstrated a preference for the recruitment of recent graduates and often used temporary agencies to secure new staff. AceCall was able to trade upon its close relation to AceCorp by suggesting to new recruits that AceCorp, which was generally seen as a highly prestigious organization to work for, actively sought to recruit directly from AceCall. The career opportunities that AceCall presented may therefore partially account for why so many graduates (more than 50 per cent of all staff) were employed within the call centre. They may also shed light on why so many CSRs reported that they felt over-qualified for the post yet remained at the call centre. Functionally, call centre managers acknowledged the importance of the mix of intellectual and social skills that graduates presented (as discussed by Callaghan and Thompson 2002) and also tended to emphasize the fact that they felt that graduates were more likely to fit into the working atmosphere. AceCall was careful to position the call centre as distinct from other similar workplaces. This was achieved by stressing the link with AceCorp and drawing attention to the atmosphere and socializing which were considered to be important aspects of the call centre by managers and many CSRs.

In many respects the differentiation of AceCall from other call centres represents the symbolic construction of the call centre as a desirable community of practice. Thus legitimate peripheral participation attained the status of not merely a process of becoming a competent CSR, but of joining a privileged community with respect to other employment opportunities. This positively impacted upon wider organizational objectives, such as achieving low turnover rates and labour discipline. Thus, whilst AceCall sought to differentiate itself as an organization from other call centres, and therefore draw a distinction between itself and other organizations as communities of practice, it also, through the extensive use of team working, differentiated itself internally, thereby creating a constellation of communities of practice.

Legitimate peripheral participation at AceCall

Legitimate peripheral participation at AceCall initially sought to provide an orientation to the telephone system, the computer software and standard procedures. The training method employed was for newcomers to shadow old-timers, and listen in to customer interactions of more experienced CSRs, to see how they dealt with various enquiries. The period of shadowing a colleague lasted for approximately two weeks. 'Sitting with Nelly' has proved to be an effective training technique for the acquisition of a number of skills and abilities required to complete routine tasks. This period was marked by the arrangement of two paired CSRs (newcomer and old-timer) sitting in close proximity to each other, sharing access to a computer and both connected to the same telephone line. This arrangement was practised only during the period of initial training. The tasks carried out by call centre agents were highly complex and involved human and computer interaction, and the training attempted to break these tasks down into a very simple routine structure. For example, on answering a telephone call the CSR would have a pre-prepared script that would detail exactly what the opening lines of the interaction would be. The CSR would then follow a flow diagram, which would detail appropriate responses to questions, enquiries and requests that were received. However, each interaction had to be recorded by the agent in a meticulous fashion and appropriate data placed on to the database whilst the call was in progress. The interrogation and manipulation of this database were the key skill that defined the ability of the call centre agent to function efficiently. The database was extremely complex in nature and familiarization was a difficult task. Whilst the database was used for standard procedures, it also had to be relevant to non-standard enquiries and therefore the complexity of the database increased exponentially. Initially many CSRs found interaction with the database bewilderingly difficult. Often the CSR would need to extract information from the database whilst conducting an interaction on the telephone with the customer or client. Mistakes made by new CSRs were highlighted by team members. The advice often given was that, in order to correct these mistakes, CSRs should think about the work routines whilst not working, to ensure that they were always at the forefront of their minds.

The informal training provided within the context of the team consisted of a growing level of participation in the everyday work routine of the call centre. It was common for attention to switch from specific routine procedures to more *ad hoc* techniques of managing customer interaction after the first week or so of a new CSR's employment. For example, it was suggested to me that if I could try to plan ahead whilst taking a customer call I could 'win [myself] more time to play with later' (advice given by Rajesh, team colleague, recorded in fieldwork journal). Furthermore, newcomers were provided with guidance on how exactly their tasks should be performed. For instance, CSRs were encouraged to use first names when on calls with customers; saying the name of the client three times in any call was suggested to build rapport with clients. Usually an old-timer would take a call, with the newcomer listening in but remaining silent. The next call would then be taken by the newcomer with the old-timer listening in, but ready to assist if necessary. As newcomers became more competent the level and frequency of instruction would be reduced and often restricted to commentary from old-timers once the call had been concluded. This process continued until newcomers were deemed to be proficient enough to handle calls on their own without old-timers listening in. This usually took between three and four weeks. Specific call coaching allowed old-timer CSRs to provide examples of customer interactions with focus given to the pace, tone and pitch of the verbal interaction. Newcomers would then be observed and corrected if necessary. Beyond the coaching of specific speech patterns, newcomers' dress, deportment and general attitude to work were all considered to fall within the remit of the training process. An experienced CSR told me that although customers and CSRs never meet in person, smart business attire was required in the call centre to ensure that CSRs 'looked' and therefore '*felt* the part' (comment made by Rajesh, emphasis added). This demonstrates that at AceCall a central concern was to ensure that newcomers not only knew the correct technical procedures but, even more important, through growing structured participation learned how such interactions should be carried out.

The initial period of CSRs' employment was widely regarded within the call centre as the most difficult. Despite the construction of AceCall as offering desirable employment opportunities, labour turnover of new CSRs was high; for example, from any particular recruitment drive managers expected to lose around 70 per cent of new staff. One of the newcomers who left, Liz, maintained close links with the call centre through mutual friends, and I was able to talk to her later in an off-site location about her experiences:

Matthew. So tell me about the events that led up to you leaving.

Liz. Well, I enjoyed the training, although it was tough, but it was just like they said, 'That's it now, out you go' . . . and you feel like 'Shit, it's me who's answering the calls.' I just didn't know what to do or what to say. I felt really stupid.

Matthew. Didn't the people you were working with help you?

Liz. Yeah, yeah. Don't get me wrong, they were great, really nice people, but there are only so many times you can ask someone the same thing without feeling really dumb. In the end I thought, this just isn't worth it.

> (One-to-one conversation during social evening, recorded in
> notebook, later transcribed to fieldwork journal)

Through informal discussions with colleagues I was able to ascertain that generally the initial period of employment within the call centre is considered the most demanding. It was noted how often newcomers responded to such demands by seeking to create small groups as a form of spontaneous collective labour, a finding which echoes that of Korczynski (2003). These would often take the form of newcomers grouping together at break times, or socializing after work, and can be partially explained by the shared experience of being a new CSR. Despite the waning of such groups over time, old-timers still spoke about other members of staff 'who had joined at the same time', an indication of the strength of bonds formed between CSRs as new recruits. I was told that often it was 'touch and go' (general discussion with Tina, recorded in fieldwork journal) as to whether new recruits would make it through their initial training period. In some respects this seems to explain why little attempt is generally made by old-timers to get to know temporary staff. Furthermore I learnt that whilst other call centres were not considered as 'tough' in terms of becoming proficient, high turnover, especially of new staff, was common. I was able to discuss the transition from training to work with the call centre manager:

> *Matthew*. It seems that the transition from training to working can be really stressful.
>
> *Amanda*. Yeah, I know. It's difficult to get the balance right, but I do think that you really need to be a certain 'kind' of person to do the job well. You have to be fairly tough.
>
> *Matthew*. To deal with difficult calls?
>
> *Amanda*. That's one aspect of the job, but it's better if staff find out early that the service centre is not for them, rather than later.

The response from the call centre manager illustrates how the process of legitimate peripheral participation within the call centre effectively constituted a continuing recruitment process. The initial 'shock' of being thrust into taking calls, without the reassurance of an old-timer listening in, was often cited as the cause of considerable anxiety.

Sexuality, gender and achieving work targets

Whilst the daily routine of taking calls and referring problems meant that CSRs often got to know staff in other organizations, from early on CSRs were encouraged to develop and nurture relationships with clients. This was done in a number of ways, but usually involved CSRs making general conversation with clients and third-party personnel. These interactions extended beyond the normal scope of customer interaction and involved the exploration of themes of common interest. The attainment of a level of informality between CSR and client was perceived as a sign that a relationship had been formed. Within the team to which I was assigned, the imperative to construct relationships with clients was systematically mobilized by the team leader and reinforced by competition between team members. Tina, the team leader, skilfully encouraged the male members of her team to construct artificial relationships with female clients by appealing to team members' sense of competitive machismo:

> *Tina.* Right. Venkat, Rajesh, Matt and Ben, by the end of the day I want to know how many phone numbers you've got, and I want new ones as well. Venkat, darling, that means Sally P. from Swindon doesn't count.
> *Rajesh.* What does the winner get?
> *Tina.* A list of women's phone numbers, idiot. Are you thick or just queer?

In this case the acquisition of telephone numbers was suggestive of a level of informality with clients, achieved largely through the flirtation of male CSRs with specific female clients. In this sense the construction of relationships was part of a strategy to better manage customer interactions and thus became a requirement of CSRs, or a team-based norm. The development of such relationship-building skills was carefully nurtured through the process of legitimate peripheral participation within the team. During training, for example, new male CSRs would almost always be paired with experienced male CSRs, and hence exposed to the ways in which such relationships were built and maintained. Although the development of relationships with clients is a key aspect of many service occupations, it was apparent from the example of AceCall that the required mode of relationship building assumed an overtly sexualized character. Initiated by the team leader, this mode of relationship building became compulsory through the use of ritualized competition between male CSRs. Those who could not or wished not to participate were ridiculed and bullied. Participation involved taking part in this form of competition, but also accepting the legitimacy of relationship building as a key aspect of the work routine. Despite the potential for being an invasive and possibly humiliating way of working, male CSRs reported that they enjoyed this aspect of their work, as 'it doesn't really seem like work, and it's just having a laugh' (interview with CSR). The internalization of this form of emotional labour (Hochschild 1983) as 'having a laugh' was again transmitted through the machinery of legitimate peripheral participation within the team.

Whilst male CSRs indicated tacit acceptance of their role in the building of client relationships, the role was not restricted merely to male members of the team. The team leader often singled out Jenny and Liz, the two female CSRs who were part of the team, as being particularly skilled in terms of building and maintaining client relationships.

> *Liz* (to Tina). I've got this problem call. It's been logged by Andy D. from Swindon. He's being really awkward, because I want to close it for the figures but technically it's not really fixed . . .
> *Tina.* What's the problem?
> *Liz.* It's a server problem, a small error, but it keeps recurring . . .
> *Tina.* What have you done with it?

Liz. Er, well, nothing, really. Andy said that a fix was being worked on by [third-party support organization] but it might be a few weeks. He wants the call kept open until it's properly fixed.

Tina. Hold on . . . (Shouts) Jenny!

Jenny. Yeah?

Tina. How's your love life with Andy D.? He's one of yours, isn't he?

Jenny (laughing). Well, yeah, he's pretty cool. We have a chat every now and then . . .

Tina. Do us a favour, darling. Get him on the phone and tell him to stop being an ass and close this call of Liz's!

The extract above, taken from the field journal, demonstrates how the development of relationships with the specific clients became an expected norm, an activity which new CSRs were expected to participate in and gain mastery over. As the observations above illustrate, worker sexuality was often mobilized on behalf of the organization in order to effect smoother interactions. In this sense the development and maintenance of pseudo-sexualized relations between CSRs and clients became a key strategy in terms of how the team sought to achieve its performance objectives. Not all members of the team, however, saw the levity and potential for fun in relationship building:

> *Lizzy*. . . . it's OK, I guess. I know you lot like it [referring to male CSRs] but sometimes they don't know when to stop.
>
> *Researcher*. What do you mean?
>
> *Lizzy*. Sometimes the banter, you know, goes too far. They [the clients] get too personal, and I just try to change the subject.

The development of such relationships was of direct benefit to the team and to Ace-Call, since the informality allowed CSRs to divert away from established procedures when the commercial need arose. For example, in the case of problems which required extensive third-party support, a CSR was able to ask the client not to log the fault officially, so that it did not appear as an 'open' call.

Both female and male CSRs were required to engage in such relationship building. However, the actual way in which this was achieved was itself distinctly gendered (see Brannan 2005b for a fuller exploration). For male CSRs relationship building was based on competition to form bonds based upon banter between themselves and female clients and frequently took the form of joking and flirting. Often male CSRs would boast about their sexual attractiveness, reaffirming the positive self-image of male CSRs reinforced through humour, exaggeration and story-telling tactics learned from old-timer CSRs, and transmitted to newcomers through structured participation in such rituals. Male CSRs reported that they saw this process as a positive affirmation of their status as men within the team and a boost to their ego. In contrast, female CSRs would be expected to 'get to know' male clients, requiring a different strategy involving the sharing of personal information in a way that was very different from their male counterparts. The pairing of female newcomers and female old-timers within the team meant the newcomers were provided with an established practice to draw upon in shaping their own customer interactions. Thus men and women doing the same job became 'different sorts of workers' (Guerrier and Adib 2004: 348).

Conclusion

This chapter has explored the process of legitimate peripheral participation in communities of practice in a call centre from an empirical perspective. This approach has been adopted with the intention of contributing more empirically informed texture to the growing debate surrounding the concept of a community of practice. The chapter has drawn upon ethnographic fieldwork, which has been sensitized to the lived experience of new CSRs as they become part of the call centre community of practice.

The concept of a community of practice yields great explanatory power in attempting to explain and understand the process of becoming a proficient CSR, specifically when the lens of legitimate peripheral participation is utilized. However, the findings presented in this chapter suggest that, with respect to modern complex organizations such as AceCall, the concept of a constellation of communities of practice is particularly useful. Significantly, in the case study example this operated in at least three different dimensions. First, AceCall sought to differentiate itself from other local and national call centres. This was achieved through the positioning of AceCall as being closely related to AceCorp whilst offering a 'fun' (Kinnie *et al.* 2000) working atmosphere. This helped to establish the organization as a different and desirable community of practice. This might be conceptualized as a vertical community of practice that extended throughout the organization. Second, AceCall differentiated itself internally between different teams, which became inextricably linked with the client organizations they served. This reinforced the primacy of specific client requirements and cemented workplace identities, crucially incorporating the customer into the process of legitimate peripheral participation, reinforcing the status of the team whilst excluding other teams and clients. Such communities might be conceptualized as being arranged on a lateral axis throughout the organization. Finally, newcomers were often observed to form spontaneous collective groupings around the shared experience of being a new member of staff, raising the possibility of a temporal dimension to a community of practice forged within a cohort of recruits.

It is argued here that the organization was able to define the boundaries for specific communities of practice and was able to manage them in ways which effectively contributed to its overall business objectives; for example, as a form of labour discipline or to reduce employee turnover. Furthermore, the subjective aspects of specific communities of practice were subtly manipulated by the organization to foster an air of competition between different teams.

Whilst the literature on emotional labour has frequently noted the significance of sexuality and gender in the conduct of work tasks, that on communities of practice has much less often recognized their centrality to the experience and organization of learning through legitimate peripheral participation. This chapter outlines the ways in which, at AceCall, gendered and sexualized relationships with clients and other third parties were crucial to managing emotional labour and, thus, were integral to the completion of routine tasks and achieving performance targets. Key aspects of the legitimate peripheral participation of newcomers within teams entailed learning to cultivate relationships of these kinds and, more generally, to accept the legitimacy of such forms of social interaction. Competition, ridicule and banter among team members were harnessed by team leaders to encourage the cultivation of gendered and sexualized relationships with clients, and thus the achievement of company aims. These processes were constructed differently for male and female CSRs, reflecting stereotyped gender differences in the way CSRs were expected to present themselves to clients.

Finally, this chapter draws attention to the ways in which the process of legitimate peripheral participation may be structured along lines of power. Inequalities of power within and between companies, teams and cohorts shaped the participation of CSRs in AceCall. These differences were further positioned within wider power differences in labour markets, gender relations and sexual encounters. This chapter suggests, therefore, that studies of processes of legitimate peripheral participation might usefully be focused upon issues of power, in the sense of exploring the boundaries placed upon participation and non-participation and the terms under which participation is facilitated.

Key questions to consider

1   How do social factors – such as gender, ethnicity, class and age – shape relationships within communities of practice?
2   How is solidarity within communities of practice influenced by rivalry, competition and conflict with other groups?
3   In what ways do novices cope with the stresses and demands of their initial entry to communities of practice?
4   How do 'old-timers' motivate, monitor and discipline newcomers to communities of practice?
5   What are the advantages and disadvantages of ethnographic research methods in studying communities of practice?

References

Adkins, L. (1992) 'Sexual work and the employment of women in the service industries', in Savage, M. and Witz, A. (eds) *Gender and Bureaucracy*, Oxford: Blackwell.

Bain, P. and Taylor, P. (2000) 'Entrapped by the "electronic panopticon"? Worker resistance in the call centre', *New Technology, Work and Employment*, 15 (1): 2–18.

Brannan, M. J. (2005a) 'Workplace Resistance in Call Centre Environments', unpublished Ph.D. thesis, submitted to Wolverhampton University.

Brannan, M. J. (2005b) 'Once more with feeling: ethnographic reflections on the mediation of tension in a small team of call centre workers', *Gender, Work and Organisation*, 12 (5): 420–39.

Callaghan, G. and Thompson, P. (2001) 'Edwards revisited: technical control on call centres', *Economic and Industrial Democracy*, 22 (1): 13–37.

Callaghan, G. and Thompson, P. (2002) '"We recruit attitude": the selection and shaping of routine call centre labour', *Journal of Management Studies*, 39 (2): 233–54.

Guerrier, Y. and Adib, A. (2004) 'Gendered identities in the work of overseas tour reps', *Gender, Work and Organization*, 11 (3): 334–50.

Hochschild, A. R. (1983) *The Managed Heart: Commercialization of Human Feeling*, Berkeley: University of California Press.

Kinnie, N., Hutchinson, S., and Purcell, J. (2000) '"Fun and surveillance": the paradox of high commitment management in call centres', *International Journal of Human Resource Management*, 11 (5): 964–85.

Korczynski, M. (2003) 'Communities of coping: collective emotional labour in service work', *Organization*, 10 (1): 55–79.

Lave, J. and Wenger, E. (1991) *Situated Learning: Legitimate Peripheral Participation*, Cambridge: Cambridge University Press.

Sturdy, A., Grugulis, I. and Willmott, H. (2001) *Customer Service Empowerment and Entrapment*, London: Palgrave.

Taylor, P. and Bain, P. (1999) 'An assembly line in the head: the call centre labour process', *Industrial Relations Journal*, 30 (2): 101–17.

Wenger, E. (1998) *Communities of Practice*, Cambridge: Cambridge University Press.

11 The learning trajectories of 'old-timers'

Academic identities and communities of practice in higher education

Nalita James

Key themes in this chapter

- Multiple communities of practice
- Shifting and uncertain identities
- Cross-cutting allegiances
- Learning trajectories of old-timers
- Impact of changing managerial strategies

This chapter will explore tensions between the different identities, and trajectories of identification, that constitute the participation of academics in communities of practice within higher education. It will suggest that their participation cannot be 'merely "read off" from a given context, but may take many forms, and may encompass individual practices of modification and resistance' (Halford and Leonard 1999: 103). The multiple, uncertain and shifting character of academics' participation in, and experience of, communities of practice will be highlighted. It will be suggested that the positions, authority and careers of 'old-timers', or knowledgeable participants, are often less predictable, clear-cut and fixed than Lave and Wenger (1991) and Wenger (1998) imply. They may be faced with difficult choices between alternative, more or less incompatible or incommensurate, ways of being a knowledgeable participant. These decisions may be hedged around by constraints imposed by the distribution of material resources, cultural capital and personal opportunities. In addition, their learning trajectories may be critically shaped by the imposition of managerial strategies that generate on-going changes within employment relations, which have the effect of reconfiguring and redefining the communities of practice of which they are part. Their roles as old-timers within communities of practice, therefore, may be shaped by institutional and societal contexts over which they have little or no control.

The chapter will develop these themes through an exploration of the stories of two academics, who have been given the pseudonyms Jane and David. It examines the ways in which their changing locations and perspectives have become part of their learning trajectories, emergent identities and forms of membership (Lave and Wenger 1991). The stories presented here are taken from a larger study that examined how academics moved into, out of and through communities of practice, and how they transformed and reconstructed their identities and understandings of their lives (see James 2003 for a detailed account). A small number of case studies cannot, of course, be representative of British academics as a whole. However, a biographical methodology yields rich and detailed insights into the ways in which processes of identification and participation are generated and constituted (Saunderson 2002). The analysis presented below will move between Jane's and David's own words, vignettes of their actions and my interpretation of the concept of communities of practice and its relevance to higher education. It should be added that the words of Jane and David quoted here were obtained from in-depth interviews conducted by e-mail. This chapter will, therefore, seek to 'inject further empirical reality' (Fuller *et al.* 2005: 54) into the study of communities of practice.

Legitimate participation of old-timers

Not only has academic work provided conditions for identity formation, but also it has ensured that knowledgeable participants develop individual identities that are located and embedded in defined communities (Henkel 2000). Lave and Wenger's work (1991) has placed emphasis on the significance of belonging to communities of practice and of learning as part of the process of becoming a full member. In this sense they see the old-timer as someone who, through membership, becomes a full participant in the cultural practices of the community. This indicates, as Hodkinson and Hodkinson (2003) do, that Lave and Wenger recognize the significance of locating the individual within communities of practice. Thus individual stories are important in developing the identities of a community of practice and its members. As such, Jane and David's stories are grounded in the complexities of their particular experiences but also reveal more general processes. It is, therefore, possible to see them 'as both distinctive individuals and embedded in the communities of primary importance to them' (Henkel 2000: 250–1).

Lave and Wenger (1991) describe communities of practice in a way that tends to imply their practices are coherent and consensual. Wenger (1998) offers a definition that draws on harmonizing categories such as 'mutual engagement', 'joint enterprise' and 'shared repertoire'. These conceptualizations ignore the dynamic processes involved in the formation and reproduction of communities of practice. Communities of practice can be located in different space–time contexts, generating different and competing conceptions of the world within and between members. They may be characterized by varying degrees of consensus, diversity or conflict among those who identify themselves, or are identified by others, as belonging to those communities (Contu and Willmott 2003). As Huzzard (2004) notes, power is articulated through social practices and the relationships on which such practices are built. These generate individuals' self-concepts and constitute the institutions in which the self is embedded. Such practices can operate to either facilitate or impede participation processes. When it comes to illustrating situated practice in communities of practice, Lave and Wenger (1991) do mention issues of power and control, but overlook the significance of wider institutional contexts for their internal operations. Instead, they favour a focus on relations between community members and their significance for processes of identity (re)formation (Contu and Willmott 2003; Fuller *et al.* 2005).

Jane and David are senior academics working in departments of psychology in two post-1992 higher education institutions in the UK. They have been in their current jobs for over five years and are in mid-career. They are chartered members of their professional body as well as programme leaders for accredited professional training postgraduate courses in psychology. They not only hold disciplinary skills and knowledge but also are perceived as full participants in the cultural practices of higher education.

In this sense they are 'old-timers' rather than novices, having both held a variety of administrative, teaching and research roles and responsibilities. Their academic identities are rooted in the multiple communities of practice of which they are members, including those located in and around their departments, institutions, intellectual disciplines, professional bodies and practitioner organizations. Jane's and David's stories, then, provide an opportunity to examine the value of Lave and Wenger's (1991) work for an understanding of participation in higher education. Furthermore, their learning trajectories facilitate an exploration of the way in which global developments in higher education have been accompanied by a set of changes within academic institutions that has created a more structured environment (Henkel 2000; Bundy 2004) and impacted on forms of academic participation that are neither static nor stable (Taylor 1999; Rowland 2002). Their stories illustrate their social location as community members within a wider set of institutional, national and international relationships. They also show how conceptualizations of their own beliefs, experiences and values about what it means to be an academic in higher education are filled with tensions. These lead them to engage in different modes of participation and non-participation that describe 'conflict in the space between activity and identification, where there is a moment of mulitplicious identifications or *identificatory possibilities'* (Hodges 1998: 273, emphasis in original).

Academic participation and identity construction

Lave and Wenger's (1991) view of communities of practice as dispersed, and Wenger's (1998) later emphasis on the harmonizing categories of joint enterprise, mutual engagement and shared repertoire, suggest that communities of practice are networks or groups which regulate and make meaning of individual's lives, both inside and outside the workplace (Tight 2004). However, academics work in a number of overlapping communities of practice. They may belong to networks forged around disciplinary, research, teaching, departmental and institutional practices, each with its own sense of joint enterprise, mutuality and shared repertoire (Hodkinson and Hodkinson 2004). In these contexts, members develop day-to-day practices – behavioural and discursive, cognitive and emotional, explicit and tacit – and sets of ontological and epistemological assumptions about what they are doing (Trowler and Knight 2000). These are articulated in and through speech communities and shared modes of discourse (Barton and Tusting 2005).

Lave and Wenger's (1991) focus on relations between members of communities of practice, how they are internally co-constructed by members and their significance for processes of identity formation, glosses over what is a fractured, dynamic process of formation and reproduction in higher education (Rowland 2002). As Saunderson (2002: 379) notes, academics' experiences have now become 'couched within . . . a dramatically changed and changing method, praxis and pedagogy of UK higher education institutions in the twenty-first century'. Bundy (2004) observes that the impact of global developments on higher education, including a marketized private economy and a reduction in public sector provision, has led to the restructuring of academic institutions. British higher education is undergoing a rapid process of profound change, generated by a series of interconnected sources of transformation that are reshaping the organizational, pedagogical, institutional and cultural forms and practices of academia (Nixon *et al.* 2001: 229).

Successive UK government policies towards higher education have included severe budget cuts, rapid growth in student numbers, a shift of student funding towards fees and loans, the rise of a regulatory state to which institutions are accountable and the imposition of quality assurance measures in which teaching and research are subject to performance indicators (Walker and Nixon 2004; cf. Larner and Le Heron 2005). These measures have created a more structured, bureaucratized and centralized environment (Bundy 2004). They have also resulted in the heightened marketing and 'branding' of institutions. Linked to these measures has been a move away from collegiality and towards a kind of managerialism, undermining academic freedom in terms of the autonomy and integrity of disciplines (Menard 1996). The new managerialism regards higher education as 'a commodity-providing service in which needs and priorities can be measured and monitored' (Bundy 2004: 165). It imposes strategies and systems in which academics now have to participate in, and compete with, 'a multitude of values and objectives – economy, efficiency, utility, public accountability, enterprise and various definitions of quality' (Henkel 2000: 47).

The result of these changes is that academic identities, and forms of participation by academic old-timers in communities of practice, are being restructured and redefined (Saunderson 2002). For Jane and David these developments pose questions about the continued dominance of their disciplinary community, manifested in a collective intellectual project, in academic identity formation. Traditionally, academics have conceived disciplinary communities and disciplinary forms of knowledge as sustaining recognizable identities, cultural attributes and a sense of personal commitment. These have been described as 'a way of being in the world, a matter of taking a cultural frame that defines a great part of one's life' (Becher and Trowler 2001: 47). In her story Jane places great emphasis on the stability and the centrality of the discipline in constructing her academic identity and membership of the disciplinary community.

> I feel that I am a psychologist and will always be a psychologist even if I were not formally working as a psychologist . . . it is my role to help keep the discipline alive by adding to our body of knowledge and sharing this with students . . . I guess I may be saying that what actually matters to me most about being a . . . psychologist is the subject matter of psychology itself.
>
> (Jane)

However, whilst the disciplinary community still provides a strong source of intellectual identity, it has also become 'a tangible social, as well as an epistemological, construct' (Henkel, 2000: 189). The obsession with standards, outcomes and quality control in higher education means that academics now have an increased investment not only in their own institutions but in 'the various networks and structures that comprise their particular fields and subject-specialisms' (Nixon *et al.* 2001: 228). Jane and David are both programme leaders on professional training courses, which are accredited by their professional body, that regulate the supply, delivery and management of professional education. As a consequence of the marketization of higher education, generating overt competition for resources and students, they are required by their departmental communities of practice to access this professional community of practice. Jane's and David's participation has become dictated by a new managerialism that sees their programmes as a commodity. As a result, participation in the regulation of the professional roles of psychologists as practitioners provides academic psychologists with greater leverage within institutional contests. However, this in turn, causes increasing tensions with other disciplines. As Jane notes:

> There is . . . tension in the professional status of psychology as perceived by those in academic institutions who resource it, and those academics from non-professional disciplines. You could argue that being able to call on accreditation thresholds, for example, is helpful – but it also can, I think, cause a little resentment among colleagues from other disciplines . . . who can feel outmanoeuvred.
>
> (Jane)

Nonetheless, Jane and David maintain their obligations to their professional body. It is a community of practice they see as significant in the structures and substance of their academic participation and sense of identity, as they participate in its education and training within explicit professional requirements, including the assessment of knowledge, skills and experiences (James 2003). However, each engages in a very different mode of participation, which affects their sense of belonging and identity construction.

For Jane, her participation is a further opportunity for her to look for a sense of belonging; to hold on to her participation as a member in the disciplinary community, underlining how her membership is of primary importance to her in shaping an identity that is also professionally legitimated.

> It's my identity with the discipline that is at issue. For example, my participation [in the professional body] engenders a strong sense of disciplinary identity . . . and is centred around ensuring the discipline is producing well qualified academics and practitioners, and the means to 'train' them.
>
> (Jane)

However, David recognizes that his participation in the professional body is limited by the social structure and traditions that organize this community of practice. These result in a form of participation in which he appears to feel marginalized, outside the dominant social structure, even though he wants to become more involved in the practices of this community. As Hodges (1998: 285) notes, 'marginalization as a larger social effect, can be structured into participation in a community of practice, manifesting itself as repetitions of . . . isolation'.

> I would like to get more involved with the practitioner side of things but they are making this very difficult for us academics. They are erecting hurdles that prevent an interested academic from becoming any more than that.
>
> (David)

As Lave and Wenger (1991) acknowledge, by bringing their whole selves into a community of practice, new members change the interrelationships between existing participants, including novices and old-timers. They also impact on the balance between the community of practice and the wider context, including other communities of practice. The potential challenges posed by new members may be further enhanced when, as does David, they bring with them already formed knowledge, expertise, skills, values and experience in cognate fields. In short, when they enter as novices but already have established old-timer credentials elsewhere. Whether David's legitimate peripheral participation poses a threat to old-timers in this particular case is not clear. Nevertheless, his case should, at least, alert us to the possibility that dynamic tensions, rather than consensus and stability, may characterize entrance to legitimate peripheral participation and the trajectories of old-timers.

As Lave and Wenger (1991) also observe, membership requires participation in accordance with the traditions and values that organize a community of practice. In higher education, participation by academics is very likely to be shaped by their identification with both the moral and the conceptual frameworks embedded in the discourses that constitute their communities of practice (Kogan 2000). Thus, for example, disciplinary communities of practice entail command over linguistic forms, intellectual rhetorics and methodological precepts (Barton and Tusting 2005). However, competitive pressures, external threats, challenges and regulation are undermining David's commitment to the discipline of psychology. He comments negatively about his identity construction and participation in the disciplinary community. He recognizes personal conflicts and tensions that surround his perceived membership, which impact on his identity construction and self-esteem. He sees himself working on the edge of the disciplinary community, as he feels that he no longer has a strong social capital within it and that his standing is diminishing. For David this marginalization leads to a transformative shift in his community participation – a shift towards its margins, creating conflictual identities.

> Early on I didn't know what to expect. Now I see ceilings, inevitable limitations (based on my knowledge of my personal skills, abilities, but limitations). So these things are changing all the time . . . sometimes negatively . . . sometimes one can be marginalized, sometimes from the discipline. Being an academic psychologist impacts on these things – in academia one is rather safe, one has status, but one is always being evaluative because of the relationship between freedom and responsibility! . . . I think being an academic psychologist fits less well with my career – at least in the last few years. I now seem to spend too much of my time doing non-academic and non-psychological tasks and responsibilities . . . When asked what I do, I would now never say, 'I'm a psychologist,' I would say, 'I'm a lecturer . . . ' The notion of a psychologist is too diverse and disparate to have any meaning to me.
>
> (David)

Jane's and David's stories also highlight how Lave and Wenger's (1991) understanding of communities of practice neglects the impact of external pressures in the wider organization where they are located and the dynamic processes of their formation and reproduction (Contu and Willmott 2003). The restructuring of higher education has created greater competition for resources and funding, in which teaching and research have become subject to targets and performance indicators. Jane's evaluation of how she sees herself located within the disciplinary community indicates that institutional structures and processes are creating conflict between actively participating in the wider disciplinary community and accommodating entry into the research community. She is in no doubt, however, that within higher education in general, and in the scheme of her own priorities, less value is placed on teaching than on research activities.

> my experience defines research as a more fundamental aspect of my identity than teaching.
>
> (Jane)

A focus on the tension between old-timer roles in teaching and in research points us towards the crucial significance of managerial strategies in setting the context of communities of practice. Teaching and research have become separate functions, driven by separate reward structures. The tension between them increasingly undermines the coherence of academic practice (Rowland 2002). In higher education the new managerialism has been elevated to 'a dominant position . . . with the intention of reshaping and redirecting academic activities through funding formulae, audit regimes and forms of control similar to those operating in the commercial world' (Bundy 2004: 165). In this wider socio-economic and political context, aspects of academic identities and community participation have been restructured and compromised by what Marginson (2000: 193) has described as the new style of research management, which 'colonizes the identities of researchers themselves' and in which academic research work is managed and regulated. In the UK research context this is illustrated by the Research Assessment Exercise (RAE). The RAE is a managerial device that prioritizes effectiveness and efficiency over academic purpose and values (Henkel 2000). In the form of peer review, it harnesses the normal activities of disciplinary communities of practice in order to achieve managerial objectives of surveillance, discipline and productivity. David's earlier comments reflect the conflicts he experiences between academic freedom and academic responsibility. He recognizes the struggle to remain research-active, in terms of making a unique contribution to the field, whilst at the same time reconciling the pressures of the institutional community to participate in the RAE.

> Now I suppose it's a matter of comparing oneself with other psychologists and in other subject fields . . . I perceive my identity in the context of past and present research, publications, plaudits . . . areas of research such as virtual reality and spatial work where I suppose I see myself as one of only a few hundred with real depth of expertise in the field.
>
> (David)

For Jane the RAE raises further concerns about remaining a full participant in the cultural practices of the disciplinary community whilst being research-inactive (in RAE terms). This is where Lave and Wenger's (1991) analysis does not fully account for the contradictions that can be structured into communities of practice through power relations embodied in managerial hierarchies and within communities of practice themselves. The RAE is organized on the basis of marginalizing difference, as academics struggle for inclusion and recognition of research work that is regulated by narrow classifications of what counts and does not count (Lucas 2004).

The imposition of the RAE means that Jane has become marginalized in her disciplinary community. Instead of being able to engage fully with the practices of the disciplinary community, her non-participation has created a transformative shift away from being a researcher, towards an accommodative identity construction as an academic manager (Trowler and Knight 2000). In these circumstances the taking up of an identity is complex because it involves a constant social negotiation that is never permanently settled or fixed, and can be understood through the practices with which academics engage. For Jane there is also a concern that her non-participation in the research community will actually close any future possibilities of maintaining her academic identity as a psychology teacher.

> I think I have reached the point where the next logical move within the institution would actually take me out of academic psychology . . . It would involve very little, if any, teaching, and little time to keep up to date with things. It would also . . . make my . . . identity 'manager', not 'psychologist', and since I have left behind opportunities to retain psychological identity as researcher, little in terms of academic psychologist would be left . . . However, the cost of developing in this direction [i.e. towards institutional roles heavy in admin.] has been a loss of research momentum. So elements of potential academic identity based on research expertise in applied settings, consultancy, participating in the RAE, etc., are now probably beyond me!
>
> (Jane)

This shift can be characterized as a process of 'dis-identification' in which Jane, an old-timer, has begun to reconstruct an identification within the context of conflict and exclusion (Hodges 1998). So, although Jane holds a strong commitment to the discipline, sustaining her membership is dependent upon her participating in ways that she feels she will find difficult to do. In essence it would mean 'negotiating a boundary and finding ways to move between two worlds' (Henkel 2000: 249). These changes to Jane's identity and practice further illustrate how her continuing membership in the disciplinary community is threatened by the RAE; 'a legacy that cannot be evaded' (Hodkinson 2004: 17). A hierarchical ordering has emerged in which Jane and David struggle to retain the value of their work (Lucas 2004). It means that Jane's and David's experiences have become structured by a system of managerial control in which external standards and quality assurance procedures are handed down (Rowland 2002).

Although Jane and David subjugate their individuality, as they find themselves subject to regulation and control, their stories indicate that they are not passive in their participatory practices; their agency also determines the nature of their participation (Billet 2004). They have had to learn to belong in new settings, and so to adapt, develop and modify their 'whole person in the process' (Fuller *et al.* 2005: 66). It is beyond the scope of this chapter to discuss in detail how their stories engender identities and subjectivities that incite different ways of engaging in the social world, as they bring with them different social and cultural backgrounds and discursive patterns. It is interesting to note, however, the ways in which Jane's community membership within the discipline is further extended to account for her related experiences in other life domains. For example, her personal experiences as both a mother and a feminist have impacted on her teaching, helping her to make sense of her academic life. She recognizes how the settings and activities in which she participates are 'engendering' of her academic identity as a psychologist. Hence Jane's academic identity is located within communities of practice outside the workplace. It can be argued that female academics' identity construction is not solely located in their central community of practice but is influenced by structural factors related to their gendered location (Trowler and Knight 2000).

The diversity of old-timer identifications

The stories of Jane and David, presented only in truncated form here, suggest a number of important general issues that are relevant to an understanding of the identities and learning trajectories of old-timers in communities of practice. First, the example of higher education suggests that old-timers may simultaneously belong to multiple communities of practice. These may not only span different spheres of life – such as family, leisure, politics and work – but may also be generated by the various practices entailed in a single occupation, job or employment role. Where these exist, multiple memberships may overlap to a greater or lesser degree. Some may be supportive of one another; others may compete or undermine one another. The same co-workers may be encountered in different communities of practice, engaged in different practices and purposes. Allies in one context may be rivals or competitors in others. In some cases the status of old-timer may carry across all, or a number of different, communities of practice; in others, old-timers may occupy segregated, even fractured, positions of authority and prestige. In some cases, elevation as an old-timer in one context may entail decline in another. Membership of one community of practice may offer greater material and symbolic rewards than the others. Where old-timers enjoy multiple memberships of communities of practice they may well encounter difficulties in maintaining their standing in all of them. Nevertheless, they may also have the option of shifting the weight of their identifications from one community of practice to another as circumstances change. Where this occurs it is most likely to involve movement from a higher to a lower-status network. However, not all old-timers occupy such complex positions. Some are members of just one community of practice offering a single role. It is clear, then, that the lives, attitudes and experiences of old-timers who occupy a single unified community of practice are likely to be very different from those who negotiate cross-cutting and competing allegiances within several (see Jewson on social networks elsewhere in this volume).

A second theme to emerge from the above discussion concerns the potential diversity of the learning trajectories of old-timers. Although the concept of learning trajectory is central to Lave and Wenger (1991) and Wenger (1998), they have been criticized for failing to develop a sufficiently complex and nuanced theory (see Fuller elsewhere in this volume). The stories of Jane and David illuminate some important aspects of this issue. Old-timers who occupy multiple communities of practice may well have more complex learning trajectories than others, including opportunities to make lateral moves into adjacent networks and groups. They may be prompted to do this by a variety of pressures; including oversubscribed senior posts, blocked career channels, shifts in managerial demands, opening up of new career opportunities and failure to achieve personal success. Old-timer trajectories may even entail a sequence of moves between nested communities of practice, with prior membership of previous networks required for entry to the next. However, lateral moves may also represent a form of 'downsizing', brought on by limited success in membership of higher-status communities of practice. In shifting sideways old-timers may, therefore, have to relinquish treasured personal identifications and long-term investments in learning. Moreover, experienced practitioners in one field who enter adjacent communities of practice as newcomers may pose particular difficulties for established old-timers (cf. Elias and Scotson 1994 on established–outsider relationships; also Owen-Pugh in this volume). Their status may be ambiguous and uncomfortable for all concerned. Their imported expertise and experience may constitute a challenge to established orthodoxies. They may threaten existing old-timers and disturb relations between old-timers and first-time rookies. Lateral moves of old-timers may, therefore, be resisted by gatekeepers who control access of newcomers.

A third theme which jumps out of the accounts offered by Jane and David is the impact of external managerial constraints and pressures on perceived and actual membership of communities of practice. Communities of practice typically function within an organizational, institutional or professional context that defines the broad parameters of work tasks, available resources and distribution of rewards. The autonomy claimed by communities of practice often sits uneasily with the prerogatives claimed by management. Changes in the forms and objectives of managerial controls can have a major impact on the viability of the membership of particular old-timers within some or all of the communities of practice which constitute important aspects of their identity. The case of the RAE is particularly interesting because it entails co-opting the traditional social relationships of independent peer review within disciplinary communities of practice in order to achieve wider managerial objectives of surveillance, discipline and regulation. Arguably, the participation and identity formation of academics in higher education is being reconstructed in the context of the new managerialism and the economies of performance. A sense of meaning and identity is being generated within a space that is bounded and shaped by communities of practice that have, themselves, become co-opted as vehicles of regulation and management of academics whilst ignoring values traditionally enshrined in academic practices. These developments raise questions about the extent to which old-timers within academic communities of practice are capable of undertaking struggle to shape their own identities or whether they are simply hostages to external events (Rowland 2002).

A fourth theme that emerges from the stories told by Jane and David is the uncertain, ambiguous and unsettled character of the identities and self-images of old-timers within communities of practice. It might be said that academics are particularly prone to chronic anxiety about their professional standing; their self-image relies to such a large degree on what they think others are thinking about their work, often indicated by secondary clues. However, leaving aside the specifics of higher education, there is a more general point to be made here. The arts of impression management frequently seek to bridge a gap between ideal performances specified in dominant discourses and the actualities of real situations (Goffman 1959). Old-timers, like other members of communities of practice, are aware not just of being less than perfect in their practices and performances, but of being less than they could be or even less than is demanded by the occasion. The erratic and fitful quality of the self-images of old-timers may stimulate self-criticism and reflexivity, energizing their on-going learning trajectories within their community of practice. However, they may also motivate old-timers to search for and pursue lateral and downsizing learning trajectories in alternative communities of practice.

Conclusion

Lave and Wenger's (1991) theory, and Wenger's (1998) analysis, in part offer a framework in which to understand the nature of higher education as *multiple* communities of practice in which academics engage. Yet their analysis tends to assume consensus and continuity. It overlooks the impact of power and control in dynamic settings such as higher education and its social location within a wider set of institutional contexts that impact on the internal operations of communities of practice. Trowler and Knight (2000) have argued that the diversity and dynamism of higher education's cultural configuration can be derived from its communities of practice. Nonetheless, it can be argued that the external control and reorganization of institutional structures in higher education has been significant in determining the reformation and existence of its communities of practice, their nature and their boundaries.

The stories of Jane and David provide insights into how the new managerialism in higher education has created shifting boundaries that generate emerging new forms of participation and identity formation, resulting in their feelings of growing insecurity within their disciplinary communities of practice. Menard (1996: 18) suggests that there has been a 'meltdown of disciplinary boundaries', leading to a hierarchical ordering, where teaching is less valued over RAE activity, to the point of disturbing the values and structures within which academic identities have been sustained (Henkel 2000). In turn, this creates vulnerabilities within academic identities as institutional structures and processes impact negatively on their identity construction (Saunderson 2002). Those old-timers experiencing insecure identifications and pressured self-images may seek to shift their learning trajectories laterally within the various communities of practice open to them. In this process they encounter both obstacles to movement and a cost in the form of losses of status and self-respect.

In applying Lave and Wenger's concept of community of practice to higher education, attention must be paid to how the wider socio-economic climate has impacted on higher education institutions, and by implication the relationship between the institution, the discipline and individual academics' participation. Increasing demands for external accountability and the exercise of managerial control and power in the establishment of regulatory frameworks (Sachs 2004) have become institutionalized within the everyday practices of those communities within which Jane and David participate. Within these parameters, Jane and David renegotiate, redefine and relocate their self-images, personal identifications and social statuses as old-timers within various communities of practice. Their stories suggest that, far from achieving a fixed, stable and secure position, old-timers may experience on-going processes of change in their learning trajectories.

Key questions to consider

1   What are the implications of membership of multiple communities of practice for the identities of participants?
2   What factors influence the learning trajectories of old-timers?
3   What are the practical and emotional processes involved in shifting membership from one community of practice to another?
4   What impact do different types of managerial strategies have on the formation and membership of communities of practice?

References

Barton, D. and Tusting, K. (eds) (2005) *Beyond Communities of Practice: Language, Power and Social Context*, Cambridge: Cambridge University Press.

Becher, T. and Trowler, P. R. (2001) *Academic Tribes and Territories*, 2nd edn, Buckingham: Society for Research into Higher Education and Open University Press.

Billett, S. (2004) 'Workplace participatory practices: conceptualising workplaces as learning environments', *Journal of Workplace Learning*, 16 (6): 312–24.

Bundy, C. (2004) 'Under new management? A critical history of managerialism in British universities', in Walker, M. and Nixon, J. (eds) *Reclaiming Universities from a Runaway World*, Buckingham: Open University Press.

Contu, A. and Willmott, H. (2003) 'Re-embedding situatedness: the importance of power relations in learning theory', *Organization Science*, 14 (3): 283–96.

Elias, N. and Scotson, J. (1994) *The Established and the Outsiders*, first published 1965, rev. edn, London: Sage.

Fuller, A., Hodkinson, H., Hodkinson, P. and Unwin, L. (2005) 'Learning as peripheral participation in communities of practice: a reassessment of key concepts in workplace learning', *British Educational Research Journal*, 31 (1): 49–68.

Goffman, E. (1959) *The Presentation of Self in Everyday Life*, repr. edn, London: Penguin.

Halford, S. and Leonard, P. (1999) 'New identity? Professionalism, managerialism and the construction of self', in Exworthy, M. and Halford, S. (eds) *Professionals and the New Managerialism in the Public Sector*, Buckingham: Open University Press.

Henkel, M. (2000) *Academic Identities: Policy Change in Higher Education*, London and Philadelphia: Jessica Kingsley.

Hodges, D. C. (1998) 'Participation as dis-identification with/in a community of practice', *Mind, Culture and Activity*, 5 (4): 272–90.

Hodkinson, P. and Hodkinson, H. (2003) 'Individuals, communities of practice and the policy context: schoolteachers' learning in their workplace', *Studies in Continuing Education*, 25 (1): 3–21.

Hodkinson, P. (2004) 'Research as a form of work: expertise, community and a methodological objectivity', *British Educational Research Journal*, 30 (1): 9–26.

Huzzard, T. (2004) 'Communities of domination? Reconceptualising organisational learning and power', *Journal of Workplace Learning*, 16 (6): 350–61.

James, N. (2003) 'Teacher Professionalism, Teacher Identity: How do I see Myself?' Unpublished doctorate of education thesis, School of Education, University of Leicester.

Kogan, M. (2000) 'Higher education communities and academic identity', *Higher Education Quarterly*, 54 (3): 207–16.

Larner, W. and Le Heron, R. (2005) 'Neo-liberalizing spaces and subjectivities: reinventing New Zealand universities', *Organization*, 12 (6): 843–62.

Lave, J. and Wenger, E. (1991) *Situated Learning: Legitimate Peripheral Participation*, Cambridge: Cambridge University Press.

Lucas, L. (2004) 'Reclaiming academic research work from regulation and relegation', in Walker, M. and Nixon, J. (eds) *Reclaiming Universities from a Runaway World*, Buckingham: Society for Research into Higher Education and Open University Press.

Marginson, S. (2000) 'Research as a managed economy: the costs', in Coady, T. (ed.) *Why Universities Matter: A Conversation about Values, Means and Directions*, Sydney: Allen & Unwin.

Menard, L. (1996) *The Future of Academic Freedom*, Chicago: University of Chicago Press.

Nixon, J., Marks, A., Rowlands, S. and Walker, M. (2001) 'Towards a new academic professionalism: a manifesto of hope', *British Sociology of Education*, 22 (2): 227–44.

Rowland, S. (2002) 'Overcoming fragmentation in professional life: the challenge for academic development', *Higher Education Quarterly*, 56 (1): 52–64.

Sachs, J. (2004) 'Sitting uneasily at the table', in Walker, M. and Nixon, J. (eds) *Reclaiming Universities from a Runaway World*, Buckingham: Society for Research into Higher Education and Open University Press.

Saunderson, W. (2002) 'Women, academia and identity: constructions of equal opportunities in the "new managerialism" – a case of lipstick on the gorilla?' *Higher Education Quarterly*, 56 (4): 376–406.

Taylor, P. (1999) *Making Sense of Academic Lives*, Buckingham: Society for Research into Higher Education and Open University Press.

Tight, M. (2004) 'Research into higher education: an a-theoretical community of practice?' *Higher Education Research and Development*, 23 (4): 395–411.

Trowler, P. and Knight, P. T. (2000) 'Coming to know in higher education: theorising faculty entry to new work contexts', *Higher Education Research and Development*, 19 (1): 27–42.

Walker, M. and Nixon, J. (eds) (2004) *Reclaiming Universities from a Runaway World*, Buckingham: Society for Research into Higher Education and Open University Press.

Wenger, E. (1998) *Communities of Practice: Learning, Meaning and Identity*, Cambridge: Cambridge University Press.

12 Unemployment as a community of practice

Tales of survival in the new Germany

Vanessa Beck

Key themes in this chapter

- Communities of practice outside the workplace
- Societal contexts of communities of practice
- Unemployment and loss of community of practice membership
- Responses to loss of community of practice membership
- Personal agency and social support

The majority of texts that utilize the concept of communities of practices deal with the workplace or various learning contexts, such as the chapters in this volume by Brannan, James, Goodwin and Unwin. Yet the original development of the framework also included a case study of Alcoholics Anonymous, thus moving outside formal work contexts. Communities of practice may be said to exist all around us; we participate and experience them in everyday situations, whether at work or in our private lives. Although this is not a plea for an all-encompassing usage of the concept, there are good reasons for extending the framework beyond situations that are easily recognizable as learning contexts. For the purposes of this chapter unemployment has been chosen as the area of investigation. It will be questioned whether the unemployed can form communities of practice and, if they can, what conditions are necessary to develop such communities. In addition, the impact of macro-social and cultural changes on the aspirations and the capacity of the unemployed to form communities of practice, as well as the potential positive effects of participating in such a community, are considered. It will be argued that at least some of the unemployed can form communities of practice and utilize them to enhance their ability to cope with redundancy.

Communities of practice theory has been criticized on the grounds that it pays insufficient attention to the power relations both within communities and between communities (Paechter 2002: 71). In this context an important issue is whether participation in a community of practice is voluntary or enforced. For example, the interest of an apprentice who has been able to choose their apprenticeship and placement will be greater when compared with a youth who has not had such a choice. This is not to say that learning and inclusion will not take place in the latter case but the literature on motivation would suggest that people who value their work are more motivated (Ilacqua and Zulauf 2000: 172). For the unemployed, these considerations are important for two reasons. First, it has not explicitly been considered how withdrawal or forced removal from communities of practice, such as workplace groupings of co-workers, can take effect. However, as will be shown, literature on unemployment has traditionally looked into such consequences, and this can be applied to the specific frame of analysis that communities of practice constitute. Second, the unemployed are generally considered to have low status and therefore have few possibilities to influence or exert power over their own situations, let alone contribute to social groupings, such as communities of practice. In fact, isolation is said to be a typical response to, and consequence of, unemployment (Jahoda 1982). For these reasons, the current analysis of the unemployed is considered an important contribution to an in-depth understanding of communities of practice. The concept is tested in relation to those on the margins of the labour market and possibly of society, thus delimiting its applicability. To this effect, the three dimensions of a community of practice as defined by Wenger (1998: 73) – namely mutual engagement, a joint enterprise and a shared repertoire – will be taken as the criteria of what constitutes a community of practice.

This chapter draws on examples from East Germany to trace the potential importance of the communities of practice framework for the understanding of unemployment. In their original development of the model Lave and Wenger (1991) considered five very diverse examples of communities of practice, located in highly industrially developed as well as tribal societies. They made no comment on the significance of these widely varying societal contexts for communities of practice and how they are established. However, any student of the German Democratic Republic (GDR) cannot fail to recognize the enormous importance of the overall organization of the communist economic, political and cultural regime for the formation and experience of small groups at the workplace. Under the GDR regime workplaces were often organized as large co-operatives, in which the work collective was a fundamental unit of society that some employees experienced as a 'second family' (Iganski 2000: 151). Benefits and disadvantages of the now defunct system have been described elsewhere (see Flockton and Kolinsky 1999). The combination of the long-term effects of a change in the economic system and the persistence of high unemployment rates is, however, ongoing. Germany has been troubled by unemployment since the early 1990s and extensive reforms were implemented in 2004 (e.g. Hartz reform, Agenda 2010). Despite, or possibly as a result of, these changes, and whilst policies start taking effect, unemployment reached new heights of over 13 per cent (see www.destatis.de), which are only partially explicable by seasonal fluctuation. The main variation in the unemployment quotas is between the West (ranging from 6 per cent to 10 per cent) and the East (between 16 per cent and 20 per cent). Within the GDR unemployment is perceived as even harsher than these figures indicate. This is because in the past unemployment was virtually unknown, because of feelings of relative deprivation *vis-à-vis* the West and because of the persistence of the problem despite subsidies and policy reforms.

This chapter will be illustrated by, and the analysis developed through, the experiences of two unemployed women in the former East Germany. Their stories emerged in research in-depth interviews conducted by the author, from which the quotations included below are taken. This biographical 'case study' approach was favoured in order to explore both negative withdrawal symptoms from work-based communities of practice and the establishment and/or reinforcement of other communities of practice whilst unemployed (for more information on the overall study see Beck 2000, 2003). The two women are referred to here by the pseudonyms Tanja and Nadine.

Tanja and Nadine

Tanja is 57 years old, married, with two adult sons. She is a qualified chemist (*Diplom-chemiker*) and a patent engineer. Until shortly after German unification she worked for Leuna, one of the biggest chemical companies of the GDR. At the time of interview she had been unemployed for eight years, although this had been interrupted by a retraining scheme, giving her an additional qualification as an 'assistant for management and organization', and short-term work creation schemes. In the main, such schemes are not related to qualifications held by an unemployed individual and, in practice, are often a means to renew entitlement to unemployment benefits. The use of such schemes has been scaled down considerably under labour market reforms but they were a key ingredient of the so-called second labour market until 2004. The second labour market refers to all schemes that are partially or fully funded by the regional or national state and its labour market institutions, such as the job centre. Initially, the second labour market was intended as a stepping stone into full employment in the first labour market, but lack of progress in improving unemployment rates has made it a more permanent feature (see Beck 2003: 181). Possibly due to her more advanced age, Tanja seemed to cope better with unemployment when compared to Nadine. The period she had to bridge until reaching retirement is more manageable, and throughout the interview Tanja was able not only to reflect critically on the changed circumstances since unification, particularly for women, and to put forward strong views on the events, but also to make jokes about developments. She, thus, gave the overall impression of being relaxed and in control of her situation.

The second interviewee, here called Nadine, is 44 years old. She was a chemical laboratory worker, also employed by Leuna, where she worked in quality control. She is single and has no children. She has experienced two spells of unemployment. The first lasted two years and, at the time of interview, she had been unemployed for a further spell of eight months. In between she had also participated in a second labour market work creation scheme. The interview with Nadine was shorter that that with Tanja. Her responses were precise but not elaborated upon and there were very few indications of what her views were on the overall developments since unification. Nadine, thus, seemed far less vocal and self-confident, giving the overall impression that she was not coping too well with her unemployment. However, whilst she admitted to being depressed, she felt that there was no point in self-pity and was therefore determined to struggle on. Both interviewees clearly expressed a desire to find employment, a typical response among East German unemployed women, independent of age, financial or personal situation. The two interviewees can provide insight into some of the conditions under which unemployed individuals cope well with their situation whilst also allowing an analysis of the conditions under which it is possible to establish or become involved in communities of practice.

Many East Germans perceived unification as a take-over by the West and, following initial euphoria, discontent increased. An increasing number felt themselves to be second-class citizens (Walz and Brunner 1997: 13 f.); different preferences and values continue to exist in two parts of the new country. Such feelings are likely to be reinforced by statements such as that of the head of the national employment agency (Bundesagentur für Arbeit, BA), who claimed that his institution could not help any individual who was older than fifty-five, lived in the east or had a qualification not required by industry. In Tanja's view, for example, her life was still strongly influenced by values she had learned and lived in the GDR. She felt that she could not and did not want to learn the values systems dominant in current-day Germany.

> I cannot change society but how can I use the means available to me that I stay healthy, to educate my children healthily, in this society coined by egoism, that does not feel shame to portray egoism as the true core, as the driving power of society. ... I find it frightening when a society no longer has humanitarian aims and instead says: well, I even want to inspire envy. Well, for me that is inexplicable. . . . I have to say that I try to maintain what is worthwhile maintaining from our humanitarian upbringing under socialism and to be a living example to my children. And to open their eyes that this society does not honour humanitarian values.

These remarks indicate the way in which whole societies may, or may not, be perceived as characterized by 'joint enterprise', 'mutual engagement' and 'shared repertoire'; that is, the attributes of communities of practice identified by Wenger (1998). They also highlight the way in which Tanja feels that she has been involuntarily removed from a social order that she experienced as a community of practice (such as a society with humanitarian values), and the consequences of partially involuntary participation in another community. Tanja felt that whilst she could not change society she could influence her own situation and health by insisting on her values and by passing them on to her children. There is, thus, still a distinct East German identity and value system more than fifteen years after unification (Woderich 2000). The quotation above suggests that opinions and habits are not easily changed and that even the next generation, who have not necessarily experienced the GDR consciously, are at least partially instilled with values from the socialist era. There is also an implicit notion that social cohesion in general is decreasing, paralleling findings about the disintegration of society as a whole in the West (see Putnam 2000 on the United States). We shall later see that strong social networks nevertheless exist and have become an important foundation of potential communities of practice for the unemployed that contribute to constructive coping strategies.

When people participate in what they experience as communities of practice in most contexts of their lives – at work and socially – they become a habitual mode of response. Consequentially, they try to establish communities of practice when faced with new situations, such as being made redundant. Traditionally, negative 'learning' effects of unemployment have been at the forefront of societal perceptions of the unemployed; for example, stereotyping them as being isolated and lazy. However, this chapter will suggest that this image is not necessarily an accurate portrayal. Positive learning can take place within unemployment, both at the individual and at the group level. This chapter will therefore do two things. First, it will suggest that the communities of practice model has analytical usefulness far beyond the workplace and, in fact, has strong implications for those who are removed from work-based communities. These include the learning effects of expulsion from work-based communities of practice as well as attempts to create new social relationships of a similar kind beyond the workplace. Second, it is suggested that both negative and positive learning processes, and communities of practice, can be established within unemployment.

Communities of practice and social environmental approaches to unemployment

Although the literature has rarely dealt explicitly with issues surrounding withdrawal or removal from communities of practice, they have long been an issue that other fields of research have investigated. Social environmental approaches, in particular, have considered the social implications of employment and unemployment, moving interactive patterns into the focus of their attention. As part of such approaches, 'latent function analysis', or 'deprivation theory', is interested in aspects of employment of which the unemployed are deprived. Of relevance are: reduction of social contacts, lack of participation in collective purposes, absence of an acceptable status and its consequences for personal identity, absence of regular activity and the experience of time (Jahoda 1982: 39). The central notion is that what produces the psychological distress of an unemployed individual is the deprivation of these latent factors, which, in employment, sustain well-being and, incidentally, are central to the establishment of communities of practice. The five 'latent functions' mentioned by Jahoda explain a range of dimensions within the communities of practice framework. Thus, although some analyses of unemployment suggest that there is little evidence that employment provides more than the manifest benefit of financial security (Winefield 1995: 176), the communities of practice literature provides evidence to counter such arguments. Deprivation theory also explains the typical initial shock that many unemployed people experience as a result of being made redundant; that is, as a result of losing out on the mentioned aspects of their (working) lives.

Tanja explained the impact unemployment had on her in the context of having just qualified herself further. She became unemployed at the same time as taking her final exams as a patent engineer.

> I did my job and finished the additional qualification. I achieved a good degree and in the middle of the final exams: the dismissal. Well, for me it was unbelievable. I still know how I – well, I have to say that it was very hard, yes. And I have, I perhaps took, well, almost two years, it took me, to deal with it emotionally, what – well, I just couldn't understand it, you know. Because in principle I was a person for whom work was almost . . . well, I don't want to say that I neglected my family, but work was at least equally important.

The feeling that an important section of an individual's life is no longer available to them can, thus, reinforce the shock of being made redundant. The more important employment is in an individual biography the more significant the shock can become. Based to some extent on a stage theory approach to unemployment (Zawadzki and Lazarsfeld 1935), it has been suggested that initial extreme reactions to redundancy balance out as the unemployed become more familiar with their situation (Clasen *et al.* 1998). In effect, learning processes enable coping. The adjustment depends on internal and external factors: 'Strong resources and weak constraints foster adaptive coping strategies that mediate better psychological and physical well-being than weak resources and strong constraints' (Jerusalem and Mittag 1995: 178). Analysis of the unemployed can thus provide insights into the effects of forced removal from a community of practice. Traditionally the unemployed have been seen as isolated. However, in this chapter it will be argued that withdrawal into isolation, relying on individual resources, and a more positive, group-based learning and exchange of experiences are both possible responses.

Negative experiences of unemployment

The forced removal from established communities of practice within the workplace can be a harsh experience. The positive implications of participation for an individual's identity (see, for example, James in this volume) can also become constraining and damaging. On being made redundant, questions to be faced could include: whether and how to remain involved in the employment-based community of practice; what other communities of practice are available to replace the work-based ones; what new communities of practice can be found or established. In addition, the unemployed can be forced into marginal, involuntary participation in training and/or welfare-to-work schemes. Linking participation in schemes to the continued payment of benefits, or their withdrawal for non-attendance, can be affective as well as restrictive in terms of motivation or learning disposition. The usefulness of such schemes, both with regard to the skills required on the labour market and for the motivation of the unemployed individual, can be very varied (see Lafer 2004: 121).

The unemployed thus often contrast the warmth and interaction of a well established community of practice in the workplace with the isolation and lack of support that can accompany unemployment. Nadine mentioned that she felt it was easier for her to be made redundant at a time when the entire section of her company was being closed down because it was not an isolating experience.

> For me it was comforting to know that we all had to go. If it had been individuals, as it had in part been previously, where only three or four ever had to go, that would be more depressing. But because it affected everybody I didn't perceive it as too bad.

Such common experiences can become the basis of a shared repertoire and mutual engagement, some of Wenger's characteristics of a community of practice. However, for this to happen, continued contact is essential. It is therefore noteworthy that Nadine went on to report how she experienced very negative feelings six to nine months later, when isolation, lack of confidence and reassurance affected her both as a result of the social transformations entailed in German unification and as a result of unemployment.

> First the *Wende* [literally, the 'turnaround': colloquial for changes associated with the end of the socialist regime and of unification]. Yes, then it did – then especially circles of colleagues, circles of friends, people you go for coffees with, competition developed somehow. . . . Yes, and now (sighs) [i.e. unemployed] . . . Perhaps it was partly my own fault: I withdrew too much. My self-esteem had sunk and so I put up the barricades for a while. I only have relatively few contacts: there are two, three friends with whom I can talk about everything or a lot of things. Circles of friends, yes, they still exist but the contacts are very loose.

The combined effects of unification and unemployment were thus too strong for most of her networks to survive. Nadine's difficulties in maintaining close friendships may have been reinforced by the fact that she had no family of her own. Overall, findings suggest that partners and children are the most direct source of support and comfort for unemployed women. Unemployment was thus harsher for those who had previously relied more on social and/or work-based contacts, such as the so-called second family. Tanja equally revealed some negative feelings, though these were not as strong when compared with Nadine's experience, whilst also indicating the existence of contacts via her husband. Interviews included questions about current feelings towards unemployment, in particular feelings of guilt for being in the situation, since attribution and perceptions of control have an effect on how individuals cope with unemployment. In response Tanja stated that she did feel uncomfortable in groups of people who were still in employment.

> Well, I don't have any feelings of guilt but sometimes, I must say, I don't feel at ease when I go out with my husband and he meets colleagues and everybody has work and I haven't. I don't feel comfortable then.

Such sentiments are frequently voiced by the unemployed and can mean two interconnected things. First, it is difficult to have to admit to being unemployed in public, because it is associated with not having social status, an occupation, and not being needed. Second, and as a result, it is difficult to be confronted with groups who still have all of these things, owing to their continued employment, thus making the unemployed individual feel like an outsider to the community of the employed.

When trying to overcome her isolation Nadine attempted to comply with the activities and routines that she perceived to be expected of the deserving unemployed. These included writing applications, seeking advice at job centres and other (communication) centres for the unemployed, taking part in training events and buying a computer to make her applications look right. She could, thus, be said to have attempted to enter a new community of practice, that of the unemployed, by learning appropriate activities (joint enterprise), sharing experiences (mutual engagement) and developing the skills and techniques of job searching (shared repertoire). The learning process had been indirect, influenced not only by her own views on unemployment but also the advice provided by the job centre and other advice centres for the unemployed. However, this had been unsuccessful in two distinct ways. First, she had not found new employment, despite having sent out a large number of applications: her own estimation was hundreds in the last few months. Her attempts to locate a new joint enterprise with other unemployed individuals thus failed to achieve its goal, although it had demonstrated her determination to find work. Second, she did not get a sense that there is a tangible community of practice to which she could be admitted and feel part of. The lack of mutual engagement and shared repertoires became very clear in her description of her contacts with friends: no new contacts with fellow unemployed individuals were mentioned. Her experience is, thus, an example of a negative development which has resulted in lower self-reported levels of well-being. Overall, there is thus here some support for negative perceptions about unemployment. In the following section, however, we will look at some more positive responses to unemployment where constructive social coping strategies have been developed or learnt.

More positive experiences with unemployment

Despite the harshness of the experience of unemployment, interviews have revealed that positive aspects can also exist. Following the indicators used in deprivation theory (Jahoda 1982), social contact and meaningful interaction, as well as purposeful use of time, are important aspects of being in work of which the unemployed can be deprived, and therefore may need to 'replace' or compensate for losses. A standard question in the semi-structured interviews that were conducted in East Germany was, therefore, whether contacts with friends and colleagues had changed in any way since becoming unemployed. Tanja's response shows that the ties with her old friends were very strong and that she had, moreover, managed to make new friends.

> Well, with me the old circle of friends has maintained itself, because we established it when we were young and based on our interests, but I have to say this circle has been extended with people that I have now got to know on these [labour market] schemes. And where there is now a need from both sides because similar problems affect this new group. So that my circle of friends has become bigger, yes, that's how I have to say it. And those in this area, that I have now got to know, with similar problems, and where the interests are similar, too, and that there is, shall we say, an exchange of experience, yes, with new problems.
> *Interviewer.* Do you help each other out?
> *Tanja.* Yes, sure, we reassure each other, we meet up and, let's put it this way, exchange our experiences in the fight for employment. (Laughs.) Yes, now, not as competitors but as – we encourage each other and advise on strategies and, yes, various things. There are always new legal regulations, you really cannot read that much. One finds out about it from this direction and the other from there, so that one always has to try, with the current strategies on the labour market – well, what do I know? – to stay up to date.

Importantly, Tanja's contacts are founded on a group of long-term friends, giving her solid support and possibly the security to go out and meet new people. This combination of old and new contacts gives Tanja access to central characteristics of a community of practice: there is mutual engagement in terms of jointly learning about the requirements of the labour market; a joint enterprise is found in searching for employment as well as, in more personal terms, in maintaining interests; and the length of friendships and joint experience of unemployment provides shared repertoires. However, they underwent a mutual, simultaneous learning process rather than one consisting of newcomers and old-timers. Hence, in some respects, such groups of unemployed individuals cannot necessarily be considered communities of practice. Nevertheless, the exchange of information that one person alone would not be able to obtain, and the feeling of not being alone in what is perceived as a very difficult situation, enables the development of positive coping strategies. This ability to maintain old contacts and make new ones, to exchange information and learn from each other, does not negate the individualized experience that unemployment usually constitutes. Moreover, it does not suggest that there are no individual activities. On the contrary, it could be suggested that the establishment of such networks could depend on individuals' personal initiative. This means that the relationship between an individual's initiative – their *agency*, in sociological jargon – their ability to learn from others more experienced than themselves, and the learning processes that may ensue for both newcomers to a group and the old timers, have not been fully explored. Ultimately, however, the establishment of coping strategies based on social networks and personal initiative can result in civic communities that have strong social capital (see Beck 2005). The implication here is that a community of practice conceptual framework may be applicable only to established or 'straight' sections of society whereas other concepts such as social networks or social capital can also explain looser, less structured learning experiences (see also Stephenson 2001 on social capital among street children).

A common point made especially in the immediate aftermath of unification was the suggestion that individuals socialized under socialism would be more reliant on a paternalist state and would expect more extensive provision (see Pfaller 1997). If such a position were assumed, it could also be argued that communities of practice are used as safety nets that allow communal decisions to be made without the individual having to expose themselves too much. Empirical results can show, however, that such lines of argument can be simplistic in that a culture of dependence cannot necessarily be assumed to be characteristic of communities of practice of the unemployed. Whilst it may exist in some, this is not generally the case. Although Tanja indicates that she is happy to learn from others and not see them as competitors in her search for employment, she also suggested that she is proactive in trying to stay up to date with developments. The following quotation from her interview reinforces this point. The mutual exchange of information and exchange of strategies show that a degree of social learning has taken place that allows East Germans – even those like Tanja who disagree with some of the fundamental values of the new state – to learn skills and capacities that they require to further their own case. Tanja thus explained that she had learned to influence the job allocation system that the job centre uses. Talking about looking for employment, she stated:

> Well, I don't expect that anybody looks for me, I will search myself. I have even noticed that the profile for employment that can be imported into the computer, the AIS [employer information system used by the job centre]. The placement officer enters what one does and what one can do. And because I never had a response I asked, when I was unemployed again, whether I was in the AIS at all? I'd been unemployed for five years and never had any response. And he said, yes, you are on there. And then I had a bit of time and looked for myself on the internet and found myself and got such a fright: I wouldn't have employed myself! Well, it wasn't my profile at all, my abilities and, generally, what I had previously done. And then I had a look what was listed for others, for men, yes, who are also patent engineers, and everything that it said about them, and took notes, and went back to the job centre and demanded: that, that and that need to be included. Oh well, there were discussions, and not a week went by after it had been changed and I had a response.

Tanja's observations indicate the importance of the state's involvement for the unemployed. The provision of accurate information to employers about job seekers, as well as information about potential job openings to the unemployed, cannot be taken for granted. In addition to services for the individual, many labour market schemes are also run by the job centre. Although schemes are rated, and funded, according to their success in placing the unemployed in the first labour market, less quantifiable results, such as increases in the self-esteem of participants, have been recognized. Recent reforms of labour market institutions and advice centres – such as the merging of the social benefits agency and job centres – has given further impetus to encouraging and supporting the strengthening of personal agency. Services are now intended to be tailored to the individual and could, potentially, reinforce the more positive responses to unemployment that have been outlined above.

Conclusion

This chapter considers the implications for individuals of being forced out of communities of practice within a workplace by being made redundant. Although much has been written about the positive aspects of communities at work, the issues surrounding involuntary removal from them have rarely been considered within the framework of the theoretical model. Social environmental approaches to unemployment have, in contrast, investigated the individual and social implications of unemployment and have consistently shown the negative consequences. The problems associated with unemployment were outlined using examples from a study of unemployment in the former GDR. Empirical research findings have highlighted important shortcomings in drawing upon theories of communities of practice to examine the situation of the unemployed. There are limitations of its usefulness outside a formal and, in the main, work-based learning environment. Furthermore, account must be taken of both the influence of the individual and social contexts on the ability to establish communities of practice, whether they be within or outside work.

Under which conditions do the unemployed form communities of practices? Positive responses are possible when unemployed individuals are able to overcome isolation and maintain or re-establish contacts and communities outside the workplace. The examples suggested that in such difficult situations mutual learning, rather than there being 'apprentices and old-timers', does occur and can provide important support and reassurance. The communities of practice framework provides limited possibilities to analyse such mutual learning processes, as it gives few indications of how knowledge and skills are created without the existence of established communities.

The case study approach utilized provided insight into the specific individual and social conditions of East German women and their ability to cope with unemployment as well as the impact on this ability that the existence or establishment of communities of practice may have. As part of a social environmental approach, unemployment can be considered to be a forced removal from a work-based community of practice. In part this explains why, traditionally, the unemployed are considered to be isolated and suffering negative effects of redundancy. Indications to support these findings, and therefore the importance of individual resources and constraints in coping with unemployment, were apparent in Nadine's case. She showed signs of depression and found it difficult to find support mechanisms to help her cope with her situation. Her circumstances did not include an established circle of friends outside of employment and she thus found it difficult to access alternative communities in which she could learn effective coping strategies. In contrast, Tanja's case is characterized by a context that enables mutual engagement, joint enterprises and shared repertoires. Her situation showed that more positive, often group-based learning and exchange of experiences can be a possible response to unemployment. It was also indicated that the unemployed do not desperately attempt to build communities of practice on the basis of the desire to re-enter the labour market and that they may, in fact, be more successful in establishing communities that are not work-based but interest-based as means to construct coping mechanisms.

It is difficult to establish clearly what a community of practice for the unemployed might be and how this would differ from social networks or indications of social capital. However, this chapter can come to indicative conclusions on the conditions that lead or contribute to the creation of communities of practice. These would include strong friendships and networks based outside the workplace and established prior to unemployment, and the support and comfort provided by family relations. Other factors that would need to be further explored could include age, gender, kinship, qualifications and the overall social cohesion of the societal context. In the case of East Germany, the enforcement of work-based relationships and support mechanisms by the former socialist state could have left those who relied on them exclusively without individual resources to develop their ability to cope with unemployment. On the other hand, quotes in this chapter suggest that the former socialist state was more attuned to creating circumstances in which work-based communities of practice became central to the labour process. Further comparative research into the specific political and societal contexts in which communities of practice exist could therefore highlight the importance of contextual factors to such learning processes.

Key questions to consider

1   How widely, and in what contexts, are communities of practice found outside the workplace?
2   What impact do different political and economic regimes have on the formation and character of communities of practice?
3   What are the personal and social effects of being deprived of membership of work-based communities of practice?
4   What factors shape the coping strategies that people deploy when deprived of membership of work-based communities of practice?

References

Beck, V. (2000) 'Managing unemployment: experiences and strategies of women in the new *Bundesländer*', in Flockton, C., Kolinsky, E. and Pritchard, R. (eds) *The New Germany in the East: Policy Agendas and Social Developments since Unification*, London: Frank Cass, pp. 138–251.
Beck, V. (2003) 'Female unemployment in the east: or, how to stay in the labour market', E. Kolinsky and H-M. Nickel (eds) *Reinventing Gender: Women in Eastern Germany since Unification*, London: Frank Cass, pp. 172–89.
Beck, V. (2005) 'Social dimensions of unemployment and their (potential) continuation in unemployment', paper given at the *International Labour Process Conference*, University of Strathclyde, 21–23 March.
Clasen, J., Gould, A. and Vincent, J. (1998) *Voices within and Without: Responses to long-term Unemployment in Germany, Sweden and Britain*, Bristol: Policy Press.
Flockton, C. and Kolinsky, E. (1999) *Recasting East Germany*, London: Frank Cass.
Iganski, B. (2000) 'The meaning of women's "second family" for current patterns of discontinuity in rural East Germany', in Cooke, P. and Grix, J. (eds) *East Germany: Continuity and Change*, Amsterdam: Rodopi, pp. 151–61.

Ilacqua, J. and Zulauf, C. (2000) 'The new learning environment and adult developmental needs', *Journal of Adult Development*, 7 (3): 171–8.

Jahoda, M. (1982) *Employment and Unemployment*, Cambridge: Cambridge University Press.

Jerusalem, M. and Mittag, W. (1995) 'Self-efficacy in stressful life transitions', in A. Bandura (ed.) *Self-efficacy in Changing Societies*, Cambridge: Cambridge University Press, pp. 177–201.

Lafer, G. (2004) 'What is skill? Training for discipline in the low-wage labour market', in Warhurst, V., Grugulis, I. and Keep, E. (eds) *The Skills that Matter*, Basingstoke: Palgrave, pp. 109–27.

Lave, J. and Wenger, E. (1991) *Situated Learning: Legitimate Peripheral Participation*, Cambridge: Cambridge University Press.

Paechter, C. (2002) 'Masculinities and femininities as communities of practice', *Women's Studies International Forum*, 26 (1): 69–77.

Pfaller, A. (1997) *The German Welfare State after National Unification*, Bonn: Friedrich-Ebert-Stiftung.

Putnam, R. (2000) *Bowling Alone*, New York: Simon & Schuster.

Stephenson, S. (2001) 'Street children in Moscow: using and creating social capital', *Sociological Review*, 49 (4): 473–619.

Walz, D. and Brunner, W. (1997) 'Das Sein bestimmt das Bewußtsein, oder: Warum sich Ostdeutsche als Bürger 2. Klasse fühlen', *Aus Politik und Zeitgeschichte*, 51 (97): 13–19.

Wenger, E. (2000) 'Communities of practice and social learning systems', *Organization*, 7 (2): 225–46.

Wenger, E. (1998) *Communities of Practice: Learning, Meaning and Identity*, Cambridge: Cambridge University Press.

Winefield, A. (1995) 'Unemployment: its psychological costs', *International Review of Industrial and Organizational Psychology*, 10: 169–212.

Woderich, R. (2000) 'Allgegenwärtig, ungreifbar. Zur Entdeckung ostdeutscher Identitätsbildung in Befunden der Umfrageforschung', *Berliner Debatte Initial*, 11 (3): 103–16.

Zawadzki, B. and Lazarsfeld, P. (1935) 'The psychological consequences of unemployment', *Journal of Social Psychology*, 6: 224–51.

13 Communities of practice in their place

Some implications of changes in the spatial location of work

Nick Jewson

Key themes in this chapter

- The changing spatial location of work
- Spatial dimensions of communities of practice
- New types of workplace
- Virtual space/time and real space/time
- Technologies of the self

It is axiomatic that social relationships exist in space and time; the social is always spatial and temporal. This chapter examines the implications of current changes in the places and locations of employment relations – the 'workscape' (Felstead *et al.* 2005) – for the formation and maintenance of communities of practice. It focuses specifically on office work, although many of the trends discussed here apply more broadly. The analysis draws on original research data generated by two ESRC-funded research projects (see Felstead and Jewson 2000; Felstead *et al.* 2005).

Much recent debate on the spatio-temporal location of communities of practice has focused on the viability of virtual communities of practice. In this context, a central issue has been whether the medium of electronic communication is too 'thin' to bear the weight of the 'thick' messages characteristic of communities of practice. Put another way, can the lived experience of legitimate peripheral participation and situated learning be reproduced in the attenuated sociability of virtual worlds? These debates have often focused on technical facilities that might enhance collaboration, such as portal architecture, discussion forums, digital repository systems, e-learning resources and virtual collaboration tools (e.g. Kondratova and Goldfarb 2004). Another prominent theme has been the role of leaders and 'leadership' (e.g. Bourhis *et al.* 2005).

This chapter will not argue that these arguments are wrong, or even wholly irrelevant. Rather, it will be suggested that the terms of the debate have not highlighted crucial aspects of key developments in contemporary workscapes. The viability of virtual communities of practice can be assessed only in the light of a broader analysis of the social relations embedded within the spaces and places of contemporary employment. Thus it will be seen that some trends in the socio-spatial organization of work, notably the emergence of new kinds of office spaces, are *increasing*, not diminishing, the 'thickness' of social interactions among co-workers, thereby potentially *facilitating* the formation and maintenance of communities of practice. Furthermore, whilst the rise of distance working via information and communication technology (ICT) is most certainly a reality, and does pose significant challenges for the maintenance of communities of practice, its impact is *mediated* by the wide variety of real social environments in which it is deployed. Hence virtual working generates a variety of different disciplinary regimes and lived experiences, each with its characteristic constraints and opportunities, which reflect the diverse range of real contexts in which ICT functions. This chapter, then, represents a plea to frame the debate over virtual communities of practice within a wider context.

The next section of the chapter considers the perspective on space and locality adopted in key texts on communities of practice. This is followed by an examination of themes emerging from the literature on virtual communities of practice, leading to a further section which poses an alternative agenda of questions and issues. The chapter continues by outlining current changes in the spatial location of work. This is followed by three sections which reflect on particular aspects of the workscape, including the 'collective office', working at home and working on the move. The chapter ends with a brief conclusion.

Participation and place

This section briefly outlines the perspective on the spaces and places of communities of practice presented in some of the key texts in the field. Lave and Wenger (1991) argue that learning is a situated activity. Newcomers learn through 'legitimate peripheral participation', that is, regular and progressive participation in circumscribed but real occupational tasks and practices, under the guidance, discipline and surveillance of established members of a community of practitioners. Gradually the involvement of novices increases in scope, responsibility and autonomy until they emerge as full members of the community of practice. Learning is conceived as an integral part of practice itself. Moreover, in becoming old-timers, novices not only master techniques and knowledge but also enter into a social identity by passing from peripheral to central membership of a community.

It might be thought that this conception of learning necessarily implies spatial proximity and face-to-face relationships. However, Lave and Wenger (1991) eschew a simple geographical determinism. Indeed, they do not dwell on issues of space and locality to any great extent. They recognize, particularly in their discussion of meat cutters (1991: 55), that the spatial layout of the workplace can have implications for the access of novices to the rungs of the learning ladder that lead to community membership. The landscape of work may facilitate or impede observing and being observed. However, at the conceptual level, they are keen to dispel notions that 'peripheral' and 'central' should be conceived in spatial terms (1991: 36–7). They argue that these concepts refer, above all, to participation in social relationships. Moreover, they argue that their use of the term 'community' does not necessarily imply physical co-presence but, rather, requires participation in an activity system, through which members share understandings about their practical tasks and the symbolic meanings of their activities (1991: 98).

Although Wenger (1998) includes a chapter on 'locality', spatial issues are not central to this text either. He recognizes that physical distance between members can be a reason for communities of practice to wither or fail. He explores the implications of the trend in contemporary societies for people to occupy multiple communities of practice, each with their distinctive times and places. However, as in Lave and Wenger (1991), it is argued that communities of practice are not defined or determined by a particular spatial form but, rather, their places and times are shaped by the active participation of participants within a system of social relations.

> My argument is not that physical proximity, institutional affiliation, or frequency of interaction are irrelevant, but rather that the geography of practice cannot be reduced to them. Practice is always located in time and space because it always exists in specific communities and arises out of mutual engagement, which is largely dependent on specific places and times. Yet the relations that constitute practice are primarily defined by learning. As a result, the landscape of practice is an emergent structure in which learning constantly creates localities that reconfigure the geography.
>
> (Wenger 1998: 130–1)

Wenger *et al.* (2002: 113–38) explore issues of space and place more directly in their discussion of the challenges of geographical dispersion for what they call 'distributed communities of practice'. They explore ways in which distributed communities of practice can be made effective across time zones, continents and multinational organizational units. They admit that the attenuation of casual, unplanned contacts – 'in the hall, in the elevator, at meetings, or in the lunchroom' (2002: 116) – is a problem because physical proximity facilitates connectivity, including that of marginal members. In distributed communities of practice, technology has to replace face-to-face interaction, even though tele-conferences and web sites do not fully convey tacit aspects of informal networking. However, the authors suggest that this problem can be overcome by careful design of the forms and frequency of virtual contacts. Moreover, they recommend that virtual contacts should be supplemented by face-to-face interactions – visits, meetings and opportune encounters – wherever possible.

It can be seen, then, that although these key texts highlight the crucial importance of intense social relationships, forged in practical and emotionally charged participation, communities of practice are not conceived as inextricably linked to a particular spatial form and it is not envisaged that they could flourish only in face-to-face, co-present relationships.

Participation in virtual communities of practice

Communities of practice conducted via on-line interactive technologies are widely advocated as a strategy for enhancing knowledge management within large-scale, transnational corporations (see, *inter alia*, Ardichvili *et al.* 2003; Hildreth *et al.* 2000; Lindstaedt 2004; Kimble *et al.* 2000a, 2000b). Increasing interest is reflected in a burgeoning nomenclature, including terms such as 'virtual', 'online', 'computer-mediated', 'electronic' and 'distributed' communities (Cothrell and Williams 1999; Wasko and Faraj 2000; Wenger *et al.* 2002; Kimble *et al.* 2000a). There has been some confusion about which types of relationships qualify for inclusion (Congar *et al.* 1999; Wellman and Gulia 1999; Hildreth *et al.* 2000; Igbaria and Tan 1997). We should be clear, therefore, that this chapter defines virtual communities of practice as those in which relationships are conducted wholly or primarily through electronic means of communication, such as e-mail, mobile phones, e-learning environments, internet chat rooms and video-conferencing. This section briefly examines the issues raised in the literature on this phenomenon.

It is widely acknowledged that participation in virtual communities of practice frees members from many constraints of time and space. Electronic technology allows people in different places and time zones to communicate and interact at the same time (synchronically) or discontinuously over a period of time (asynchronically). Electronic networks thus dramatically change the terms of access to, and conduct of, participation in communication (Sassen 2002). However, the literature also identifies difficulties confronted by members of virtual communities of practice. Prominent among these are: technical limitations; establishing trust; communicating knowledge; learning through sensing; and coordinating with management.

The vulnerability of ICT to technical failures is a familiar story that need not delay us here. It is worth noting, however, that technical problems can be exploited, manufactured or even simulated by those who wish, for one reason or other, to avoid making contact with others (Felstead *et al.* 2005: 172). Technical breakdowns may mask social tensions.

Establishing trust is critical within any community of practice, because members are expected to share tacit knowledge, new ideas and treasured repertoires of practice. Lack of trust may impede information flows and generate resistance to sharing. Informal, personalized interaction cues – such as body language, verbal hesitation, voice tone, dress, demeanour and facial expression – typically play a major role in forging intimate ties. However, electronic communication often does not facilitate the breadth of informal and intuitive non-verbal communications characteristic of face-to-face contact. Such problems may be intensified when virtual communities of practice span cultural boundaries between nations, ethnicities and religious groups. Ardichvili *et al.* (2003) suggest that the willingness of members to engage in mutual sharing depends on the presence of norms of reciprocity. Where knowledge is perceived within the group to be a public good there is greater willingness to participate in its development and use. Where knowledge is construed as a private asset, collaboration is less forthcoming.

Even if relationships of trust are established, virtual communities of practice may encounter difficulties in communicating some kinds of knowledge and skills. Kimble *et al.* (2000a) suggest that formal, codified, 'hard' knowledge can be transmitted relatively easily but 'soft', tacit, intuitive aspects of interaction within communities of practice may be more difficult to reproduce. The latter may include the narratives and non-formal discourses which are central to legitimate peripheral participation and situated learning. They require a shared repertoire of responses that are rooted in the lived experience of everyday interactions, expressed in nuanced and artful performances.

A related issue is whether the loss of direct sensory experience involved in much ICT affects the learning processes of members of communities of practice. Sight, sound, touch, taste, feel and smell may all be relevant not only to learning skills but also, critically, developing a sense of identity within the group.

The rise of virtual communities of practice has also highlighted issues about managerial control (e.g. see Bourhis *et al.* 2005). The visible presence of staff in designated places during fixed hours has long been a fundamental aspect of strategies of managerial control, facilitating surveillance, co-ordination and discipline (Joyce 1987; Baldry 1999; Baldry *et al.* 1998; Felstead *et al.* 2003). When members of communities of practice are geographically dispersed, it becomes much more difficult for supervisors to monitor their work rate and to ensure that their output meets the requirements of the organization. The self-motivated and self-directed character of all communities of practice often poses a dilemma for management; these difficulties are compounded when members are no longer subject to the controls embedded in conventional work-places (Vaast 2004).

This brief overview, then, has raised a number of issues of current debate about the functioning of virtual communities of practice. It is not the aim of this chapter to dismiss these but, rather, to place them in a different context or framework.

An alternative perspective

It is the contention of this chapter that much of the literature on communities of practice generally, and virtual communities of practice in particular, oversimplifies current trends in the places of work and, as a result, fails to register some of their most important implications. The issues and concerns reviewed above are certainly import-ant. However, a full understanding of their import requires them to be framed within a broader perspective on the development of the contemporary workscape.

First, it should not be assumed that virtual working *replaces* physical workplaces. The growth of ICT does not necessarily lead to the disappearance of factories and offices; indeed, it makes possible the emergence of new kinds of workplaces, such as call centres (see Brannan elsewhere in this volume). There is a heroic, utopian literature that predicts the 'death of distance' (Cairncross 1997; Rifkin 2000) and which portrays the internet as a wholly new kind of reality (e.g. Rheingold 1993). However, although ICT has grown enormously in the workplace, only a small proportion of the labour force work mainly, let alone solely, in cyberspace. A much larger proportion use virtual work spaces *in conjunction with* offices and factory spaces. Electronically mediated social interaction emerges, then, alongside and interwoven with physical workplaces. Our focus should be on the implications of relationships *between* virtual and physical work-places for communities of practice. Thus a number of studies suggest that even where virtual communications are in place, face-to-face contact remains a crucial aspect of their effective functioning (Kimble *et al.* 2000a, b; Hildreth *et al.* 2000). Evidence suggests that occasional face-to-face gatherings energize a virtual community of prac-tice, leading to a burst of online enthusiasm and activity, gradually fading until the next meeting. Paradoxically, therefore, it appears that the more virtual a community of practice becomes the more important it is that members meet in person.

Second, it should not be assumed that the only significant change in the workscape that has occurred since the 1980s concerns the invention of cyberspace. A major shift is occurring in the *physical* spaces of work *alongside* the emergence of virtual work space. To a significant extent, this has been made possible by the same technology that gener-ated web working. However, rather than the death of distance, in some contexts at least the impact of new technology on physical workplaces may well be to heighten the intimacy, immediacy and socio-psychological reach of face-to-face relationships between co-workers. The emerging 'collective office' – discussed below – facilitates legitimate peripheral participation and the formation of self-directed communities of practice via direct face-to-face contact. It is a reminder that, although technology may determine the outer boundaries of what is possible, it rarely determines the detailed practices of its application. How technology is used, and for what purposes, remain a socio-political decision.

Third, it is often noted that virtual communications are instantaneous, stretch across great distances and transcend spatial and temporal contexts. What is less often recognized is that the act of participating in such communication networks is *always* contextualized in real time and space for those involved. E-mails are read at a desk, on a train, or in a hotel lobby; mobile phone calls are made on a beach, at a party, or in a car speeding down a highway. The constraints and opportunities of these real places and times profoundly shape the way in which people participate in virtual communities of practice. Precisely *because* ICT is ubiquitous and portable, the real material and social contexts in which members of virtual communities of practice operate vary enormously. For convenience, they can be grouped into two clusters – the private spaces of residential households and the public spaces of travel outside home and office – but these harbour many different and contrasting locations. Each offers distinctive constraints and opportunities; each requires their users to learn skills appropriate to managing the particular site in which they find themselves at any one moment. The challenge for researchers is to excavate the significance of real time/space contexts for virtual encounters.

Current trends in places of work

A revolution is under way in the spatial location of work. Employment relationships and activities are threading their way throughout more and more of the times and places of our lives. The effect is that work and non-work are being blended in time and space in new ways. The linear, sequential, pattern of going to a place called 'work' to undertake paid tasks, and then at the conclusion of 'working hours' leaving occupational duties behind, is increasingly redundant. For some this trend opens new personal choices about how, when and where to work. For others it opens up new possibilities of work intensification. For many, it entails both.

This trend represents a startling reversal in the direction of change during the previous two hundred years. Industrialization replaced the household economy of the pre-modern era with the separate spaces, times and social relationships of home and work. Places of employment were increasingly differentiated from other spatial locations. Ever greater numbers of people were employed in specialized locations, hedged around by legal and administrative regulations and characterized by distinct social codes, psychological attitudes and aesthetic sensibilities. Work became a place, not just a task.

In the newly emerging factories and offices, managerial strategies focused on the visibility and presence of the work force within fixed and designated workstations. The co-ordination of the division of labour, measurement of output performance, surveillance of behaviour, disciplining of attitudes and control over stock were all greatly enhanced by having a place for every worker and every worker in their place. For white-collar staff this principle was manifested in the 'personal office'. 'Personal offices' confined employees to fixed cubes of space that were theirs and theirs alone (Felstead *et al.* 2005). Although office design changed over the decades – for example, from 'cellular' to 'open plan' – this key spatial arrangement remained intact.

In the twenty-first century this socio-spatial order is breaking down. Electronic technologies have made it possible for white-collar staff not to be present at their employers' premises over long periods of time whilst engaged in productive work. The conduct of their activities depends on access to a network of electronically mediated channels of communication that have become ubiquitous, portable and cheap; in short, an electronic envelope. Consequently, many tasks can be completed at home, on the move, or even during leisure time. Furthermore, in an era of global competition and cost cutting, there are good reasons to encourage staff to work outside the office. The stretch of ICT across twenty-four/seven enables work intensification. Employees can be expected to function outside 'office hours'. Moreover, office space is an expensive and inflexible asset. Use surveys regularly show that, even during conventional working hours, 'personal offices' are not occupied for large amounts of time. Fluctuations in the business cycle are not easily matched by disposing of, or acquiring, new premises. Furthermore, when staff work at home, some overhead costs – such as heating, lighting, catering and furnishings – may be transferred to the worker. Although some activities, such as team meetings and client presentations, may still require attendance at company premises, if employees can be facilitated to work outside the office for part of the time the savings can be enormous.

These cost imperatives have driven the rise of 'collective offices'. In 'collective offices' space is allocated to those who need it when they need it, and then reallocated to others when it becomes vacant. Staff are required either to book hot desks and hot rooms in advance or to find a vacant place from those available when they arrive in the building. Workstations and spaces left unoccupied for longer than a few minutes become available for someone else to use. Concierge and facilities managers typically have the task of organizing and policing the system, including frustrating attempts by individuals to reclaim spaces for their sole personal use, or 'stalling' (Goffman 1959).

Use of hot desks (booked in advance for specified periods) and touchdown desks (available on a 'drop in' basis) are good indices of the rise of collective offices. Thus, for example, the Location of Work Survey (Felstead *et al.* 2003, 2005), found that in 2002 a third of large organizations (31.3 per cent) made use of hot desks, a quarter (27.8 per cent) reporting increased use over the previous five years and nearly half (44.6 per cent) planning greater use in the future. Two-fifths (43.3 per cent) reported use of touchdown desks, with a similar proportion (43.9 per cent) planning further use. Numbers were significantly higher in the private than in the public sector.

The Labour Force Survey (LFS) and the census both suggest sharp increases over the last thirty years in the number of people working at home for at least some of the time. Both sources indicate that the numbers working mainly or solely at home are relatively modest; the 2001 census, for example, suggested that 9.2 per cent of the work force (2.2 million people) 'work mainly at home', up from 3.4 per cent in 1981. However, more people use their home as an occasional place of work. In the 1998 LFS over a fifth (21.8 per cent) of the employed work force reported working at home 'sometimes'. Such figures suggest that working at home has become a major supplement to other places of work, but that the numbers becoming full-time home-located workers are limited.

Business travel by car, train and plane has increased enormously in the last half-century, with managerial and professional workers clocking up more than double the miles of manual workers (Doyle and Nathan 2001). As a result, working 'on the move' has become part of life for increasing numbers of people. American Telephone & Telegraph (AT&T) estimate that half their staff will be on the road at any one time and half work independently of any fixed location, the key to these changes being the provision of laptops to employees. A survey of business users of motorway service stations and intercity trains (Felstead *et al.* 2005: 59–60) revealed that respondents regularly and routinely worked in trains, cars, planes, service stations, business centres, hotel bedrooms, hotel lobbies, temporary hired meeting rooms, station platforms and airport lounges as well as clients' and employers' premises and their own homes.

The conclusion to draw from this evidence is that the location of work is becoming increasingly diverse and heterogeneous. Different members of the same occupation, organization or community of practice can combine working times and spaces in different ways; the same individual may construct a shifting combination of localities over the course of a working week. ICT has made it far easier to work outside the confines of employers' premises. As a result, there is an extension and diffusion of work activities into and through other aspects of life, such as family and leisure activities. However, for most employees electronic technologies have not entirely replaced offices and factories but, rather, supplemented them and reshaped them. Although working at a distance is on the rise, face-to-face contacts remain central aspects of working lives and are intensified in new kinds of office spaces.

What, then, are the implications of these trends for the creation and maintenance of communities of practice? The answer, outlined below, is that working in 'collective offices', at home and on the move, pose contrasting challenges.

Communities of practice and 'collective offices'

Collective offices prioritize 'change over stability, process over structure, mobility over stasis, and uncertainty over predictability' (Felstead *et al.* 2005: 80). They enable and encourage potential members of self-directed communities of practice to come into contact, discover common interests, shape the agendas of their work, develop the parameters of their sense of expertise, and evolve the texts, devices and disciplines of their common projects. The defining features of communities of practice – 'mutual engagement', 'joint enterprise' and 'shared repertoire' (Wenger 1998: 72–85) – are all stimulated and facilitated in the mêlée of the collective office.

In collective offices, the need to find a workstation – whether it be hot desk, hot room, touchdown desk, seat in the atrium, couch in the lobby or table in the coffee bar – generates constant mobility and flows of personnel, over short and long time periods. Individuals who succeed in this environment develop a capacity for self-initiated planning and self-discipline in matching tasks to appropriate spaces and in anticipating future needs through the booking system. It also means that workers, of different grades, skills and functions, are constantly bumping into one another as they move through the building. This way of working gradually becomes an ingrained habit, bodily disposition and psychological attitude. Informal and unplanned encounters between juniors, seniors, operational staff, administrative personnel, novices and old-timers become commonplace. Order is imposed on the working environment by employees themselves, not given to them in the organization of space.

Personal offices emphasized the hierarchy and deference of traditional bureaucratic disciplines. They incorporated panoptic surveillance and disciplinary regimes that emphasized order, compliance and docility (Foucault 1977). In collective offices, too, visibility is high, but it does not take the form of centralized inspection from the watchtower of authority. Rather the collective office is characterized by 360 degree, decentralized observation of everyone by everyone else. Observation of co-workers by co-workers, of all types and grades, is enormously increased. The panoptican is replaced by a 'polyopticon' (Felstead *et al.* 2005: 84).

It is the avowed intention of the designers of collective offices that new ideas, practices and projects arise out of the unsupervised and unfettered encounters of people circulating within the building (see, for example, Law 2001). Mobility is intended to foster serendipitous cross-fertilization of thoughts and perspectives. Business gets done through brief, informal, chance encounters rather than drawn-out formal meetings.

'Bumping into' others becomes a way of making connections and networking. Over-hearing, eavesdropping and observing are valued as ways of absorbing information, gossip, expertise, tacit knowledge and indications of where the action is or is going to be (Felstead *et al.* 2005: 86–7). Such encounters may have a high level of redundancy but also provide stimulating ground for coalescing and cultivating communities of practice (cf. Wenger *et al.* 2002: 49–64).

In the collective office employees are expected to devote themselves to participation almost as much as task-based activity. Through participation in the relationships of the office, practice is driven, refined and developed. The socio-spatial relations of collective offices facilitate the 'totalizing' direction of contemporary managerial strategies of control that seek to 'colonize the self' (Gabriel 2003). They encourage wholehearted involvement in workplace conviviality, intense bonding with co-workers in informal settings, blurring of the boundaries between the ties of work and non-work, and the performance of personality as a key career asset. The design and aesthetic of the workplace seek to realize the metaphor of the corporation as family or community. Indeed, the architects and designers of collective offices frequently use the rhetoric of community to draw an analogy between work spaces and villages. Hence terms such as 'streets', 'neighbourhoods' and 'village greens' replace corridors, departments and canteens.

Entering collective office spaces for the first time can be disturbing for those not used to this way of working. It entails learning how to learn in a new way. Most succeed in mastering this environment by developing a greater sense of self-discipline and self-awareness – a reflexive personal responsibility combined with identification with co-workers. It should not be thought that workers always comply with the requirements of collective office space. Resistance can take various forms (Felstead *et al.* 2005). Nevertheless, the self-direction, self-discipline, participation, sociability and open communication characteristic of collective offices provide fertile conditions for *cultivating* communities of practice (Wenger *et al.* 2002).

Communities of practice and working at home

One of the main venues for virtual working, and hence for participating in virtual communities of practice, is the home. Working at home brings members of com-munities of practice into close proximity with the social relations of family, domesticity and leisure. In order to function effectively in this context they are required to reconcile the competing demands of two different spheres of life, based on contrasting values, ethics, beliefs and practices.

The differentiation of home and work, as a result of the breakdown of the pre-modern household economy, has had enormous implications for identities, selfhood and socio-psychological dispositions. It has been critical for the social construction of age, gender, sexuality, marriage, parenting, leisure, labour, time, space, neighbourhoods, urbanism, welfare provision and government policies. House and home are the locus of relationships of gift exchange and emotional dependence which, even though sometimes fraught with ambivalent tensions, are different from the contractual, mar-ket-based relationships of employment. Bringing work into the home – including the work of maintaining employment-based communities of practice via virtual links – juxtaposes two very different ways of life.

Those who work at home are subject to well established pressures, including a sense of isolation from co-workers, the absence of externally enforced structure to their working day, the need to fend off interruptions from family and friends, the deprecating banter of colleagues and the necessity of exercising very high levels of self-discipline (Felstead and Jewson 2000). Their most commonly preferred coping strategy is to create a clear physical and aesthetic segregation within the home between working places and domestic places (Felstead *et al.* 2004, 2005). Ironically, this strategy typically re-creates the personal office within the home, replete with appropriate décor, decoration, furnishings and ambience. Commercial manufacturers have been quick to supply the accoutrements of the 'home office'.

Detachment of the workstation from the rest of the home is not always feasible because of limitations of space. Even when achieved, it by no means resolves all the problems. Working at home poses particular obstacles to the development of the legitimate peripheral participation, mutual engagement, joint enterprise and shared repertoire of a functioning community of practice (Wenger 1998: 73). Home-located workers may feel they are invisible, forgotten or disparaged as not serious participants by other members of the community of practice precisely because of their spatial location. Those who work at home frequently feel conscious of missing out on the gossip, information, stories and rituals generated by 'hanging out' with co-workers and clients. Home location provides few opportunities to supplement virtual interactions with opportune 'bumping into' encounters. To invite a fellow member of a community of practice into the home is a big step. Home is a private sphere and such a visit might be deemed inappropriate by those involved and other household members.

Those who succeed in working at home adopt specific 'technologies of the self' in managing these stresses; that is, a series of interconnected skilful practices, intended consciously and reflexively to organize the course of everyday life, that are imposed on the self by the self (Foucault 1988; Rose 1990). These include such practices as: marking spatial and temporal boundaries around workstations; using personal cues to switch between domestic and employment activities; defending working space and time from the invasion of other household members; developing the confidence to intrude work commitments into the plans of other household members (for details, see Felstead and Jewson 2000: 120–60).

The technologies of the self adopted by home-located workers tend to be individualized, rather than following a common formula. This is partly because household circumstances vary but also because there is relatively little opportunity to compare notes with others in the same situation. Technologies of the self are also often gendered, with the familiar pattern of 'juggling' diverse tasks in fragmented times and spaces more commonly associated with women than men. The latter are more likely to command uninterrupted, linear, time slots.

Working at home, then, contrasts sharply with the experience of the collective office, even though both venues are increasingly common in the workscapes of contemporary employees. The opportunity, capacity and motivation to participate in a community of practice are likely to be shaped differently in each case. Increasingly, however, workers participate in communities of practice not only in the office and at home but also while travelling. Travel time is increasingly factored in as work time in the schedules of professional, managerial and administrative workers. However, working 'on the move' represents yet another set of challenges.

Communities of practice and working 'on the move'

Working 'on the move' entails carrying out tasks, such as participating in virtual communities of practice, whilst occupying transitional spaces; that is, spaces that are temporary, fleeting and often shared (actually or potentially) with strangers. These include transport facilities – such as planes, cars, trains – and stop-over points – such as hotels, service stations and departure lounges (Laurier 2001; Felstead *et al.* 2005). Specific locations vary greatly; for example, journeys by car pose quite different opportunities and challenges to those by train (Urry 2006). In general, however, whereas the constraints of working at home arise from location in the personal, private sphere of life, those of working on the move arise because of the impersonal nature of public spaces and places. These call for a different set of technologies of the self.

Some of the technologies of the self deployed by those working on the move are tactical. Thus, for example, a critical initial requirement is that of securing temporary access to a space that is wired to the electronic envelope. Such locations are increasingly provided in public places, such as railway stations, pubs and airport lounges. However, access is often limited, noisy and crowded. Obtaining a suitable slot may call for 'stalling' techniques; that is, laying a temporary, personal claim to the sole use of a specific, public space. This may be achieved by leaving possessions on empty seats, spreading out across several spaces, or occupying strategic positions, such as aisle seats, that block unwelcome latecomers. Having obtained a suitable place, it is necessary to defend it from unwanted incursions, such as small-talk from fellow passengers. Strategies of 'civil inattention' (Goffman 1959: 222–30) construct social distance from those in the immediate vicinity; for example, by pointedly ignoring their presence or by giving off clues that indicate interaction is unwelcome. Books, newspapers, documents, laptops and mobile phones may be deployed in these performances as well as in actually carrying out work tasks.

Other technologies of the self adopted by those who work on the move are more strategic. Travel is notoriously subject to unpredictable delays and disruptions. Preparing for these contingencies involves 'planful opportunism' (Perry *et al.* 2001). This may include: carrying a wide range of devices to facilitate a variety of types of potential work capabilities; recruiting office-based third parties as agents or proxies to provide updated information; navigating personally favoured routes that constitute familiar paths and short cuts; seeking out favoured seats, hotel rooms or restaurants; occupying locations with the least possible public visibility and noise.

Those working on the move are also careful to match the work they do to the places available to them whilst in transit. Journeys may be undertaken by a variety of different means or by a combination of means. Cars, planes and trains all have their different 'learning affordances' (Billett 2001). For example, travellers may seek to match the duration and required concentration of tasks to available times and places. They may use voice mail and similar stacking facilities to store up responses to other community of practice members. They may take care to avoid confidential communications in highly public places and take measures to maintain a professional or businesslike image in presenting to others (for details see Felstead *et al.* 2005: 136–75).

Being on the move may make it possible to meet and greet other members of the community of practice while 'passing through', unlike working at home. 'Bumping into' members may be promoted by adopting travel routes and stop-overs known to be frequented by others. Such venues may have the benefit of a liminal or carnivalesque quality, being neither home nor office, leading to a relaxed atmosphere that helps promote trust.

Conclusion

As a result of the rise of electronic forms of communication, the last twenty years have witnessed great changes in the spatial location of work and employment, reversing many trends of the previous two centuries. One thread of change is transforming the social relationships of offices, arguably making them more conducive to the mutual engagements, joint enterprises and shared repertoires that Wenger (1998) identifies as the defining features of communities of practice. At the same time, opportunities to engage in work, and participate in communities of practice, have escaped the boundaries of office and factory and have been diffused throughout the times and places of everyday life. As a result, the private sphere of the home and the public sphere of transitional places have increasingly become the real context in which virtual connections are made. The specific characteristics of these diverse contexts shape whether, what and how participation in communities of practices takes place.

Current debates in the managerial and technical literature about the viability of virtual communities of practice often fail to address these broader strategic developments in the spaces and places of work. Hence widely discussed obstacles to the development of communities of practice within cyberspace, outlined above, need to be placed in a wider social context. As far as work is concerned, virtual reality does not herald the arrival of a self-contained, hermetically sealed, new world of human consciousness. ICT is embedded within existing *social* relations of employment. It certainly is enabling major changes in the way work is done, but the driving forces are the familiar constraints and opportunities of the social relations of management and markets. Technology makes possible a range of options, but it does not determine whether, how and by whom these possibilities are taken up.

In contemporary Britain the direction of change appears not simply to be from one type of workplace to another but rather towards greater heterogeneity in the spaces and times of work. This calls for a chameleon-like quality, involving the capacity to switch between sharply contrasting locations, moving into and out of quite different ways of behaving. It also requires the capacity to stitch together these different localities into one seamless work regime. Participation in a community of practice, therefore, may call for the ability not only to command but also to bridge a range of contrasting real-world contexts.

As we have seen, after a long period in which employment relationships and tasks were largely confined behind the walls of factories and offices, work is now spreading out across time and space. It is intruding into, and even colonizing, other spheres of life, such as family and leisure. These developments make achieving a satisfactory work–life balance much more challenging. They require individuals to take responsibility for drawing boundaries around different parts of their lives which once were dictated by the spatial and temporal organization of the workplace.

All these developments highlight the changing mix of generic skills and knowledges required to participate in communities of practice in the twenty-first century. Successful involvement entails developing a repertoire of technologies of the self, adapted to cope with the demands of a range of different real-world contexts. Participating in a community of practice in the collective office, at home and on the move each calls for distinct skills and performances. However, a common thread underlying all of these contexts is the requirement, on the one hand, to acquire a sense of collective identity as group member and, on the other, to develop a personal sense of responsibility grounded in self-motivation, self-organization and self-discipline. The places and times of communities of practice increasingly demand a particular kind of subjectivity among members.

In conclusion, then, the viability of virtual communities of practice is a reflection of their context. The keys to their success or failure do not lie simply in their internal design, organization and management, important though these may be. They crucially depend on the *juxtaposition* of real spaces and virtual spaces, office spaces and cyber-spaces, public places and private places. Virtual modes of working depend upon the integration of increasingly diverse and novel relationships forged in work and non-work contexts. Furthermore, negotiating this increasingly fractured workscape entails developing a wide range of *personal* skills, and the capacity appropriately to deploy and redeploy them within a mosaic of shifting and contrasting situations. These competences and practices are embedded within individuated identities and performances of the self. Thus, learning through legitimate peripheral participation in virtual communities of practice is dependent on the prior acquisition of a range of contrasting and deep-rooted technologies of the self.

Key questions to consider

1   What are the implications of electronic information and communication technologies for the formation, maintenance and meaning of communities of practice?
2   What personal disciplines are required to sustain participation in communities of practice while working 'at home', 'on the move' and in 'collective offices'?
3   What learning processes are involved in acquiring the technologies of the self required by new ways of working?
4   What are the personal and social characteristics of people who most readily adapt to contemporary changes in the spaces and times of work?
5   Are the demands of work-based communities of practice increasingly intruding into other spheres of life, such as family, home and leisure?

References

Ardichvili, A., Page, V. and Wentling, T. (2003) 'Motivation and barriers to participation in virtual knowledge-sharing communities of practice', *Journal of Knowledge Management*, 7 (1): 64–77.
Baldry, C. (1999) 'Space – the final frontier', *Sociology*, 33 (3): 535–53.
Baldry, C., Bain, P. and Taylor, P. (1998) 'Bright satanic offices: intensification, control and team Taylorism', in Thompson, P. and Warhurst, C. (eds), *Workplaces of the Future*, London: Macmillan.
Billett, S. (2001) 'Learning through work: workplace affordances and individual engagement', *Journal of Workplace Learning*, 13 (5) 209–14.
Bourhis, A., Dubé, L. and Jacob, R. (2005) 'The success of virtual communities of practice: the leadership factor', *Electronic Journal of Knowledge Management*, 3 (1): 23–34.
Cairncross, F. (1997) *The Death of Distance: How the Communications Revolution will change our Lives*, London: Orion.

Congar, T., Noyes, J. and Kimble, C. (1999) 'CLIMATE: a framework for developing holistic requirements analysis in virtual environments', *Interacting with Computers*, 11: 387–402.

Cothrell, J. and Williams, R. L. (1999) 'Online communities: helping them form and grow', *Journal of Knowledge Management*, 3 (1): 54–60.

Doyle, J. and Nathan, J. (2001) *Whatever Next? Work in a Mobile World*, London: Industrial Society.

Felstead, A. and Jewson, N. (2000) *In Work, at Home: Towards an Understanding of Homeworking*, London: Routledge.

Felstead, A., Jewson, N. and Walters, S. (2003) 'Managerial control of employees working at home', *British Journal of Industrial Relations*, 41 (2): 241–64.

Felstead, A., Jewson, N. and Walters, S. (2004) 'Images, interviews and interpretations: making connections in visual research', in Pole, C. (ed.), *Seeing is Believing? Approaches to Visual Research*, Oxford: Elsevier, pp. 105–22.

Felstead, A., Jewson, N. and Walters, S. (2005) *Changing Places of Work*, Basingstoke: Palgrave Macmillan.

Foucault, M. (1977) *Discipline and Punish*, Harmondsworth: Penguin/Peregrine.

Foucault, M. (1988) 'Technologies of the self', in Martin, L. H., Gutman, H. and Hutton, P. H. (eds) *Technologies of the Self: A Seminar with Michel Foucault*, Amherst, MA: University of Massachusetts Press.

Gabriel, Y. (2003) 'Glass palaces and glass cages: organizations in times of flexible work, fragmented consumption and fragile selves', *Ephemera*, 3 (3): 166–84.

Goffman, E. (1959) *The Presentation of Self in Everyday Life*, repr. edn, London: Penguin.

Hildreth, P., Kimble, C. and Wright, P. (2000) 'Communities of practice in the distributed international environment', *Journal of Knowledge Management*, 4 (1): 27–37.

Igbaria, M. and Tan, M. (eds) (1997) *The Virtual Workplace*, Hershey, PA: Idea Group.

Joyce, P. (1987) *The Historical Meanings of Work*, Cambridge: Cambridge University Press.

Kimble, C., Hildreth, P. and Weight, P. (2000a) 'Communities of practice: going virtual', in Malhotra, Y. (ed.), *Knowledge Management and Business Model Innovation*, Hershey, PA, and London: Idea Group.

Kimble, C., Feng, L. and Barlow, A. (2000b) 'Effective Virtual Teams through Communities of Practice', Research Paper 2000/9, Glasgow: Strathclyde Business School, University of Strathclyde.

Kondratova, I. and Goldfarb, I. (2004) 'Virtual communities of practice: design for collaboration and knowledge creation', *Proceedings of the European Conference on Products and Process Modelling (ECPPM)*, Istanbul, Turkey, 8–11 September.

Laurier, E. (2001) 'The region as a socio-technical accomplishment of mobile workers', in Brown, B., Green, N. and Harper, R. (eds) *Wireless World: Social and Interactional Aspects of the Mobile Age*, London: Springer.

Lave, J. and Wenger, E. (1991) *Situated Learning: Legitimate Peripheral Participation*, Cambridge: Cambridge University Press.

Law, A. (2001) *Open Minds: Twenty-first Century Business Lessons and Innovations from St Luke's*, New York: Wiley.

Lindstaedt, S. N. (2004) '(Virtual) communities of practice within modern organizations', *Journal of Universal Computer Science*, 10 (3): 158–61.

Perry, M., O'Hara, K., Sellen, A., Brown, B. and Harper, R. (2001) 'Dealing with mobility: understanding access anytime, anywhere', *ACM Transactions on Computer–Human Interaction*, 8 (4): 323–47.

Rheingold, H. (1993) *The Virtual Community: Homesteading on the Electronic Frontier*, Reading, MA: Addison-Wesley.

Rifkin, J. (2000) *The Age of Access: How the Shift from Ownership to Access is Changing Capitalism*, London: Penguin.

Rose, N. (1990) *Governing the Soul: The Shaping of the Private Self*, London: Routledge.

Sassen, S. (2002) 'Towards a sociology of information technology', *Current Sociology* 50 (3): 365–88.

Urry, J. (2006), 'Inhabiting the car', *Sociological Review*, 54 (1): 17–31.

Vaast, E. (2004) 'O brother, where art thou? From communities of practice to networks of practice through intranet use', *Management Communication Quarterly*, 18 (1): 5–44.

Wasko, M. M. and Faraj, S. (2000) '"It is what one does": why people participate and help others in electronic communities of practice', *Journal of Strategic Information Systems*, 9: 155–73.

Wellman, B. and Gulia, M. (1999) 'Virtual communities as communities: net surfers don't ride alone', in Smith, M. A. and Kollock, P. (eds) *Communities in Cyberspace*, London: Routledge, pp. 167–94.

Wenger, E. (1998) *Communities of Practice: Learning, Meaning and Identity*, Cambridge: Cambridge University Press.

Wenger, E., McDermott, R. and Snyder, W. M. (2002) *Cultivating Communities of Practice: A Guide to Managing Knowledge*, Boston, MA: Harvard Business School Press.

14 Conclusion

Further developments and unresolved issues

Jason Hughes, Nick Jewson and Lorna Unwin

In many ways the original idea of communities of practice is a noble project with humane objectives. It raises the prospect of liberating the creative and self-directed impulses of workers of all kinds and at all levels in carrying out their everyday daily tasks. It celebrates the knowledge, skills and contributions of front-line employees to the very existence and effectiveness of the organizations in which they are employed or engaged. It seeks approaches to learning that aim to liberate and empower individuals, and to improve the effectiveness of organizations. However, the contributors to this book also indicate that there are many unresolved issues and problems associated with the concept and that much further work remains to be done. We conclude, therefore, with a brief review of the scope for future developments that emerge from the chapters in this volume.

One of the most fundamental issues, referred to by Fuller at the end of Chapter 2, concerns the appropriate levels of analysis to adopt in studying communities of practice. Put differently, how are we to discern and disentangle the complex, interwoven societal contexts within which communities of practice are located? This calls for an analysis of the micro, meso and macro layers of social relationships within which communities of practice are situated and between which they mediate. Communities of practice may be found at any, all or none of these levels. They may span, or be contained within, differentiated layers of vertical and horizontal social relationships, such as teams, departments, institutions, organizations, economic sectors, national and global interdependences. Moreover, as societies become more structurally differentiated during long-term processes of development, communities of practice change in form because their context has changed. This issue is so fundamental that, one way or another, it surfaces in all the contributions to the book. It is one that is becoming of increasing salience within the study of learning processes (Unwin *et al.* 2007).

This leads on to our second point: the need for a developed political economy of communities of practice embedded within a political economy of learning. In much of the literature, communities of practice are depicted as free-floating social entities whose fate is determined by internal processes. A political economy approach, in contrast, is concerned with how communities of practice fit within the overall economic, political and cultural systems of different types of society (cf. Ashton 2004; Ashton *et al.* 2000; Whitley 2000; Keating *et al.* 2002). How, for example, do different historic settlements between markets, the state, welfare systems and voluntary sector institutions, characteristic of different historical types of capitalism, influence the structure and functioning of communities of practice? How do communities of practice sit within different types of vocational education and training systems? How are communities of practice distributed between different economic sectors and industries? How do communities of practice sit within the runaway processes of global economic change characteristic of 'modernity' (Giddens 1991, 1992; Bauman 2000)? What external forces bear down on the operation of communities of practice? In this volume Hughes, Goodwin, Unwin, James and Beck touch on some of these questions in various ways.

Questions concerning the societal context of communities of practice draw attention to another theme that emerges from a number of contributions. Several comment upon, or empirically observe, the significance of 'constellations' of communities of practice within contemporary societies. These include chapters by Fuller, Owen-Pugh, Brannan, James and Jewson (on social networks). Constellations refer to multiple communities of practice that are interlinked, overlapping or nested in some way. One individual may simultaneously belong to several, all generated in and by their employment role. (The term 'constellation of practice' is also used by Wenger [1998: 126–28] in a slightly different way.) As Jewson notes, increases in the structural differentiation of societies increase the likelihood that constellations of communities of practice will emerge. The presence of multiple communities of practice generates a number of interesting processes that deserve further study (cf. Österlund 1996; Fuller and Unwin 2003, 2004a; Engeström 2004). They may facilitate multiple learning experiences and trajectories. They often create potentiality for lateral mobility, and hence enhanced agency, rather than a straightforward trajectory from novice to old-timer. They may generate conflicts and tensions in the lives of individuals and the functioning of organizations as a result of cross-cutting and shifting alliances and rivalries between their members.

A crucial issue that receives surprisingly scant attention in Lave and Wenger (1991), Wenger (1998) and Wenger *et al.* (2002) is the importance of the wider social memberships that are intrinsic to the identities, meanings and purposes – and shape ways of acting, thinking and feeling – of members of communities of practice. Prominent among these are age, sex, gender, religion, nationality, ethnicity and class. The only social divisions *conceptually* recognized within the theoretical model, however, are those of generation, or cohort. Hence, for example, Wenger (1998: 149–63) discusses 'identity in practice', using terms such as 'individuals', 'persons' and 'the collective'; he does not discuss men and women, old and young, black and white, rich and poor. It is as if members of communities of practice are standard interchangeable units rather than human beings rooted in specific biographies. Chapters by Owen-Pugh, Goodwin, Unwin, Brannan, James and Beck explore some of the ways in which performance within communities of practice is shaped by, embedded in and experienced through these aspects of social identifications. The biographical methodology adopted by James and Beck also points us towards these issues.

The obverse of these concerns is that, ironically, there are also doubts about the conceptualization of individuals within the communities of practice model, reflecting aspects of the widely discussed structure–agency debate in social science (Giddens 1984). A number of authors seek to rescue proactive, creative, purposeful, reflexive agents from over-deterministic structural perspectives in learning theory (cf. Billett 2004; Hodkinson *et al.* 2004). In this volume, issues about subjectivity and the subject are salient in the contributions of Billett, James, Owen-Pugh, and Beck. In his chapter, Billett argues that the distinctive feature of Lave and Wenger's (1991) work is the development of a social theory of learning that incorporates personal agency within its framework. In this perspective, an important area of research and study is that of the meanings, interpretations, affective states and emotions that individuals attach to their experience of membership within communities of practice. It should not be assumed in advance that these are necessarily positive or negative, empowering or constraining, alienating or liberating, exciting or frustrating. Owen-Pugh, in her chapter, evaluates three theories that seek to make sense of the experiential qualities of personal agency. Jewson's chapter on virtual communities of practice conceptualizes self-directed learning in terms of 'technologies of the self'. The work of Elias, which informs the chapters by Goodwin and Owen-Pugh, offers another distinctive 'solution' to the structure–agency 'dilemma'.

These questions lead us into another theme which, it is widely recognized, is not dealt with adequately in the paradigmatic texts, that is, inequalities and asymmetries of power. Inequalities of power characterize relationships between participants *in* communities of practice; they also shape relationships *between* different communities of practice, and between communities of practice and other social groupings. They may be generated by the dynamics of internal relationships within communities of practice, and/or reflect wider social divisions, such as those noted in the previous paragraph. Although Lave and Wenger (1991), Wenger (1998) and Wenger *et al.* (2002) refer to these issues, they do not adequately build them into the theoretical framework. Chapters by Fuller, Billett, Jewson and Owen-Pugh on social networks explore and evaluate alternative theoretical perspectives. Empirical studies by James, Brannan, Beck, Unwin and Goodwin indicate some of the ways in which these themes may be researched empirically.

The presence of social divisions and power inequalities within communities of practice points us towards another set of under-examined issues, that is, conflict and collaboration, resistance and control. Once again, these matters appear in the paradigmatic texts in the guise of struggles between cohorts, that is, novices and old-timers. However, chapters in this book by Engeström, Owen-Pugh, James, Brannan, Beck, Unwin and Jewson on networks, suggest that the scope and forms of conflict can be much broader than simply the displacement of old-timers. There are struggles between participants to exert control over different aspects of practice, struggles to regulate entry and exit, and struggles by communities of practice as a whole to exert power over others. The unfolding dynamics of these clashes of purposes can rarely be controlled by one party, leading to a constant stream of consequences and outcomes that are unintended, unanticipated or undesired by any of the disputants. This suggests a rich field of further investigation into the performance of communities of practice.

One of the most important ways in which divisions, conflicts and struggles are played out within communities of practice is through the policing of boundaries, thereby regulating the selection of newcomers, promotion to old-timer status, disciplining of practice and regulation of the labour supply. The occupational groups designated by social scientists as 'professions' – characterized by collegiate rather than client, employer or state control over their work – have historically been highly adept at these processes. This issue, then, directs attention to the critical significance of strategies of inclusion and exclusion within and between communities of practice. However, as Fuller acknowledges in this volume, the concept of 'boundary' is unclear and insufficiently developed in the key texts. Jewson's chapter on social networks proposes an alternative approach. Chapters by Owen-Pugh, Goodwin, Unwin, Brannan, James and Jewson on spatial changes in places of work present a variety of empirical investigations into how boundary lines are drawn, maintained and traversed in diverse circumstances. It is interesting, in this context, to compare what Johnson (1972) calls 'trait theories' of professions with those that focus on the dynamics of relational interdependences. Wenger (1998) offers a trait theory of communities of practice. By contrast, chapters by Jewson, Owen-Pugh and Goodwin draw, *inter alia*, on the work of Elias in order to develop a relational perspective.

An aspect of communities of practice that has come to the fore throughout the book is that of the relationships between novices and old-timers, and their respective learning trajectories. Although Wenger (1998) modified and refined the account of these relationships portrayed within Lave and Wenger (1991), as Fuller notes, further work remains to be done on this topic. Empirical research and theoretical analyses suggest that the potential learning trajectories of both novices and old-timers are more diverse, fragmentary and uncertain than the early texts suggest. This, in turn, picks up on many of the issues we have raised in this section. Thus constellations of multiple communities of practice make possible lateral moves and/or careers that travel through a series of nested networks. Members may, therefore, pass through a series of roles in which they repeatedly appear as novices and old-timers, albeit with increasing levels of knowledge. Conflicts and divisions – such as those of ethnicity, gender or class – may divide old-timers and direct their learning trajectories. There are more ways to be an old-timer than the model suggests, reflecting increasing specialization of skills and knowledge. Moreover, learning is often two-way, involving exchange between newcomers and established authorities (Fuller and Unwin 2004b). Chapters by Owen-Pugh, Goodwin, Unwin and James explore these issues.

Another area of uncertainty, raised in Fuller's chapter, is whether communities of practice are conservative or radical, backward-looking or transformative. Wenger (1998) remarks that they may foster resistance to change rather than innovation, and counsels against idealizing them. However, he does not offer a theoretical account of the conditions which shape their development. Nevertheless, the paradigmatic texts, and the consultancy movement more generally, project an optimistic and upbeat account of the benefits to organizations and individuals of sharing knowledge within communities of practice. An important area of investigation, therefore, is to find out under what circumstances communities of practice defend established truths and under what circumstances some or all of the members come up with novel ideas and procedures. Struggles, conflicts and inequalities within the context of multiple communities of practice may be one source of impetus to develop new ideas (cf. Engeström 2001; Fuller and Unwin 2003, 2004a). Do external pressures – such as market forces – or internal divisions – such as tensions between novices and old-timers – spark defensive responses or 'blue skies' thinking? It is also interesting to consider what level of novelty is achieved; for example, single, double or triple-loop learning (Argyris and Schon 1978). Hughes points us towards the importance of the managerial prerogative and power relations in determining the capacity for innovation characteristic of communities of practice. Jewson's chapter on social networks suggests that the answer to these questions lies in an analysis of the detailed configurations of network relationships between participants.

These issues highlight how knowledge, skills and practices are conceptualized in the key texts. The entire model is one of transmission and reproduction of knowledge, rather than creation or invention. It is not a theory of innovation. In this context it is interesting to note that Edwards (2005) has carried out a review of the extent to which the concepts 'community of practice' and 'learning through participation' are being used in projects in the Economic and Social Research Council's Teaching and Learning

Programme (TLRP), which runs from 2000 to 2011. Edwards (2005: 49) found that the concept of 'learning through participation' was 'used more widely as a structuring metaphor in projects concerned with post-compulsory education and training than with school-based studies' and was particularly prevalent in studies of workplace learning. This is not surprising, given the empirical foundation of Lave and Wenger's work outside formal educational settings. The key point in Edwards's review, however, is that where projects have drawn on Lave and Wenger's work they place far less emphasis on knowledge creation (Edwards, 2005: 51). Edwards argues that socio-cultural and activity theory frameworks (see Engeström in this volume) have greater capacity to recognize both the importance of cognitive processes in learning and how people learn new practices. This connects back to Young's (1998: 179) concern that, although Lave and Wenger's work poses a much-needed challenge to school-centric and psychologically-centric perspectives on learning, 'Its weakness is that it can play down the importance of what is learned, the question that lies at the heart of curriculum debates and the justification of formal schooling.'

The discussion of knowledge innovation raises more general questions about sources of change in communities of practice that signal further areas where more research is required. The key texts foreground generational turnover as the main source of change. Not enough consideration is given to other impetuses. Do communities of practice have a collective limited life span? If so, what are the forces making for vitality and regeneration, atrophy and decay? How does the transformative potential of communities of practice ebb and flow during this life course? What external forces most commonly disturb, disrupt, relaunch or rejuvenate communities of practice? More fundamentally still, how useful is a model of learning based on long-term generational transmission in a world where restless forces constantly tear up established ways of life and demand new responses? In this book, chapters by Hughes, Engeström, Owen-Pugh, Unwin and Beck and both contributions by Jewson all touch upon these issues.

A number of theoretical questions also remain that call for further consideration. Among the most important of these, as Fuller notes in her chapter, is the status of the 'learning as participation' paradigm itself (Hager 2004). Should 'learning as participation' be regarded as an alternative or supplement to 'learning as acquisition'? How might non-formal learning through legitimate peripheral participation be reconciled with more formal classroom-based approaches? What is the relationship between context-relevant, practice-based, task-focused knowledge and more abstract, relatively context-free, reflexive knowledge in situated learning?

An issue that is unlikely to be at the forefront of the concerns of practitioners, but which is of interest to social scientists, is to look at the body of theory and evidence that constitutes the communities of practice model through the lens of the sociology of knowledge. Clearly, there are connections between communities of practice as a consultancy project and developments in managerial strategies in the late twentieth century, particularly those associated with debureaucratization, cultural management and the 'colonization of the self' (Gabriel 2003; Willmott 1993). There are also interesting parallels between communities of practice, 'communitarianism' and the idea of 'social capital' (Etzioni 1993; Putnam 2000). All three reached prominence as practical social movements, attracting the attention of policy makers, during the 1990s. All seek to turn away from earlier debates about 'rights' towards an emphasis on 'duties', 'responsibilities' and 'participation'. All move the focus away from the purposes and goals of organizations and societies, which are taken as read, towards an emphasis on disciplined, collective means of attainment. All invoke a largely intuitive and normative notion of 'community', arguably thereby smuggling moral principles and assumptions about order and altruism into social science analysis. These questions are touched on in chapters by Fuller, Hughes and Jewson on networks.

Finally, Hughes's contribution to this volume directs us to two critical, overarching issues which repeatedly emerge throughout the book: on the one hand, the relationship between theory and evidence, and on the other, the relationship between knowledge and practice. The first of these, the relationship between theory and evidence, raises questions about what would constitute evidential support for the theoretical model, and, moreover, what kind of methodology would enable us to assess, revise and amend the communities of practice framework? The second issue, the relationship between knowledge and practice, is necessarily framed in terms of the salience of the managerial and consultancy project, which seeks to market the concept of communities of practice as a commodity. It is ironic, given the emphasis on situated learning in Lave and Wenger (1991), that we are inevitably drawn to ask the question, what kind of knowledge is learned from a highly commercialized practice?

Our list of unresolved issues by no means exhausts the lines of enquiry and topics for debate raised by the concept of communities of practice. However, we hope that we have done enough here to suggest that the idea is one which is rich, complex, multi-stranded and deserves to be the focus of intensive further theoretical analysis and empirical research.

References

Argyris, C. and Schon, D. (1978) *Organizational Learning*, Reading, MA: Addison-Wesley.

Ashton, D. (2004) 'The political economy of workplace learning', in Rainbird, H., Fuller, A. and Munro, A. (eds) *Workplace Learning in Context*, London: Routledge, pp. 21–37.

Ashton, D., Sung, J. and Turbin, J. (2000) 'Towards a framework for the comparative analysis of national systems of skill formation', *International Journal of Training and Development*, 4 (1): 8–25.

Bauman, Z. (2000) *Liquid Capitalism*, Cambridge: Polity Press.

Billett, S. (2004) 'Workplace participatory practices: conceptualizing workplaces as learning environments', *Journal of Workplace Learning*, 16 (6): 312–24.

Edwards, A. (2005) 'Let's get beyond community and practice: the many meanings of learning by participating', *Curriculum Journal*, 16 (1): 49–65.

Engeström, Y. (2001) 'Expansive learning at work: toward an activity theoretical reconceptualization', *Journal of Education and Work* 14 (1): 133–5.

Engeström, Y. (2004) 'The new generation of expertise: seven theses', in Rainbird, H., Fuller, A. and Munro, A. (eds) *Workplace Learning in Context*, London: Routledge, pp. 145–65.

Etzioni, A. (1993) *The Spirit of Community: The Reinvention of American Society*, New York: Simon & Schuster.

Fuller, A. and Unwin, L. (2003) 'Learning as apprentices in the contemporary UK workplace: creating and managing expansive and restrictive participation', *Journal of Education and Work*, 16 (4): 407–26.

Fuller, A. and Unwin, L. (2004a) 'Expansive learning environments: integrating organizational and personal development', in Rainbird, H., Fuller, A. and Munro, A. (eds) *Workplace Learning in Context*, London: Routledge, pp. 126–44.

Fuller, A. and Unwin, L. (2004b) 'Young people as teachers and learners in the workplace: challenging the novice–expert dichotomy', *International Journal of Training and Development*, 8 (1): 31–41.

Gabriel, Y. (2003) 'Glass palaces and glass cages: organizations in times of flexible work, fragmented consumption and fragile selves', *Ephemera*, 3 (3): 166–84.

Giddens, A. (1984) *The Constitution of Society*, Cambridge: Polity Press.

Giddens, A. (1991) *Modernity and Self-identity: Self and Society in the late Modern Age*, Cambridge: Polity Press.

Giddens, A. (1992) *The Transformation of Intimacy*, Cambridge: Cambridge University Press.

Hager, P. (2004) 'The conceptualization and measurement of learning at work', in Rainbird, H., Fuller, A. and Munro, A. (eds) *Workplace Learning in Context*, London: Routledge, pp. 242–58.

Hodkinson, P., Hodkinson, H., Evans, K., Kersh, N., Fuller, A., Unwin, L. and Senker, P. (2004) 'The significance of individual biography in workplace learning', *Studies in the Education of Adults*, 36 (1): 6–24.

Johnson, T. J. (1972) *Professions and Power*, London: Macmillan.

Keating, J., Medrich, E., Vollkoff, V. and Perry, J. (2002) *Comparative Study of Vocational Education and Training Systems*, Leabrook, SA: NCVER.

Lave, J. and Wenger, E. (1991) *Situated Learning: Legitimate Peripheral Participation*, Cambridge: Cambridge University Press.

Österlund, C. (1996) *Learning across Contexts: A Field Study of Salepeople's Learning at Work*, Aarhus: Psykologisk Institute, Aarhus Universitet, Denmark.

Putnam, R. D. (2000) *Bowling Alone: The Collapse and Revival of American Community*, New York: Simon & Schuster.

Rainbird, H., Fuller, A. and Munro, A. (eds) (2004) *Workplace Learning in Context*, London: Routledge.

Unwin, L., Felstead, A., Fuller, A., Ashton, D., Butler, P. and Lee, T. (2005) 'Worlds within Worlds: the Relationship between Pedagogy within the Workplace', Learning as Work Research Paper 4, Leicester: Centre for Labour Market Studies.

Wenger, E. (1998) *Communities of Practice: Learning, Meaning and Identity*, Cambridge: Cambridge University Press.

Wenger, E., McDermott, R. and Snyder, W. M. (2002) *Cultivating Communities of Practice: A Guide to Managing Knowledge*, Boston, MA: Harvard Business School Press.

Whitley, R. (2000) *Divergent Capitalisms: The Social Structuring and Change of Business Systems*, Oxford: Oxford University Press.

Willmott, H. (1993) 'Strength is ignorance, slavery is freedom: managing cultures in modern organizations', *Journal of Management Studies*, 30 (4): 515–52.

Young, M. F. D. (1998) *The Curriculum of the Future*, London: Falmer Press.

Index